A Longing Like Despair

A Longing Like Despair

Arnold's Poetry
of Pessimism

Alan Grob

DELAWARE

Newark: University of Delaware Press
London: Associated University Presses

Associated University Presses
440 Forsgate Drive
Cranbury, NJ 08512

Associated University Presses
16 Barter Street
London WC1A 2AH, England

Associated University Presses
P.O. Box 338, Port Credit
Mississauga, Ontario
Canada L5G 4L8

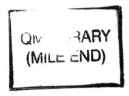

The paper used in this publication meets the requirements of the American National Standard for Permanence of Paper for Printed Library Materials Z39.48-1984.

Library of Congress Cataloging-in-Publication Data

Grob, Alan, 1932–
    A longing like despair : Arnold's poetry of pessimism / Alan Grob.
        p.   cm.
    Includes bibliographical references (p.) and index.
    ISBN 0-87413-752-7 (alk. paper)
        1. Arnold, Matthew, 1822–1888—Criticism and interpretations.
    2. Pessimism in literature.   3. Despair in literature.   I. Title.
    PR4024.G76   2002
    821'.8—dc21   2001048061

For Jay and Julie

Contents

Acknowledgments

I WOULD LIKE TO BEGIN MY ACKNOWLEDGMENTS BY PUBLICLY VOICING MY thanks for one of my great pieces of academic good fortune, the graduate requirement at the University of Wisconsin that I take twelve credits in another graduate department in addition to my major field of English. I have never come across a requirement quite like it. But being required to choose a minor, I took four courses in eighteenth- and nineteenth-century philosophy that have subsequently proven a mainstay of my scholarly career. Because when I first came to the teaching of Victorian poetry almost forty years ago, I came to it from an excellent course in nineteenth-century philosophy taught by A. C. Garnett, the affinities of Arnold and Schopenhauer seemed apparent then, as they do now, at least to me. (The Freudian connection came later.)

Ever since those earliest days, I have tried to make my case for Arnold as philosophic pessimist to innumerable friends, colleagues, and students. To those who have borne with me in this grim endeavor, I can only offer my blanket thanks. Since setting those arguments on paper, several of my colleagues have read portions of my manuscript in one of its many incarnations; and I would like to thank Scott Derrick, Helena Michie, Meredith Skura, and Ed Snow, all of whom have read and helpfully commented on parts of this work. Both in our Humanities 102 meetings and in our sessions at the Black Lab, Jack Zammito and Steve Crowell gave me philosophic instruction as I needed it and provided a model of intellectual commitment that I shall always try to emulate. During my extended labors on this project, Allen Matusow has been everything the best of friends and best of deans might be. Terry Munisteri, editor and friend extraordinaire, has patiently overseen the working out of this study in all its many guises. Bob Patten is to be especially singled out for a generosity and supportiveness that go far beyond the call of ordinary friendship and collegial duty.

For reasons that are not entirely clear to me, Texans have taken to Arnold in an exceptional way, so that I have been able to try out my ideas not far from home on audiences that were both informed

and encouraging at the two major American gatherings of Arnoldi-
ans in recent years: the Arnold conferences at Texas A&M and at
the Browning Library in Waco. Clinton Machann has patiently an-
swered my inquiries and been gratifyingly supportive of this project. David DeLaura has been teaching me about Arnold ever since
our days as graduate students at Wisconsin, and, as my own work
has developed, I have been able to take advantage of our long
friendship and avail myself of his great expertise on a number of
occasions. Don Reiman has been a sensitive and helpful reader, and
it was a special pleasure to renew an old acquaintance in the final
stages of my work. I have never met David Riede, who is the author
of the last full and serious study of Arnold's poetry, and our under-
standings of that poetry differ considerably—but as reader for both
the present work and an earlier essay of mine that appeared in *Victorian Poetry*, he has exemplified what being part of a scholarly
community genuinely means. On both occasions he read my work
carefully, let me know in no uncertain terms that he disagreed with
many of my conclusions (as I on the pages that follow will disagree
with some of his); but he praised where he felt praise was merited,
and, most important, in the end he recommended publication on the
grounds that my views, while very different from his own, deserved
a hearing. Finally—again and always—I would like to thank my
wife, Shirley, the true love who has really made the world that lies
before us into a land of dreams.

Unless otherwise noted, all references to Arnold's poetry are cited
as *Poems* in the notes and by line number in the text and refer to
The Poems of Matthew Arnold, edited by Kenneth Allott, 2d edition, edited by Miriam Allott (New York, 1979); references to the
prose works are cited as *CPW* and by volume and page number in
the text and refer to *The Complete Prose Works of Matthew Arnold*, 11 volumes, edited by R. H. Super (Ann Arbor, University of
Michigan Press, 1960–77); and references to the letters are cited as
Letters and by volume and page number in the text and refer to *The
Letters of Matthew Arnold, 1829-1870*, 3 volumes, edited by Cecil
Y. Lang (Charlottesville, University Press of Virginia, 1996–99). References to *The World as Will and Representation* are cited as
WWR and by volume and page number in the text and refer to Arthur Schopenhauer, *The World as Will and Representation* 2 vol-
umes, translated by E. J. F. Payne (Mineola, N.Y., Dover
Publications, 1969). Longer versions of the discussions of "Mycerinus" in chapter 2 and "Resignation" in chapter 3 and the discussion
of "The Scholar-Gipsy" in chapter 4 first appeared as: "Arnold's

'Mycerinus': The Fate of Pleasure," in *Victorian Poetry* 20 (1982): 1–20; "The Poetry of Pessimism: Arnold's 'Resignation,' " *Victorian Poetry* 26 (1988): 25–44; and "Arnold's 'The Scholar-Gipsy': The Use and Abuse of History," *Victorian Poetry* 34 (1996): 149–74.

A Longing Like Despair

1

Introduction

F<small>OR THOSE OF US WHO CARE ABOUT ARNOLD'S POETRY, THESE DAYS OF RADI-</small>
cal remaking of the canon are difficult ones. All around us the evidence compellingly builds of his waning standing, even as last among equals, among those three Victorian poets who a generation ago were axiomatically presupposed major by most of those who wrote on and taught them.[1] We find a dwindling number of articles dealing with his poems listed in the annual MLA bibliography; fewer and fewer pages given over to them in the major anthologies; and, as the logical inference from these facts (and still more sadly, in what we learn from our students in the advanced classes in Victorian literature we teach), we must unhappily surmise that little time is spent on Arnold's poetry in the surveys with which English majors begin their literary education. Even "Dover Beach," a poem that a generation ago Norman Holland could describe as "the most widely reprinted of any poem in the language" and, probably, "the most widely explicated," has received less and less attention in recent years.[2] (It is perhaps best known to the current critical generation of theoretically inclined critics from Gerald Graff's *Beyond the Culture Wars*, where "Dover Beach" serves as the bone of faculty-lounge contention between the Old Male Professor [OMP] who fogyishly champions its "universality" and the up-to-date Young Feminist Professor [YFP] who dismisses it as nothing more than "phallocentric discourse.")[3] More tellingly, perhaps, no full-length study of Arnold's poetry has appeared since David G. Riede's *Matthew Arnold and the Betrayal of Language* in 1988, a work that, in retrospect, we can now see disturbingly prefigures current critical tendencies by its having considerably more to say against than in favor of Arnold's poetry.[4]

To be sure, interest in Arnold has not wholly dissipated, and during the 1990s we have had two substantial biographies, two volumes of the long-awaited edition of his letters, and, most recently, an important critical study of his writings by Donald Stone (though this last focuses mainly and most successfully on the prose).[5] But even these appearances of continuing interest in Arnold can be deceiving in regard to criticism of the poetry, at least criticism as we have known it during that mature phase initiated in 1966 by A. Dwight Culler's seminal study, *Imaginative Reason* (still cited as "the most influential general study of the poems,"[6] by Arnold's latest bibliographer), that is, criticism as close reading of important (and sometimes not so important) texts, readings usually conditioned by some overriding hypothesis about Arnold's poetry generally, the excellence and interest of that poetry a premise tacitly assumed by most of those writing on it. Though the currents of a criticism so conceived have not entirely dried up, they have certainly slowed to a trickle, and, most dishearteningly, among that scattered handful of readings of Arnold's poetry recently published, more and more assume an adversarial posture that has become increasingly the rule in criticism of the traditional white, male canonical author.[7]

At my most wildly optimistic, I do not foresee any reversal of present tendencies, so deeply ingrained have they become in our criticism. Instead I can only hope that in the course of describing Arnold's poetry in what I think are new and original ways, I may reassert its claims, at least among those willing to value it, by showing it to be possessed of more philosophic depth and subtlety than it is usually credited with. Like many of those who write on the poetry, I shall choose as my starting point that widely quoted letter to his mother, written in 1869, when, his career as a poet virtually over, Arnold took stock of how posterity might judge his poetry: "It might be fairly urged," he stated, "that I have less poetic sentiment than Tennyson, and less intellectual vigour and abundance than Browning" (*Letters*, 3:347). Nonetheless, he went on to reassure his mother that there was still a powerful case to be made in behalf of his poetry, good reason for her to anticipate that her son would one day not only rank with but perhaps even surpass his rivals as claimant to the title of first poet of the age: "[Y]et because I have more of a fusion of the two than either of them, and have more regularly applied that fusion to the main line of modern development, I am likely enough to have my turn, as they have had theirs" (*Letters*, 3:347). In this assessment and prediction, Arnold showed himself to be remarkably prescient. His poetry has had its turn, and most of us who would have it ranked with or even ahead of the poetry of Tennyson and Browning have generally done so because of its sensed affinity with modernity—because, even more than theirs, Arnold's seems so obviously to have situated itself on "the main line of modern development."

In that letter Arnold never does spell out what he means by "the main line of modern development" to which he had so effectively applied his own "fusion" of "poetic sentiment" and "intellectual vigour and abundance." I would like to think though that Arnold, like many of us who have ranked his poetry so highly, would have perceived its affinity with modernity to reside in its courageous recognition of the painful cosmic circumstances of secularized man, in its willingness to render unflinchingly what Hardy, a quarter-century later, would call "the ache of modernism." In short, it seems modern in its unsparingly deep and pervasive bleakness. Of course, one has to concede that in this instance, as in many other equally crucial matters, Arnold sends decidedly mixed signals to the reader who would try to understand what he might mean by "the main line of modern development." In 1869, at the peak of his powers as a writer of an essentially forward-looking prose, Arnold (with a certain Enlightenment bravado) had already identified "the supreme characteristic" of a truly modern age to be "the manifestation of a critical spirit, the endeavour after a rational arrangement and appreciation of facts" (*CPW*, 1:25). Certainly it was in such a spirit that he had embarked on his great project of the 1850s and 1860s, his goal nothing less than the cultural transformation of Britain. But in his preface to the *Poems* of 1853, Arnold had already indicated his awareness of a more darkly ominous side to modernity, tendencies of the modern to which he knew he had already shown himself prone in his own poetry. In that preface, Arnold explained that he had chosen "one of the last of the Greek religious philosophers" (*CPW*, 1:1), Empedocles, as title character in the major poem of his preceding volume, not because exposure to that philosophy would put us in touch with the saving graces and virtues of the classical spirit, but because into his thoughts and feelings "there entered much that we are accustomed to consider exclusively modern" (*CPW*, 1:1). But the modernity that had entered into the words of that "Sicilian Greek born between two and three thousand years ago" (*CPW*, 1:1) was not the modernity of a "critical spirit" primed to aid the moderns of Arnold's own day in achieving an "intellectual deliverance," which in 1858 Arnold was to call "the peculiar demand of those ages which are called modern" (*CPW*, 1:1). Instead, Empedocles presented us with, according to Arnold, that other, more darkly ominous side of modernity, since in his thoughts and feelings "we hear already the doubts, we witness the discouragement, of Hamlet and of Faust" (*CPW*, 1:1).

As a suggested antidote to the intellectually crippling tendencies of this aspect of modernity, Arnold urged the writer of his own day who would escape its dangers to look to the example of the truly classical, to imitate those actions that served as organizing principles for the dramas of the great Greek tragedians, especially Sophocles. Moreover, to spare his readers from whatever dangers his own *Empedocles on Etna*—with its modernity of doubt and discouragement—might pose, Arnold, in a notoriously self-repudiating gesture of recantation, eliminated this perhaps greatest of his poems from the 1853 collection and from subsequent collections as well. But by 1869 Arnold, by deed if not by word, apparently reversed himself again, recanting his earlier recantation by republishing *Empedocles on Etna* in the *New Poems* of 1867. Though Arnold tells us that he did so in deference to the wishes of Robert Browning, the decision to republish almost certainly suggests what Carl Dawson has called an "acceptance of his poems on their own terms," an owning up to his own affiliations as poet with modernity in its more darkly ominous sense.[8]

Further confirmation of Arnold's willingness in 1867 to come to terms with what was darkest but deepest in his poetry was another obviously fateful publishing decision, the publication for the first time in that same collection of another indisputably modern poem of doubt and discouragement, "Dover Beach"—a poem that, despite what seems to us its only too transparent brilliance, had been unfathomably withheld from publication for at least fifteen years after its probable composition in 1851. It was as though Arnold in 1869 recognized himself as having applied his very considerable but highly dissimilar talents to two main lines of development, equally modern but virtually antithetical in character. One was the line to which he was now applying his talents as a writer of prose. On this line he would be essentially historical in orientation, implicitly future-oriented in his focus on the society coming into being, which Arnold would have organized in keeping with the claims of reason and the critical spirit. The other was the line to which he had formerly applied his now apparently waning powers as a poet, a line he had once renounced but would tacitly commit himself to once more, at least to the extent that he would not disown what he had written almost two decades earlier. On this line he had been essentially metaphysical in orientation, implicitly focused on that darkly ominous understanding of the nature of things that a godless modernity was bringing ever more clearly into view.

From the very first, his closest friends and earliest reviewers clearly recognized how fundamental to his poetry that propensity to bleakness was: J. C. Shairp complained of "that great background of fatalism or call it what you will which is behind all his thoughts";[9] Clough, in his review of Arnold's first two volumes in the *North American Review,* chided Arnold as poet for "that dismal cycle of his rehabilitated Hindoo-Greek philosophy."[10] It is a view of Arnold's poetry that has persisted even among his most recent critics—Stefan Collini, for example, who declares it to be almost axiomatic that "the dominant note of Arnold's best poetry is reflection on loss, frustration and sadness"[11]; and Paul Turner, who, in his summary chapter on Arnold in the 1989 Victorian volume of the Oxford History of English Literature, asserts with likeminded assurance that Arnold's best poems "relate, more closely than those of his contemporaries, to the problems of modern man, his bewilderment at living in an apparently pointless universe."[12] Most authoritatively perhaps, Dwight Culler, the preeminent critic of Arnold's poetry, commenting on the line from "Dover Beach" that most famously epitomizes Arnoldian bleakness, "We are here as on a darkling plain," writes: "One would not go far wrong then, if he took from this most famous of Arnold's poems its most famous phrase, and said that this is the central statement Arnold makes about the human condition." Then, returning to that same familiar letter of 1869 by Arnold to his mother, Culler would have us regard the perspective on "the human condition" expressed by "We are here as on a darkling plain" as the most compelling of all grounds for placing Arnold in "the main line of modern development": because "[i]t is only the modern poet who has followed Arnold in his vision of the tragic and alienated condition of man. In this sense, Arnold may be called a modern poet, and it is certain that he would have accepted the designation."[13]

Yet for all the prominence given it in the the commentary, the Arnoldian bleakness, the ache of modernism, has never really been put forward as the leading idea of any of the major full-length critical studies of the poetry, the primary principle of explanation, the interpreter's key. Almost invariably, the major books on Arnold's poetry have instead proposed as their explanatory principle for understanding the poetry something more positive, ameliorative, even uplifting. Over the past thirty or so years, books by our leading commentators have given us Arnold the poet as humanist, Arnold as spokesman for the aesthetic temperament, Arnold the dramatic monologist ironically undermining the dramatized show of despair, but never really Arnold the poet committed to a view of life conditioned by an overriding propensity to bleakness.[14] The closest we have come to invoking bleakness as a primary interpretive principle is in a work by the one important critic of Arnold who has taken the linguistic turn, David Riede, who at least reads the poetry as beset by troubledness, its "overt purposes" continually "subverted by a corrosive subtext" of "doubts about poetry and the poetic tradition."[15] But, for Riede, Arnold's "overt purposes" still retain a conscious and primary bent toward the positive, being impelled by "the need to find an infallible, authoritative language, a voice of God or at the very least a voice that would harmonize with the natural world."[16]

One may wonder even whether Culler, while seemingly assuring us that "[o]ne would not go far wrong" in taking "We are here as on a darkling plain" as "the central statement Arnold makes about the human condition," is not possibly hedging his bet by prefacing that seemingly bold assertion with such a curiously tentative qualifying phrase, perhaps insinuating that, while one would not go far wrong in saying so, one might not be getting it quite right either. After all, that poetic landscape for whose charting Culler's book is so justly celebrated is itself presented, in its unfoldingness, as the expression of something profoundly positive, ameliorative, even uplifting.

What Culler proposes is that we look at those recurrently symbolic features of Arnold's poetry as fundamentally expressive of a three-stage process through which both the individual human life and human history generally move, a process that, for all its vicissitudes, is ultimately optimistic in the direction toward which it points: "The first is a period of joyous innocence when one lives in harmony with nature, the second a period of suffering when one is alone in a hostile world, and the third a period of peace in which suffering subsides into calm and then grows up into a new joy, the joy of active service in the world."[17] Accordingly, for Culler, Arnold's deepest affinities are not with those writers who share his distinctively modern sense of "the tragic and alienated condition of man" but with the essentially progressive historicizers who dominated European thought in the first half of the nineteenth century, the teleologically directed mythic landscape of Arnold's poetry being basically his way of elaborating concepts like those "put forward by Herder, Goethe, Novalis in Germany, by the Saint Simonians in France, and by Carlyle in England,"[18] and, it seems hardly necessary to add, Arnold's way too of latently articulating in the poetry the progressive historicism he will manifestly enunciate in his later prose. Further reinforcing this argument for Arnold as optimistic historicizer, Culler also provides a narrative of Arnold's poetic career according to which, at its proximate midpoint in "Stanzas in Memory of the Author of 'Obermann,'" Arnold turns away from the life-negating precepts of Obermann and toward the world. This gesture Culler would have us regard as nothing less for Arnold than "the most important spiritual act of his entire life," a Carlylean moment of conversion "corresponding to the episode in the Rue St. Thomas de l'Enfer in *Sartor*," one that is at the very least a standing up and saying no that led Arnold to "put behind him the subjectivity and *Sturm and Drang* of his early poetry."[19]

The present study differs from these more positive accounts of Arnold's poetry in that its leading idea, its interpreter's key, is derived from the bleakness—or, more precisely, from the philosophy and psychology that underlie that bleakness. I shall also propose a more unified interpretation of Arnold's poetic career than that which we get in Culler, one that finds the philosophy and psychology underlying the bleakness a persistent and determining element in the poetry extending from "To a Gipsy Child by the Sea-Shore" through "The Scholar-Gipsy"—that is, through the most significant portion of Arnold's poetic career. In addition, in contrast to Culler and many of Arnold's more optimistically oriented critics, I will argue that the gloomy worldview put forward in the poetry differs fundamentally from that which is propounded in the far more hopeful later prose.

Conversely, from my perspective, the early poetry—the poems published in *The Strayed Reveller*—are not, as Culler calls them, mere "subjectivity and *Sturm und Drang*," a kind of intellectual flailing-about, but, far more substantively, the emerging expression of a philosophical point of view that is both original and sophisticated, one that receives its fullest exposition in the culminating work of that first collection, "Resignation," perhaps the most philosophically interesting poem of the Victorian period. Admittedly, after "Resignation" there may well be in "Stanzas in Memory of the Author of 'Obermann,' " as Culler suggests, something of a historicist turning toward the world and away from the life-negating views that Obermann seems to represent, and to that turning toward the world we may also be able to trace the incipient beginnings of the historicism that comes to loom larger in some of the subsequent poetry and eventually becomes the governing premise of the socially oriented prose of the 1860s. But the turn reported in the "Stanzas in Memory of the Author of 'Obermann' " is not for Arnold as decisive as Culler would have us believe, "the most important spiritual act of his entire life," a nullification of what had gone on before as mere "subjectivity and *Sturm und Drang*." Indeed, so powerfully do the psychology and philosophy of bleakness of the earlier poetry infiltrate this initial turn toward history that Arnold's

seemingly most significantly historicist poems—"The Future,"
"Dover Beach," "Stanzas from the Grande Chartreuse," "The
Scholar-Gipsy," and even "Stanzas in Memory of the Author of 'Obermann' " itself—can finally be best understood as further and
more complex variants of his poetics of bleakness.

I shall largely forgo attempting to explore and explain the psychology in which I believe the Arnoldian bleakness to be rooted until
the chapter dealing with the Marguerite poems ("Arnold in Love")
because it is in these implicitly confessional poems that the insecu-
rities and anxieties of the Arnoldian subject—a figure, I believe, not
unconnected to Arnold himself—come most transparently close to
the surface and are most easily read. But to explore and explain
what it is about his poetry that philosophically placed it in "the
main line of modern development," as Arnold apparently intuitively
recognized, I will look at this point to one who is usually regarded
as the most un-Arnoldian of guides,[20] but who, nonetheless, is probably the most perspicacious of students of the coming of modernity:
Friedrich Nietzsche, whose "History of European Nihilism"—
forbidding title—in *The Will to Power* remains the richest and wid-
est ranging account we have of the development of that line. In
analyzing the movement of thought that had culminated in his own
nihilistic project, Nietzsche pointed to a philosophic moment over
half a century earlier—the moment of philosophic pessimism—
crucial enough to the main line of modern development for him to
single it out for commendation as "a preliminary form of nihilism."[21]

But if philosophic pessimism constituted the vanguard of modernity that in the middle of the nineteenth century pushed nihilistic
denial to its farthest limits, it was a vanguard still in the wilderness,
denied entry to the philosopher's promised land by having fallen
short in one particular of nihilism's perfected philosophy of negation. The pessimist, Nietszche explained, had grasped the great and
fundamental truth at the heart of modernism: that purpose, value,
and goodness have no ontological status, that human existence was
therefore metaphysically meaningless. Yet the pessimist still clung
desperately to one last vestige of the old theism, the need for metaphysical explanation. The absolute and unconditioned were for the
pre-Nietzschean pessimist still required, presumably entailed (as
Kant assumed) by the laws of thought. We would retain a metaphysical ground even if, to make philosophic sense of the senselessness
of our existence, the pessimist "had to conceive of this metaphysical
ground as the opposite of the ideal—as evil, blind will."[22] Thus
the pessimist, Nietzsche tells us, turned his back on the only
philosophic option that truly offered the promise of freedom, the

abandonment of metaphysical explanation altogether. At that historically crucial moment, the pessimist "did not renounce the absoluteness of the ideal—he sneaked by."[23]

In his characterization of pessimism, Nietzsche clearly had in mind that first and foremost of his educators, Schopenhauer, founder of philosophic pessimism, its greatest advocate and most systematic expositor. Working, as all post-Kantian idealists did, from Kant's basic distinction between noumena and phenomena, Schopenhauer had elaborated an austerely stark metaphysics in which metaphysical agency and human consciousness are profoundly and fundamentally at variance, now and forever, in an all-inclusive opposition of an antithetically conceived will and idea. In Kant's original formulation, the noumenal—independent of space, time, and the categories—was regarded as inaccessible to the understanding and, therefore, as essentially unknowable. Kant's major successors—Fichte, Hegel, and Schopenhauer—were far less restrained by any Kantian epistemology of limits, so that for them the end of philosophic speculation was to identify and expound the nature and attributes of Kant's noumenally unknowable. Where Fichte and Hegel found in that noumenally unknowable an Absolute whose aims could reasonably be seen as at one with humanly intelligible and humanly desired purposes, Schopenhauer stood in fierce opposition to his major philosophic contemporaries, categorically rejecting any interpretation of the metaphysical Absolute that would enable it to serve as a kind of substitute for the Christian God, an ultimate ground of things teleologically beneficent in its aims and impulses. In its place as the ontological ground of things, Schopenhauer offered a metaphysical will that was "merely a blind incessant impulse," "an endless striving." In the course of its indifferent stirrings, it fostered events in the phenomenal world in such a way that our own hapless existences and futile activities were best understood as simply the unintended consequence of that "blind" will's objectifying energies.

Because the will that so blindly strives can never know satisfaction in either its noumenal being or in its phenomenal manifestations, Schopenhauer sweepingly concludes in a proposition of the most unqualified hopelessness, *"[A]ll life is suffering"* (*WWR*, 1:310). Moreover, that suffering which is an indigenous feature of all life generally is further intensified in humanity, its suffering raised to a higher pitch by the special gifts of a more acute receptivity and an intelligence able to reflect upon its own circumstances. But while the suffering imposed upon the individuated consciousness can finally be neither overcome nor transcended since it ultimately resides in the inherently conflicted nature of things, Schopenhauer does qualify his unrelievedly pessimistic argument in one important way: we can achieve a modicum of relief—if not release—by turning our metaphysical gift upon itself, by using our subjective will to deny the cosmic will. We can effectively deny the will, according to Schopenhauer, by aesthetic self-forgetfulness (a notion that draws upon Kantian disinterestedness), through a sympathetic going-out of the self in compassion, or, the most promising though most chilling remedy of all, by the pleasure-denying self-negation of the ascetic, a method closely akin to what Arnold will call resignation.

Where Nietzsche has Schopenhauer in mind, I would substitute Arnold, who could very well be characterized as the poet of pessimism just as we consider Schopenhauer its philosopher—with all due allowances for the philosophic unsystematicness that the term "poet" implies, an unsystematicness to which Arnold knew himself especially prone. This tendency to pessimism particularly characterizes Arnold's poetry before the turn to history with the 1849 "Stanzas in Memory of the Author of 'Obermann' " and, much of the time, continues to characterize it in a complex and qualified way afterwards. Because that turn is itself not sharply right-angled, not a total conversion, a still-potent element of pessimism impinges upon and shapes the outcome of many of Arnold's seemingly most explicitly historicist poems. To be sure, Arnold's poetry contains a number of significant philosophic strands, with these sometimes in tension with one another, but metaphysical pessimism seems to me the most philosophically innovative, interesting, and important among them, important to Arnold's poetry itself as its philosophically most useful principle of explanation and important, too, to the development by his readers of distinctively modern ways of comprehending the world. I therefore believe that what justifies another study of Arnold's poetry, though so much has already been done, is the perspective I have chosen, the reading of it in terms of its overriding bleakness and, especially, in terms of pessimism in the philosophically specialized nineteenth-century sense of that concept.

Pessimism, most broadly considered, as a governing philosophy of life, certainly predates the publication of *Die Welt als Wille und Vorstellung* in Leipzig in 1819.[24] No words of Schopenhauer or Arnold sound the depths of an irredeemably pessimistic hopelessness more profoundly than the conclusion of the chorus in Sophocles' *Oedipus at Colonus*: "Not to be born is best / When all is reckoned in";[25] nor than Job's curse, "Let the day perish wherein I was born,

and the night *in which* it was said, 'There is a man child conceived' " (Job 3:3)[26]—words that so deeply resonate with the pain
of human existence that Hardy's Jude will repeat them on the day
of his death as a kind of summary judgment on his own profoundly
unhappy life just ending.[27] A similarly pessimistic sense of life as
most fundamentally defined by its immense preponderance of
pain—intense, enduring, catastrophic—over pleasure—empty,
fleeting, inconsequential—is, of course, reiterated by any number
of subsequent writers: Euripides, Lucretius, and Epictetus, for example, among the ancients, and Montaigne, Racine, and Pascal
among their modern successors. Nor have the depths of pessimism
ever been sounded more searchingly or to more dismaying conclusions than in the world-weary Hamlet's near-suicidal meditation on
the "unweeded garden" of this world,[28] nor in Lear's claim that our
cries upon coming to "this great stage of fools" are a premonition
of the unbearable suffering that awaits us,[29] nor again in Lear's out-
raged rebuke of the heavens that would incomprehensibly permit
the death of the never-to-come-again Cordelia when "a dog, a horse,
a rat have life."[30] It was, almost certainly, by some such body of
texts as these that Arnold initially had his own disposition shaped
to view the world as, most centrally, a site of suffering,

Still, by the beginning of the nineteenth century, for all its many
evidences of progress, the grounds for this pessimistic sense of life
as overwhelming tribulation had, if anything, expanded, with the ordinary course of human suffering now exacerbated by a growing
feeling of cosmic perplexity and estrangement. Science, which had
promised so much—and in fairness, had made and would make
good on much of that promise—had in the wake of its triumphant
progress through recent history shaken and even brought down verities that an earlier age had assumed to be eternal, particularly
those that, over the preceding eighteen Christian centuries, had
come closest to making the world a home—or at least the world as
it might be construed if we were allowed to take into account the
ameliorative possibilities of a postmortal existence. In place of
these verities science had posited verities of its own, drawn from its
findings about a nature that, to be sure, lent itself to human mastery
in ways that once had been unthinkable, but a nature that was also
inescapably represented as matter in motion, a material and mechanistic order from which the feeling human soul or even the feeling
human psyche found itself estranged and alienated.

One need not rehearse again in detail these familiar developments. But for those who would come of age in Arnold's own
generation, probably no statement of a pessimism resting on

fundamentally cosmic grounds conveyed contemporary anxieties
more compellingly than the words of "The Everlasting No" that had
"pealed authoritatively through all the recesses of" the "Being" of
Thomas Carlyle's Diogenes Teufelsdröckh on the Rue St.-Thomas
de l'Enfer: "To me the universe was all void of Life, of Purpose, of
Volition, even of Hostility: it was one huge, dead, immeasurable
Steam-engine, rolling on its dead indifference, to grind me limb from
limb. O the vast gloomy, solitary Golgotha, and Mill of Death."[31] The
"No" that would seemingly speak everlastingly to Teufelsdröckh
emanated from a natural order given us by science, mechanistic
and material, in no way like ourselves. The crowning illustration of
our apparent scientific mastery over nature, the steam engine, was
turned bitterly by Carlyle into a symbol of a mindlessly indifferent
cosmic oppressiveness destined to thwart human enterprise at
every turn. In response to that "No" that had seemed to peal so authoritatively, Carlyle had famously told how the "whole ME" of Teufelsdröckh had stood up in indignation and defiance, declaring its
godlikeness and freedom.[32] That momentous day on the Rue Saint-
Thomas de l'Enfer was, of course, not to be a day of pessimistic succumbing to the mechanistic operations of the order of things but
rather a "Baphometic Fire-baptism,"[33] a moment of Fichtean conversion in which the ego would begin its life's work of transforming
matter into spirit.

Another work that seems typical of the mid-nineteenth century's
cosmic debate—Alfred Lord Tennyson's "The Two Voices"—also
lacks any final pessimistic succumbing of Tennyson's speaker to his
own articulation of "The Everlasting No" by the analogous "still
small voice" (4) that poses what has been traditionally the pessimist's ultimate query: "Thou art so full of misery / Were it not better
not to be?" (2–3).[34] Once again the argument that it would be better
to choose death over life appears to derive mainly from the findings
of a science that presents us with a natural order utterly indifferent
to human needs or desires, an infinite universe that in both its unending expansiveness and biological profusion continually declares
our human inconsequence in the greater scheme of things. Here,
too, our author eventually stands fast against his naturalistically
predicated despair, resisting what he had at first ominously termed
"The Thoughts of a Suicide"—Tennyson's title in an early manuscript version of the poem—by invoking, though almost belatedly,
an alternative voice whose glimmering intuitions of God and immortality are deemed sufficient reason not to give in to that seemingly

suicidal logic propounded at the poem's beginning from the evidences of science.

But the philosophic pessimism proposed by Schopenhauer presents us with a ground of our suffering that in both its omnipresence and inescapability goes far beyond anything to be found even in the most despairingly pessimistic passages of Carlyle or Tennyson. A philosopher of the greatest importance, influence, and originality, Schopenhauer is, after Hegel and Nietzsche, still considered by many historians of Continental philosophy the leading European philosopher of the nineteenth century; by the latter part of the century, he even vied with Hegel for intellectual preeminence among both the philosophers and the poets, novelists, and dramatists of the period. Moreover, in terms of the originality of his philosophic vision, Schopenhauer seems virtually sui generis among the significant philosophers of the nineteenth century. His sharp differences with and deviations from his contemporaries more than justified Joseph Oxenford's title for his *Westminster Review* essay in 1853, which introduced Schopenhauer to the British public: "Iconoclasm in German Philosophy."

The source of Schopenhauer's importance, influence, and, above all, his originality—his distinctive difference from all other nineteenth-century philosophers—lay, as Nietzsche understood, in Schopenhauer's willingness to preserve the familiar dualistic paradigm of Western metaphysics. He retained an ultimate ground, the thing-in-itself, an unconditioned that was the ground of all that was conditioned, that world of sensible appearances that included both nature and ourselves. But while providing his readers with the model to which they were accustomed, his version of the philosophically familiar was not as the traditional theistic paradigm would have it, nor even closer to home in the nineteenth century, as Kantian and post-Kantian variants on that paradigm would have it—an Absolute directing the course of things to an essentially beneficent outcome. For the conventional arrangement in which a virtually unknowable metaphysical agency directed this life to humanly desirable ends, Schopenhauer substituted an Absolute that was in itself evil and the ground of an evil that was the dominant experiential fact of this life. The unendurable unhappiness that "The Everlasting No" and the despairing voice of "The Two Voices" declared an inextricable part of our condition, Schopenhauer insisted, was not the consequence of our alienation from or homelessness in nature, our sensed inferiority to the larger and truer natural order; for, according to the philosophic pessimist, the human order and the order of nature are, in the end, both alike in their common victimage.

They are to be regarded as joint participants in a single phenomenal existence, each deriving its particular suffering from the operations of an Absolute, metaphysically distinct, that blindly wills these sufferings. Nor can there be any metaphysical escape route from the common plight, evasion of cosmic danger by a flight to an internalized immanence, as there is for Carlyle, who has the "Godlike me" of his Teufelsdröckh stand up in triumphant defiance of that principle of universal negation that he had previously regarded as irresistible. Even more implausible to Schopenhauer or any adherent of his philosophy would be any flight to transcendence, as in Tennyson, whose almost-despairing speaker in "The Two Voices" is saved from the suicide that seems to follow from the logic so impeccably set forth by the "still small voice" of the poem's earlier sections by the just-in-the-nick-of-time intervention of that alternative whispered voice that tells us that even in nature there is more than nature, that a personal and caring God hovers in the distance. For the true philosophic pessimist, from the seeming facts of a ubiquitousness of suffering that must lead us to regard evil as the ground of life, there can be no appeal. It is a position that philosophically is the end of the line: all that there is or can be.

It should be understood that I believe that to label Arnold a philosophic pessimist, as I have done, is to commend him. To link him with the great philosopher Schopenhauer is to credit Arnold as poet with an intellectual courage, audacity, originality, and philosophic acumen akin to (if plainly not of) the magnitude of his philosophic counterpart. It is, as Nietzsche understood, to place Arnold in the main line of modern development. Of course, the case for Arnold as pessimist, in the strict philosophic sense of the term, a kindred spirit of Schopenhauer's and in some way leader with him in that intellectual vanguard identified by Nietzsche, obviously cannot be made on the basis of the influence of the earlier writer on the later writer. Schopenhauer's great European vogue was yet to come; he was virtually unknown in England until the appearance in 1853 of Oxenford's unsigned article in the *Westminster Review*, and by that time Arnold's poetry of pessimism was essentially completed. When Schopenhauer did at last become an important presence in European intellectual life, Arnold would take note of the philosopher only to reject him. In his preface to *Last Essays on Church and Religion*, Arnold declared the religion of the "joy of self-renouncement" offered by Jesus superior to the Schopenhauerian pessimism currently "in fashion" (*CPW*, 8:160). But it was the Arnold of 1877 who made that declaration, the writer of the late prose, with the poetry we regard most highly long ago over and done with, the Arnold who by this time had found in the metaphysical workings of things "a stream of tendency that makes for righteousness" and not "a something that infects the world."[35]

Only Arnold the poet, then, can be termed a philosophic pessimist; and the case for likeness between the poet and the philosopher must rest finally not on any claims of direct influence but on the demonstration of a shared weltanschauung, the common assumptions, beliefs, interests, and anxieties of two writers, approximate contemporaries, drawn by a certain affinity of temperament to interpret human life and the world in much the same way at a critical juncture in the main line of modern development. This shared weltanschauung, moreover, not only links the two but also sets them apart from virtually all their major contemporaries: Tennyson and Browning, among the poets, and Fichte, Hegel, and Marx, among the philosophers, who shared the historicist faith that human existence shall be improved by an inherently necessary progress over time. But for Schopenhauer and Arnold (at least in his poetry of pessimism), the plight of humanity is neither to be explained by historical conditions nor alleviated by any historically determined improvement in our material or spiritual circumstances. Rather, we are as we unhappily are, both writers believed, because the universally unalterable metaphysical conditions of human existence have so mandated it.

It is by emphasizing metaphysical agency, and especially metaphysical agency understood as will, rather than the phenomenal consequences of the workings of that agency, that philosophic pessimism most strikingly differentiates itself from other formulations that would describe the world pessimistically. Among the attributes Carlyle is careful to tell us that are absent from that "immeasurable Steam-engine" Teufelsdröckh felt "rolling on, in its dead indifference, to grind me limb from limb"—Carlyle's principal image of cosmic oppressiveness mechanistically conceived—is "volition." Indeed volition is to be found only on the side of the angels in that Fichtean drama played out in *Sartor Resartus*. Our sense of will is for Carlyle, as it was for Fichte, the grounds of our rejoinder to the steam engine that threatens us, the primary manifestation of a freedom metaphysically constituted, the basis of a saving doctrine of striving, converted by Carlyle into a Gospel of Work, the means by which we may ultimately bend nature to our superior spiritual purposes and thereby create for ourselves a world congenial to the goods and goals of human consciousness.[36] For Schopenhauer too, as Oxenford explained to his readers in 1853, the answer to the question, "What then is the thing in itself?" was "The Will," this answer Schopenhauer declaring to be " 'the great discovery of my life.' "[37] But Schopenhauer, as Oxenford went on to explain, was no Fichtean apostle of freedom for the individual but an "absolute necessitarean," whose metaphysical will in its manifestations in the world was not liberating but binding.[38] The metaphysical will as Schopenhauer conceived of it, "the great discovery of my life," was in every way antithetical to the will as it was represented by Fichte and Carlyle, antithetical in fact to the very goods and goals of human consciousness that Fichte and Carlyle saw the noumenal will aligned with—indeed, saw as the prime agent in bringing those goods and goals to realization.

In her recent study of Victorian poetry, Isobel Armstrong finds in Tennyson's *Maud* "a Schopenhauerian universe of intentional violence and mutually antagonistic wills," a universe that comes particularly into prominence in that poem's "struggle-for-existence" passage, in which the narrator tells how "[t]he mayfly is torn by the swallow, the sparrow spear'd by the shrike, / And the whole little wood where I sit is a world of plunder and strife" (part 1, 4.124–25).[39] Certainly, the universe that the narrator of *Maud* gives us is a "Schopenhauerian universe of intentional violence" (though I do not believe that Armstrong is suggesting any direct influence by Schopenhauer on Tennyson either), the way in which nature can be expected to manifest itself as an objectification of the noumenal will. Yet in the passage from Tennyson we are never really given to understand that there is anything more than nature at work here. The one thing that would give the passage in question a truly Schopenhauerian character is never really implied: that the struggle for existence described by the narrator of *Maud* might express some ultimate metaphysical ground whose own nature bears some analogous relation to that struggle. (It has, of course, long been held by Tennysonians that the "struggle-for-existence" moments in Tennyson, most of which predate Darwin, are educible from sections of Lyell augmented by Chambers, that is, from scientific and quasi-scientific writings that deal only with nature.)

In Arnold, too, nature at times takes on a "struggle-for-existence" character: "Nature is cruel, man is sick of blood" ("In Harmony with Nature," 7). Yet what makes Arnold a more Schopenhauerian poet than Tennyson, even in passages like that from *Maud*, is a disposition to look beyond nature to a determining metaphysical agency for the ultimate explanation of the common suffering that all phenomenal existence, nature as well as man, must endure. Anthropomorphized, that agency is the malevolent God who "bade" our "severance" " in "To Marguerite-Continued";[40] or, more abstractly, it is the "unknown Powers" to whose chartering we owe our aimless and disconnected voyage in "Human Life"; or it is, most especially, "[t]he something that infects the world" of "Resignation," the determining real experienced as an alien presence whose endlessly proliferating energies are wholly inimical to our human well-being. Against this seemingly irresistibly destructive force, the only remedy Arnold can imagine is the one he finds in a nature like ourselves, in that it too must endure the general plight engendered by our common metaphysical antagonist, but a nature from which we could learn that the appropriate response to our common circumstances is to seek "to bear rather then rejoice" (270).

Among the writers of Arnold's time who most clearly convey the pessimistic spirit in their writings, probably none can help us better to understand why Arnold probably comes closer to nineteenth-century philosophic pessimism than any of his contemporaries than the great poet Giacomo Leopardi, of whom Schopenhauer himself would say that "no one has treated this subject"—"the misery of our existence"—"so thoroughly and exhaustively as Leopardi in our own day" (*WWR*, 2:588). Arnold, too, would speak admiringly of the poetry of Leopardi in an 1881 essay on Byron, granting Leopardi "the firm touch of the artist" (*CPW*, 9:229) and claiming "the full superiority of Leopardi over Byron in philosophic thought" (*CPW*, 9:230). However, Arnold then qualifies that praise (though making clear that these are plainly comparisons of poets at the highest levels) by ranking Leopardi in "poetic value" (*CPW*, 9:231) finally below not only Byron but also Wordsworth, because Wordsworth's "criticism of life" is "healthful and true, whereas Leopardi's pessimism is not" (*CPW*, 9:231). It should be remembered in this case, too, as with Arnold's judgment of Schopenhauer, that when Arnold came to make that judgment in 1881 he had found in the workings of things "a stream of tendency that makes for righteousness" and not "[a] something that infects the world." As spokesman for pessimism as a philosophy of life, Leopardi conveys the unremittingness and severity of human suffering with an eloquence and power that go beyond what we find in Schopenhauer or Arnold—who, even in the context of his bleakest poems, might justifiably have said of Leopardi what his poet-speaker says of the gipsy child: "Glooms that go deep as thine I have not known" ("To a Gipsy Child by the Sea-Shore," 17).

Still, the major sources of that suffering, however unremitting and severe, of which Leopardi writes, are for the most part traditional ones: the brevity of life and especially youth, a knowledge that is sorrow exacerbated for Leopardi by recognition of the cruel conditions under which most men labor and by the further expectation of the pains and pangs of the old age that awaits us. To this catalogue of the general sorrows of humanity should be added those particular details of Leopardi's own unhappy life that so often enter into his poetry. Perhaps the only respect in which Leopardi seems genuinely modern in his pessimism is in his analysis of our cosmic circumstances, his depiction of human life as solitary and futile, carrying on its wearisome and pointless endeavors in the vastness of an alien and indifferent universe in no way like ourselves. Even this, though, is not sufficient to justify our speaking of Leopardi as a full-blown pessimist, according to Gian Piero Baricelli, who concludes in his own philosophically informed study of Leopardi, "Pessimism becomes, therefore, a fallacious term if it is used to label Leopardi's thought in any absolute sense."[41]

Why Leopardi would be thought of as less than a pessimist "in any absolute sense" is probably best illustrated by his two greatest poems, "Night-Song of a Wandering Shepherd of Asia" and "The Broom," poems soul-wrenchingly bleak in their insistence on the irremediable painfulness of human existence, and yet poems in which Leopardi exercises an unmistakable skeptical restraint in matters of metaphysics, being careful not to look beyond nature for the ultimate grounds of life's painfulness.[42] In the first of these, Leopardi's shepherd, now "A white-haired, weak old man—/ Barefoot and half naked / With a ponderous load upon his back" (174), hardly needs more than the horrendous details of his now virtually completed life of incessant labor and excruciating pain—"Without a stop or rest / His body cut and bleeding" (174)—to justify that Job-like condemnation of life with which the poem closes: "The day of birth for creatures born is dark" (177). With only death left to complete this life—and the shepherd austerely resists drawing any Christian consolation for present sufferings from a death that, when imagined, only adds to life's terrors, "The abyss, horrid, immense, / Wherein, in falling he unremembers all" (174)—Leopardi's shepherd, in the most wonderful of pathetic fallacies, turns to the moon for some explanation of the meaning of a life of such evident misery and futility. With a kind of leap of faith intimating that the moon does "fathom" (176) life's purpose, the shepherd apparently gleans from the moon an explanation for human suffering, including his own, couched in terms very much like those Enlightenment rationalizations of evil that would justify our individual suffering on the grounds that it serves some other and perhaps greater good. The reductio ad absurdum of such a rationalization was, of course, the notorious assertion of Soames Jenyns that, given our place on the chain of being, human suffering might be justified by our serving the interests of creatures above us on the chain: "intermediate beings who have power to deceive, torment, and destroy, for the ends only of their pleasure and utility," an argument famously ridiculed by Dr. Johnson for its inherent inhumaneness: "Many a merry bout have these frolick beings at the vicissitudes of an ague, and good sport it is to see a man tumble with an epilepsy and revive and tumble again, and all this he knows not why."[43] On similar grounds— though far more poignantly—Leopardi's shepherd, too, resists acquiescing in any rationalization that would justify individual suffering by the benefits that would thereby accrue to others, rejecting such a view because of its patent unjustness from the vantage point of the sufferer:

> And I? I surely know and sense this much:
> If these eternal rounds
> And my own fragile being
> May satisfy the whims
> Of others, for me this life is only woe.
>
> (176)

"The Broom" also takes place in a philosophic atmosphere not so very different from that in which Enlightenment quarrels over the origins of evil were conducted, with Leopardi using the eruption at Pompeii much as Voltaire had used the Lisbon earthquake, to dispel the illusions of a misguided cosmic optimism. In such a setting, nature is to be understood as the indifferent but implacable antagonist of humanity, having "no more heart / Or care for human seed than for the ants" (211). Though man in his insufferable vanity may "dream / Of how the authors of this universe / Came down expressly for your sake to walk / Among you" (210), Leopardi's sobering truth is that of cosmic unconcern for our human needs and desires. To the infinite heavens "not merely man / And earth but the huge mass and infinite host / Of closer stars and our bright sun itself / Remain unknown" (210). Even in the one abstractly philosophic work by Leopardi that might seem to verge most closely on the pessimism of Schopenhauer, "Dialogue of Nature and an Icelander," an imagined exchange where nature acknowledges itself no more than "a perpetual circuit of creation and destruction, bound together in such a way that each promotes the other and the conservation of the world" (118), its mind always "on matters other than man's happiness and unhappiness" (117), this process is described and defended by nature in essentially eighteenth-century terms. The workings of the world are to be understood as something of a *concordia discors* in which accidental evil yields, according to Leopardi's spokesman for nature, a modest universal good. Moreover, it is important to remember that the speaker to whom Leopardi imputes sentiments that are obviously his own is still only nature and nothing beyond nature.

It is in going beyond nature for his principle of explanation that Arnold, more than any of his contemporaries, may be regarded as a pessimist in the "absolute sense." More than that, in his way of approaching the world, in looking beyond nature for the ground of his metaphysics, he may—for all his unsystematicness—justifiably be spoken of as a genuine philosophic poet in much the same way as Coleridge would have us regard Wordsworth.[44] That organizing metaphysical principle we find in Schopenhauer—noumenon and phenomenon antithetically conceived—is, I would argue, similarly expressed, mutatis mutandis, by the deep structures of Arnold's own poetry. Arnold, too, while conceding that our human goods and values are without ontological sanction or significance, is unwilling to concede all, to make the last and hardest act of renunciation in the Nietzschean sense and do away with the principle of metaphysical explanation altogether. Even if Arnold sometimes skeptically stipulates that the ultimately real, like that "sea of life" that expresses it, is finally "incognisable" ("Human Life," 8), he more often and more strikingly maintains that we can infer from its operations attributes that render it inherently inimical in every way to our human desires, interests, and values. Poem after poem speaks to us not only of the fundamental bleakness of our existence, its utter senselessness by any humanly meaningful measure, but beyond that of a persisting hunger for presence, a still-lingering prejudice for metaphysical explanation, the need to believe in an absolute and unconditioned, even if such an absolute and unconditioned must be construed as evil and blind, a "something that infects the world" ("Resignation," 278), an ultimate cause whose effect, needless to add, for Arnold, as for Schopenhauer, is that *all life is suffering.*

Like Schopenhauer, Arnold also shows us that he is working within the major philosophic tradition of his time by maintaining the basic idealist distinction between the noumenal and the phenomenal, one rendered with virtually Kantian exactness in the complaint by Empedocles that "mind" and "thought" are ultimately inhibiting barriers to metaphysical knowledge, that they

> keep us prisoners of our consciousness,
> And never let us clasp and feel the All
> But through their forms, and modes, and stifling veils.
>
> (*Empedocles on Etna*, 2.352–54)

More often though, the relationship between the metaphysically real and the life of consciousness oppositionally conceived is rendered figuratively, its best-known representation that familiar allegory of the "sea of life" on or in which the individuated human consciousness is either embarked or enisled. That is, for the world as idea, Arnold offers the island or vessel, the bounded circumference within which the individuated and particularized, the rationally intelligible and the humanly desiring, are to be found. But always surrounding these vessels and islands is the ontologically more fundamental "sea of life," that always enveloping and often determining region of otherness in which the individuated consciousness as vessel or island must carry on its existence, forever at the mercy of the elements, winds and waves and currents that direct and impel, constrain and estrange, oppose and sometimes even overwhelm.

In general, Arnold figuratively represents noumenal agency by that which is elemental, diffuse, and undifferentiated, and often implicitly volitional, some pulse or force or energy or, most commonly, some pure movement or flow, inexorable and all-compelling. Some representations of noumenal agency are explicitly destructive of the life of consciousness: for example, the fiery and pulsating volcanic core of Etna into which Empedocles leaps and the tempestuous "trade winds" that issue "from eternity" (58) in "A Summer Night," through whose destructive power the Madman finally founders. Even when less overtly malevolent, metaphysical reality is often depicted as alien and antithetical to the life of consciousness, indifferent to the interests and needs of the individuated human existence that lives within or upon it. Most familiarly, there is "the sea of life," which typically, as in "Human Life," drives us away from "[t]he joys," "[t]he friends," "[t]he homes," for which we yearn but which "were not destined to be ours" ("Human Life," 30). And there is that great noumenal stream of "Mycerinus," a compelling cosmic "Force" that, sublimely indifferent, "[s]weeps earth, and heaven, and men and gods along" (39), a "Force" whose tremendous scope and power Arnold will liken to "the broad volume of the insurgent Nile" (40).

But in one fundamental respect the relationship of will and idea in Arnold differs from what we find in Schopenhauer. For Schopenhauer, the metaphysical will is always humanity's great cosmic antagonist; freedom from it comes only by denial or death. In most cases for Arnold, too, the metaphysical forces that shape our world and individual lives—the "Powers," for example, that ordain "endless strife" (5) for us in "Destiny" or the "God" that our "severance ruled" (22) in "To Marguerite—Continued"—are perceived as implacably hostile. But in a few clearly important poems, Arnold sounds a note of ontological longing, a wish to overcome metaphysical estrangement and homelessness and become one with the ultimately real. In "Resignation," it is the "general life," that minimal existence of mere birth and subsistence, that the poet "craves"; in "The Buried Life," it is the "buried life" for which we feel an "unspeakable desire" (47), that normally "unregarded river" whose sole use for us is apparently to remind us of our origins and ends in the implicitly undifferentiated; and even Empedocles desires to overcome estrangement from the real by leaping into the fiery core of Etna. But even in these instances, the noumenal will is never truly humanized, never claimed to be consonant with our customary values, with justice or virtue or pleasure. When Arnold intimates that the noumenal will might be a good that we would wish to embrace and be reconciled with, that valuation derives wholly from his ontological claims for it. Excluded from the metaphysically real by the barriers of consciousness, confined to a secondary and derivative realm of phenomenal appearances, the human individual must naturally at times long for that reality of which he has been deprived. But overcoming such feelings of homelessness may require the sacrifice of the life of consciousness itself to a general life, which even in its most seemingly benign and desirable representations remains an undifferentiated and incessant flow, blind motion with no humanly intelligible purpose or direction or goal, the implicit enemy of consciousness and human existence as we know it.

In addition to a common weltanschauung that best reflects itself in the deep structures of Arnold's poetry, Arnold and Schopenhauer also share a cluster of affinities, interests, and attitudes understandably associated with such a weltanschauung. For example, both are attracted to Stoicism yet find it, in the end, deficient as a solution to our metaphysically engendered predicament. Epictetus "props in these bad days my mind" ("To a Friend," 1), Arnold tells us, and Schopenhauer praises Stoicism at large as "a very valuable and estimable attempt to use reason, man's great prerogative, for an important and salutary end, namely to raise him by a precept above the sufferings and pain to which all life is exposed" (*WWR*,

1:90). Yet while Empedocles advises Pausanias that if he were to adopt the Stoic remedy and but "moderate desire" (*Empedocles on Etna*, 2.2.386), he might achieve at least a "moderate bliss" (*Empedocles on Etna*, 2.2.391), Empedocles himself wholly ignores this advice in his own search for relief and ultimately release from the metaphysically induced sufferings of "[t]his uncongenial place, this human life" (*Empedocles on Etna*, 2.366). Schopenhauer, too, finds himself compelled to dismiss "Stoic morality" as "only a particular species of *eudaemonism*" (*WWR*, 2:159), merely another of antiquity's illusory "guides to a blissful life" (*WWR*, 2:150). For Schopenhauer, Christian asceticism is even superior to Stoicism, which "teaches only calm endurance and unruffled expectation of unalterably necessary evils" (*WWR*, 2:434), while "Christianity teaches renunciation, the giving up of willing" (*WWR*, 2:434). But the value of Christianity, he adds, "is wholly on its ethical side"(*WWR*, 1:361), carefully stipulating that it errs when it attempts to "encroach on the sphere of metaphysics proper" (*WWR*, 2:167). So, too, while Arnold is sympathetically drawn to the severe asceticism of the Carthusians, he knows the Catholic faith in which they anachronistically persist is nothing more than a "dead time's exploded dream" ("Stanzas from the Grande Chartreuse," 98).

Still more striking is a shared admiration for what in the middle of the nineteenth century must have seemed the most esoteric of religious philosophies—"the Oriental wisdom, God grant it were mine" (*Letters*, 1:87), as Arnold, discussing the Bhagavad Gita, says in a letter to Clough, while Schopenhauer, more than any other nineteenth-century writer, helped disseminate Eastern thought to European readers. Again, it is ethical practice, the renunciatory call for "abandoning the fruits of action" (*Letters*, 1:89) in Arnold's phrase, rather than metaphysical explanation that Arnold and Schopenhauer commend. Indeed, the latter rejects out of hand such a metaphysically grounded hereafter as "the reabsorption in *Brahman* or the *Nirvana* of the Buddhists" as "myths and meaningless words" (*WWR*, 1:411).

If metaphysical conditions dictate that suffering is the law of life, we would still seem to have at our disposal a far more potent remedy than resignation or any other ascetic practice to end that suffering, one both Arnold and Schopenhauer seem at least willing to contemplate. The philosophic pessimist, of necessity, must (for obvious reasons) acknowledge the possibility of suicide as a means—perhaps the only incontrovertibly efficacious means—of release from a pain surely destined to last as long as life does. Yet recommending suicide as a solution to the intolerableness of human exis-

tence is a course from which, understandably, even the most
committed pessimist must finally shrink. Schopenhauer does begin
his essay on suicide by denouncing all moral objections to or legal
prohibitions against suicide. Still, he ultimately condemns it as "a
senseless and foolish act" (*WWR*, 1:411), unpardonable not on
moral but on metaphysical grounds, murkily contending that suicide does not release us from the hold that the will to live has over
us but actually strengthens that hold.

In *Empedocles on Etna*, Arnold comes even closer to endorsing
suicide as a philosophically sanctioned solution to our existential
calamity, our confinement in "[t]his uncongenial place, this human
life" (2.366). But he too hedges, shying away from giving the choice
of Empedocles his unqualified approval, even if that approval could
be rationalized as a purely poetic assent, hence affirming nothing.
Instead, Arnold chooses to neutralize the thrust of the play's apparently dominant argument and the authority of its title character's
fearless example by presenting us with an obvious and attractive
counterargument and counterexample. Set against Empedocles and
his claims for suicide—not merely as ease from pain but as a metaphysical good—is the offsetting figure of Callicles, to whom Arnold
grants the last word in *Empedocles on Etna*, the lyrically voiced
possibility that the metaphysically determined pains of human existence may be mitigated by the mysterious powers of the mythopoeic
imagination—though it must be added that the exercise of these
powers by Callicles really changes nothing.[45]

One predictable corollary of the pessimist's metaphysics of the will
is a deep mistrust of and hostility toward the most obvious of experiential analogues to that uncontrollable cosmic impulse, the sexual
drive. For Schopenhauer the connection between the metaphysical
agency that wills our suffering and the sexual drive is quite explicit.
"The genitals," he writes, "are the real *focus* of the will" (*WWR*,
1:330), so that one logical remedy to our metaphysical bondage
quite naturally turns out to be "[v]oluntary and complete chastity"
(*WWR*, 1:380). If Arnold never quite so explicitly connects metaphysical agency and sexuality, still only a deep mistrust of the sexual impulse can explain the curiously de-eroticized and ascetic
attitudes and outcomes of so much that passes for love poetry in
Arnold: for example, the preference of the narrator for the low-
pulsed, innately virginal Iseult of Brittany over her romantically
passionate rival, Iseult of Ireland; and, most strikingly, the astonishing scenario that concludes the "Marguerite" poems, the speaker's prophecy that he and the lover with whom he has just broken

are to be reunited in a life hereafter, not as lovers but in the chaste relationship of brother and sister that Arnold would have us believe their inherently asexual and thus real natures truly require.

By the same kind of psychosexual logic, the mistrust Arnold and Schopenhauer direct at the sexual impulse carries over into a corresponding mistrust toward women. Schopenhauer's misogynistic contempt for women—"the Number Two of the human race"[46] as he calls them—is blatant and notorious. Arnold is never as reproachfully or contemptuously misogynistic as this; but he does clearly provide us with an extensive bill of particulars against women as lovers, both as companions and as sexual partners. Beginning with "The New Sirens," moving forward to the Margaret who leaves husband and children in "The Forsaken Merman," then to Marguerite herself, and finally to the faithless Iseult of Brittany, Arnold is, most often, censorious in his judgments of the women he describes. More often than not, he finds them frivolous and worldly, mocking, inconstant, and, in the most categorical and apparently severest denunciation of all, unrestrainedly passionate, "things that live and move / Mined by the fever in the soul" ("A Farewell," 21–22).

While the pessimist's program of sexual restraint (whose natural corollary is the avoidance of women) can be seen to rest ultimately on philosophic grounds, the post-Freudian reader, conditioned to a hermeneutic of suspicion, suspects that the sources of Schopenhauer's stated hostility toward sex and women were already in place long before its philosophic theorization began. Our disposition is to read pessimism of the kind we find in Schopenhauer as a projection of primal sexual anxieties, an attempt to neutralize the fears engendered by these potentially disruptive inner forces by externalizing them, translating an apparently irresistible but anxiety-producing sexual desire into the metaphysical first principle of a blind and overpoweringly turbulent cosmic will against which consciousness, by the very nature of things, can offer no truly effective resistance.

Freud himself, in his most ambitious excursion into metaphysics, *Beyond the Pleasure Principle*, had acknowledged Schopenhauer as something of a precursor, freely admitting that in developing his own theory of life and death instincts he had "unwittingly steered our course into the harbour of Schopenhauer's philosophy."[47] But even when we turn to the more customary Freudian mapping-out of the mind in terms of the categories of the conscious and the unconscious or the later refinement of that design as the ego and the id, the congruence of Freudian theory (with its unalterably tragic disposition) and pessimism (with its similarly tragic dualism of the world as will and idea) is apparent. Indeed, almost from the beginnings of psychoanalysis, the notion of Schopenhauer as a philosophic precursor—perhaps *the* philosophic precursor—to Freud, the philosopher who, more than any other, had been there before him, has been a staple of commentary on both writers. Evidence showing similarities and even biographical anecdotes implying influence or at least demonstrating likeness abounds, the most notable undoubtedly being Otto Rank's pointing out to Freud a passage in Schopenhauer that plainly anticipated Freud's claim to have been the first to recognize repression as the "bedrock of mental functioning" and thus "the cornerstone, the foundation, on which the house of psychoanalysis rests."[48] In one important respect, psychoanalysis may very well be looked upon, from the perspective of its historical evolution, as a kind of domestication of the metaphysics of the will, making manifest what had been latent in nineteenth-century pessimism, a philosophy in which Schopenhauer could in all innocence speak of "the genitals" as "the real *focus* of the will." What Freud, in effect, did was to bring home from the mystified fastness of metaphysical thinking to its true lodging place in the psychic and biological life those drives and impulses that we now recognize comprise the basis for a fundamentally sexual explanation of human experience and behavior.

Pessimism, in its philosophic sense, will be a guiding concept as we take up the poems of Arnold, but anxiety, in the psychoanalytic sense, will be a secondary but plainly crucial consideration. The two are obviously not mutually exclusive: philosophic pessimism does not simply govern one poem and psychological anxiety another; rather they are simultaneously present, inextricably interwoven correlatives, with pessimism most of the time supplying the manifest principle of interpretation and anxiety, the latent, the key to understanding what is hidden, veiled, often repressed, yet perhaps ultimately determining. For reasons of heuristic convenience, in the first part of this study I shall deal almost exclusively with the manifestly philosophic content of the early poems, beginning with the tentatively formulated metaphysics of "To a Gipsy Child by the Sea-Shore" and concluding with the fully elaborated pessimism of "Resignation" and *Empedocles on Etna*. Only with the appearance of Marguerite, when unhappiness in love leads Arnold to foreground what seem to be his deepest psychosexual anxieties and desires, shall I provide detailed psychoanalytic analysis. But even the Marguerite poems are deeply philosophic and, as philosophy, fundamentally pessimistic, thus conveying the rootedness of Arnoldian metaphysics in sexuality most transparently. Finally, I shall examine some poems in which an optimistic historicism (which clearly carries over into the later prose) seemingly emerges as Arnold's governing premise—"Stanzas in Memory of the Author of 'Obermann,'" "Dover Beach," "The Scholar-Gipsy," "Stanzas from the Grande Chartreuse," and "The Future." Here too, though, residues of an earlier pessimism and its psychosexual correlatives still remain powerfully intrusive, impeding progress, undoing hope, and causing these poems of an ostensibly forward-looking historicism to be in the end virtually indistinguishable in their spirit of negation from Arnold's earlier and more plainly manifest poetry of pessimism.

Metaphysical pessimism—not as system but as shaping weltanschauung—thus remains a relative constant in this study of Arnold's poetry. Admittedly, any encompassing label runs the risk of obscuring the intellectual multifacetedness of a poet like Arnold; but such labels do have a hermeneutic usefulness. Compared to the classificatory labels suggested by other critics—the aestheticism proposed by Madden, for example, or, far more influentially, the optimistic historicism argued for by Culler—the claim for philosophic pessimism as a general way of characterizing Arnold's poetry, I would remind us again, has one decisive advantage over these other broadly explanatory concepts: within the current of ideas made available to Arnold by his age, it is closest in spirit to what is self-evidently most central to the poetry, the malaise that suffuses it, the tragic sense that resides at its very core. To understand how deeply informing and even determining a presence that pessimistic weltanschauung is in Arnold's poetry, we can probably do no better than temporarily forgo chronology and turn briefly to two poems that seem to present us with opposing poles of Arnold's ways of experiencing and explaining the world: the first, "Human Life" and, the second, "A Summer Night."

From the claim to universality implicit in its title, "Human Life" would seem, interpretively, the most promisingly paradigmatic of all of Arnold's poems. In this broadly encompassing allegory of the suffering that lies at the heart of things, no individual would seem exempt from the predestined constraint, frustration, and denial that rule so absolutely in human affairs. Surprisingly, though, the poem begins by anticipating our being called to account by the most atypically benevolent of all of those anthropomorphized divinities who appear from time to time in Arnold's poetry. The speaker's expectation, at least initially, is that, "[l]ife's voyage done," a "heavenly Friend" (2) will ask us if we have followed that "inly-written chart" (5) kindly given us for moral guidance on our life's journey, the degree of our fidelity to it presumably serving as the basis for our postmortal disposition. But the "Friend" and the metaphysics he seems to represent are summarily banished almost as soon as they are introduced.[49] We quickly learn that the "human life" of and for which Arnold purports to speak is beset by desire and incorrigibly willful. "[F]ain" to "drive / At random, and not steer by rule" (13–14), we are unlikely to be guided by the "inly-written chart" of conscience thoughtfully provided by God as our principal navigational aid for "[l]ife's voyage." Even more disturbingly, we also learn that the "sea of life" (27), which had earlier been represented as a mapped-out-in-advance testing ground that God's anticipatory instructions would enable us to negotiate successfully, is in fact "incognisable" (8), uncharted and unchartable waters that yield no evidence of providential purpose or guidance.

If life's sea is, as Arnold now characterizes it, "incognisable," any ultimate values and final purposes unknowable, the will and wishes of a "heavenly Friend" nowhere in evidence, good sense would seem to tell us that if we are to attain happiness we might just as well follow not the dictates of conscience but the counsels of hedonism. Accordingly, we should not, as Arnold wanly puts it,

> fret and fear to miss our aim,
> If some fair coast have lured us to make stay,
> Or some friend hailed us to keep company.
>
> (10–12)

Then with one final turn, Arnold cuts through to his deepest concerns, in the process rendering the choice between hedonism and conscience essentially moot. Our lapses and transgressions, if they are that, are sins of intention and not of commission, acts we *would* but *cannot* perform. Desire *is* "weakness" Arnold insists, in a final gesture of moral disapproval. But in a phrase that powerfully coalesces the discomfort of guilty desire with the anguish prompted by the certainty of desire's inevitable frustration, he quickly adds that it is "[w]eakness! and worse, weakness bestowed in vain!" (15).

From this point forward in "Human Life," Arnold explains that the real defect in human existence (conceived as a voyage across "the sea of life") is not our propensity to transgression, that we are condemned by our wayward nature to fall short of the moral expectations of our "heavenly Friend." Life's real defect resides rather in the severe psychic costs that the figure of the solitary voyage across that sea's vastness inevitably suggests, that we are destined to experience life as enclosure, separateness, never-ending isolation. The contact with others we have hungered for is to be ultimately denied by the external and elemental constraints implicit in the figure of life as a voyage: "Winds from our side the unsuiting consort rive, / We rush by coasts where we had lief remain" (16–17).

Implicit as well in this characterization of life as isolation in a general sense are still more disheartening intimations of a sexual despair seemingly indigenous to Arnold's poetry. It is clear that human life, as Arnold imagines it, is to be not just lonely but without intimacy, without love. "[I]t is natural," Kenneth Allott, Arnold's editor, tells us in his headnote to "Human Life," "to assume that Marguerite is recalled in l.16" as that "'unsuiting consort' from whom we are riven by those course-determining winds that sweep across 'the sea of life.' " I would only add that the word "rive" itself, with its dictionary definition of "strike asunder, split, cleave," similarly recalls the Marguerite poems with their "sea" that "rolls between us" to sever and estrange.

By the closing stanza, then, the figure of the voyage has apparently been reconstituted into a conflict between human consciousness—a fragile vessel that, nonetheless, is the sole repository of whatever humane values the poem puts forward—and that greater reality into which consciousness finds itself incomprehensibly thrust and that it is compelled to obey, the alien and hostile environment of the sea, with its impelling and dissevering agencies of wind and current. From this reconstituted scenario, the "heavenly Friend," too, must inevitably be banished, replaced by an overseeing agent whose ways are more in keeping with the voyager's skeptical understanding of life as "incognisable" and his experiential sense of it as painful. As "[w]e stem across the sea of life by night" (27), we feel ourselves chartered to "unknown Powers," whose hidden purposes are plainly inimical to our own desires, forcing us to "leave behind"

> The joys which were not for our use designed;
> The friends to whom we had no natural right,
> The homes that were not destined to be ours.
>
> (25–30)

At the end of the parable, the basic elements of Arnold's pessimistically conceived metaphysical dualism seem firmly fixed. The things of the world perceived as out there are, in terms of our subjectively lived existences, known only at a distance, by the outlines of the shores we rush by, the far-off sounds of the voices of the friends who hail us, the wakes of the ships that move past us. We are never to land on the coasts that tempt us nor reach out and embrace those who, like ourselves, call longingly from the decks of their own ships that pass in the night, never to know things in their real essences, in those depths that their surfaces conceal, but only as "unmating things" ("Isolation. To Marguerite," 32). What is now primary and determining and all-pervasive in our lived experience is the other component of Arnold's dualism, an unknowable but oppressive otherness that overrules our wishes and impels us in accordance with its own inscrutable volitional principles. For all its strangeness, though, we feel this metaphysical otherness as immanently and unceasingly present, as that to which we are "chartered" during the whole of "[l]ife's voyage," as it indiscernibly impels us, like the buried life of another poem, on our life's true, though unhappy course.

To all appearances, "A Summer Night" is "Human Life" in reverse. That is, in "A Summer Night" Arnold begins where his earlier poem leaves off, in isolation among "homes that were not destined to be ours" (36), and ends in heavenly hope. However, it is not any supposed metaphysical agency that imposes the burden of solitude here but the inhospitableness of men who dwell behind "windows" that "frown" (3) upon the gazing speaker, "Silent and white, unopening down, / Repellent as the world" (4–5).[50] Relief from that burden comes quickly, however, with the sighting of an unexpected vista, "A break between the housetops" (6), that reveals, first, "The moon" (7) and then, "Down at the far horizon's rim, / Doth a whole tract of heaven disclose!" (9–10). To decipher the message encoded in the moon and stars, Arnold apparently finds it necessary to shift his attention to yet another and presumably psychologically more amenable object of poetic vision, using memory to turn the urban skyscape before him into "a far different scene," the most characteristic of all Arnoldian vistas:

> Headlands stood out into the moonlit deep
> As clearly as at noon;
> The spring-tide's brimming flow
> Heaved dazzlingly between
> Houses with long white sweep,
> Girdled the glistening bay;
> Behind through the soft air,
> The blue haze-cradled mountains spread away.
>
> (14–21)

Much here may seem semantically extraneous, an unnecessary intrusion by memory, a piling on of descriptive detail far in excess of conceptual needs. Still, a scene that recurs at such critical junctures in the poetry of Arnold as this recollected moonlit scene does plainly carries a message of its own, providing a kind of cosmological mapping-out by which Arnold expresses wishes and needs more firmly and deeply embedded than the more philosophically abstruse formulations of his poetry can ever adequately render.[51]

In Arnold's poetry, that favorite scene of a shoreline and its adjacent waters steeped in the light of the moon and the stars generally provides a catalyst to hope, a signal that desire has been kindled, that possibilities have presented themselves that might alleviate or overcome the anguished loneliness of the life we have always known. It is to be on a night "When clear falls the moonlight, / When spring-tides are low" ("The Forsaken Merman," 126–27) that the forsaken merman wishfully imagines that he and his children shall be once more drawn back to "the white sleeping town" ("The Forsaken Merman," 137) they are now dejectedly abandoning in apparent defeat. In "To Marguerite—Continued" it is only when the illumination of moonlit and "starry nights" (9) and the "lovely notes" (10) that "[a]cross the sounds and channels pour" (12) merge into a single symbolically suggestive perceptual whole that we become aware, even in our solitary enislement, of the existence of others like ourselves, doubtlessly desirable and desiring, and thus feel the kindling of our "longing's fire" (19). In "Dover Beach" it is only when "the moon lies fair / Upon the straits" (2–3) that we can envision a "world" that "seems / To lie before us like a land of dreams" (30–31) as a projected alternative to that far bleaker world construed from "[t]he eternal note of sadness" (14).

How much work this figure is asked to do is probably best illustrated in *Empedocles on Etna*, where Arnold employs the same scenic effect in both of the poem's antithetical projections of desire: with the "mild and luminous floor of waters" (2.315) forming a segment of that elementally real with which Empedocles would be united, even if he must commit suicide to do so; while "moon-silvered inlets" (2.425) are envisioned by Callicles as part of the landscape of his countervailing closing song with its intimation of salvation through faith in the mythic imagination. Undoubtedly the most psychologically intriguing of these uses of the moonlit sea occurs in "Resignation," where Arnold caps the celebratory end to a walking tour through the Lake District by the Arnold children under the supervision of their father with just this image, here plainly resonating with unspoken expectancy (though quite possibly dashed expectations in light of his father's death only a year before the poem was written): "We bathed our hands in speechless glee / That night, in the wide-glimmering sea" (84–85).

Of course, each of the two elements conjoined when the light of the moon and the stars is somehow seemingly fused with the placid surface of waters often appears separately in the poetry of Arnold with very different implications. It is upon that deep, the sea of life, that man either blindly and anxiously plies his way in the voyage of life or finds himself hopelessly and helplessly enisled. It is to that same deep also that the river of the individual life itself inexorably flows in its subterranean course until finally subsumed in that larger body of waters that consciousness knows only as death. In these independent appearances, the deep is often the destructive element, alien, chaotic, and undifferentiated, pure purposelessness, all that consciousness abhors and yet that to which it must submit. So conceived, the deep then belongs to, embodies, symbolically expresses (all seem appropriate) that which within Arnold's philosophic dualism is designated as ontologically privileged, the ultimately real, that undifferentiated metaphysical will that, only concerned with its own impulses and strivings, pursues its blindly sought-after ends, indifferent to the goals and intentions of a human consciousness that seems only an accidental presence on its vast and sometimes vexed surface of waters.

Contrastingly, stars and moon, when viewed in their isolation in the heavens and reflected upon as seeming entities in themselves, are characteristically looked to by Arnold as a model for an alternative mode of existence, within the terms of that metaphysical dualism of will and idea, fit emblems of the world as idea raised to a longed-for preeminence. In their luminousness, their sharpness and clarity of definition and outline, they represent for Arnold a vision of determinate boundaries as opposed to "the sea of life's" undifferentiatedness. In the heavens above, Arnold finds a possibly saving cosmic analogue for that desired good of a heightened consciousness, of the human self rising above flux and formlessness, capable of gaining a settled, even rational comprehension of things, and thereby achieving a life with its own truth. Moreover, however austere and unfulfilling the desiring self might find the life imaged by the heavens, it would still suffice, Arnold seems to say, if we could only attain it. Though living as the stars do may not enable us to overcome that sense of essential separateness from others that is the inevitable consequence of human individuation and its clearly circumscribed life of consciousness, by experiencing that separateness from a heavenly rather than a merely earthbound perspective, we shall learn that to be alone is not to be isolated and loveless but to be autonomous, self-dependent, free.

Just such an idealized vision of human possibility is what the sight of the "tract of heaven" (10), spied in "a break between the housetops" (6) of the claustrophobic city, leads Arnold to in "A Summer Night." It is a vision of separateness as autonomy in every way antithetical to that vision of separateness as metaphysically induced isolation and frustration found in the implicitly paradigmatic and profoundly pessimistic "Human Life." I would suggest that what enables Arnold to imagine the starlike autonomy of "A Summer Night" as a realizable human possibility is the supplementing of the perceived scene, the starry sky hovering over the housetops of the city, by that other, seemingly redundant, dramatically and thematically extraneous "far different scene" (13) of "a past night," when "[h]eadlands stood out into the moonlit deep."

Just as in "Dover Beach," "To Marguerite—Continued," and "The Forsaken Merman," in "A Summer Night," too, the conjoining of moonlight or starlight and water serves as a kind of precondition to hope, a catalyst to imagining the realization of seemingly impossible human aspirations. It would seem that such a conjoining lends a kind of momentary metaphysical sanction to such aspirations, to the wish that the split between the phenomenal consciousness (even in its idealized representation in terms of the moon and stars) and noumenal reality (its undifferentiatedness expressed through the image of the sea), with its baneful consequences for human endeavor, can somehow be healed—as the coalescence of these seemingly insuperably distant and irremediably separated elements in this glittering epiphany seems analogously to intimate that such a split can be healed. Under the spell of a moon that "lies fair / Upon the straits" ("Dover Beach," 2–3), the speaker at the window in "Dover Beach" is able to imagine that "the world, which seems / To lie before us" can be made into "a land of dreams" (30–31); when "clear falls the moonlight, / When spring-tides are low" ("The Forsaken Merman," 126–27), the forsaken merman and his children shall leave their home in the sea hopeful that the heretofore obdurately resistant Margaret will choose to return there; in "To Marguerite—Continued," on "starry nights" when music sounds across "echoing straits," Arnold's "mortal millions" may, at least, dream that their ordained severance will be overcome and they will once more be "[p]arts of a single continent" (16).

But even as the desired outcomes associated with the figure of moonlight and starlight reflected on the sea's surface of waters are being imaginatively conjured, the most hopeful of expectations quickly give way to forebodings of their inevitable frustration. It is as though we intuitively understand, even as we observe, that the reconciliation of the sea and the heavens that "stands before us" is only a trick of light, a transitory appearance at the mercy of wind and cloud and time that shall ultimately again undo it. In "To Marguerite—Continued," "The Forsaken Merman," and "Dover Beach," the great crisis poems of "the moonlit deep," hopes are raised only to be dashed; the scenario that begins in longing ends with despair renewed and even deepened.

In "A Summer Night," the burden placed on this inherently fragile representation of reconciliation and thus a catalyst to hope, the "moonlit deep," is made greater still by the speaker's acknowledgment of his own deeply felt deficiencies and needs. Using that "past night" and "far different scene" as a base point from which to assess his inner progress, he finds his inner life unchanged over time: fretful and dissatisfied then, he is no less fretful and dissatisfied now. As the only observer supposedly present on both occasions, "the calm moonlight" (26) ventriloquistically asks,

> *Hast thou then still the old unquiet breast,*
> *Which neither deadens into rest,*
> *Nor ever feels the fiery glow*
> *That whirls the spirit from itself away,*
> *But fluctuates to and fro,*
> *Never by passion quite possessed*
> *And never quite benumbed by the world's sway?*
>
> (26–33)

Unlike the poetic speaker of "Human Life," who represents himself as spokesperson for all humanity, the speaker of "A Summer Night" presents us with a second version of the Arnoldian speaker, in this latter case, describing himself as a being apart, radically different from "all the other men I see" (36), a poet without any identity, ever in flux, eddying between passion and numbness, unhappily longing that life be otherwise.

Perhaps the term that best characterizes the state of mind of the neurasthenic Arnoldian speaker (not just in "A Summer Night" but in those many other poems where he depicts himself as unsuffing and deficient) is R. D. Laing's still-useful phrase "ontological insecurity." Beset by doubts about its identity, its realness, its substantiality, the highly volatile, "ontologically insecure" self is tempted to abandon the search within for that elusive and perhaps nonexistent core of inner being that would constitute its identity and turn outward, imitatively playing a role to become "[l]ike all the other men I see," a choice as devoid of hope as that "ontological insecurity" that originally provoked the desire to be otherwise.

Furthermore, two primary threats to the ontologically insecure individual, according to Laing, are *petrification*, the apprehending of ourself as an "object without personal autonomy of action, an *it* without subjectivity,"[52] and *engulfment*, where "[t]he individual experiences himself as a man who is only saving himself from drowning by the most strenuous desperate activity."[53] The threatened dangers to the ontologically insecure cited by Laing are, of course, strikingly analogous to Arnold's own categories in "A Summer Night": the Slave, with "most men" (37) experiencing themselves as an *it*, "*benumbed*" (33) and "languidly" giving "[t]heir lives to some unmeaning taskwork" (39–40); and the Madman, literally engulfed, drowned within "the wide ocean of life" (53). Of the life options available to the ontologically insecure Arnoldian speaker, the way of the Slave is self-evidently unpalatable, to be "[u]nfreed" and "unblessed"(50), confined to a "brazen prison" (37), to perform "barren labor" (43) beneath "the sun's hot eye" (38). The Madman can at least flee a world already found "repellent" and, as a "freed prisoner," set sail "where'er his heart / Listeth" (54–55), follow his own inclinations and aims during his surely inspiriting voyage upon "the wide ocean of life." Yet in the end, this account of the Madman proves a cautionary tale, in which to choose freedom is to court destruction, such senseless Promethean defiance inevitably provoking the wrath of those "unknown Powers" that rule the Arnoldian cosmos.

Arnold understands that the Madman's voyage is a doomed enterprise: to go "where'er his heart / Listeth" is inevitably to run counter to the far more potent will of a volitionally conceived metaphysical agency utterly indifferent to the will and wishes of any merely epiphenomenal being foolhardy enough to put itself in harm's way. Out there, "[d]espotic on that sea" (57)—with "despotic" connoting both irresistible power and malevolent intent—are seemingly omnipotent forces that move implacably across the "ocean of life," forces given explicit metaphysical signification as "[t]rade-winds which cross it from eternity" (58). As in "Human Life," here too we have metaphysical agency antithetically conceived, with that which issues from "eternity" apprehended as at cross-purposes with and inimical to human desire. But in "Human Life" *all* men are voyagers, compelled to follow the course set for them because of their having been chartered by "unknown Powers," despite the longings of the heart to diverge from that predetermined course and pursue objects of its own choosing. In "A Summer Night," though, "most men" remain landbound, with only "a few" summoning the courage to become heroic voyagers. It will prove to be a disastrous choice: in following the directions of the "heart," they have misguidedly set out "for some false impossible shore," on a journey whose end is certain to be metaphysically entailed destruction, an engulfment brought about by that vast storm driven by the "Trade-winds" that emanate from "eternity": "Fainter and fainter wreck and helmsman loom, / And he too disappears, and comes no more" (72–73).

With his allegory of the Madman, Arnold inserts into "A Summer Night" a philosophic pessimism that renders his two conjectural life options—Madman or Slave—wholly irrelevant. Whichever we choose, desire is to be frustrated, longing turned into despair, by the irresistible metaphysical will Arnold terms "eternity." Yet, abetted by the metaphysically sanctioned encouragement implicit in the figure of the "moonlit deep," Arnold turns to the heavens for a third way, that of neither the landlocked Slave nor the seafaring Madman—though in the first of several undoings of that posited possibility of being like a star, Arnold seems, by the speaker's own casual computations, to rule it out before even raising it. "Most men," he tells us, "in a brazen prison live" (37), while "the rest, a few, / Escape" (51–52), but escape only to suffer a premature destruction. Adding together "Most men" and "the rest" would seem to give us a sum sufficiently inclusive to account for all humankind. For that third life option that the speaker of "A Summer Night" would have us believe is the only one that suffices, there would appear to be no known human precedents.

That Arnold apparently answers "There is another life" to the questions "Is there no life but these alone? / Madman or Slave, must man be one?" (74–75) seems a tribute to the irrepressibleness and potency of desire, given the odds generated against such an answer by the negating force of the speaker's own earlier computations. But the spirit of negation exacts its own penalties, the repressed returning only after being transformed at poem's end into a projected good that seems distressingly attenuated, in no way a solution to the problem indicated at the outset, the speaker's exclusion from community and intimacy by an unbreachably "[r]epellent" world. With the speaker's final apostrophe to the stars, these goods remain unpursued, relegated to regions where he dare not venture. For all of its elevation and grandiloquence, that apostrophe entails a lowering of sights, a huddling within the boundaries of the self to minimize risk, a forgoing of involvement with others to satisfy a vague notion of heightened self-definition—"Plainness and clearness without shadow of stain!"—a willingness to be "unpassionate," to remain "yet untroubled" (80).

It is doubtful, though, that an ideal so conceived—free of anxiety, austerely unpassionate, self-dependent and autonomous—can be sustained; that man, even if he could, would wish to possess the calm of the stars. The reason such a goal may be neither attainable nor desirable is not our human flawedness but the inappropriateness of the heavens themselves to the function they have been called upon to serve. The moon and stars may appear calm and dispassionate, not because they have achieved a kind of low-pulsed mastery over the longings that beset us on earth, but because they are in truth pulseless and possess no life at all. At a critical point in "A Summer Night" (the point perhaps at which the text deconstructively undoes itself—the revelatory *aporia*), Arnold comes close to making this very point, to declaring that the life he ascribes to the heavens, which in their inanimateness are constitutionally incapable of desiring, is inapplicable to the situation of man, the being who vainly longs. (In "Destiny," Arnold actually *defines* "man" as "[a]n aimless, unallayed desire" [8].) So tentatively and evasively formulated is that crucial passage in "A Summer Night" that it reads as if the speaker would hold back from, even nullify his seeming assertion by insinuating into his goal-directed argument a highly skeptical disclaimer implying that he really knows that it is rationally impossible ever to become like a star and thereby avert the human fate of becoming either Madman or Slave. What he implicitly tells us by speaking what "he will not say" is that man and the heavens are fundamentally unlike, that the one must inevitably desire, while the other, in its inanimateness, never can:

> I will not say that your mild deeps retain
> A tinge, it may be, of their silent pain
> Who have longed deeply once, and longed in vain.
>
> (83–85)

Still, even after communicating this undermining truth he "will not say," Arnold sets his disclaimer aside and picks up the old argument with its original fictions of vitalization and idealization, assuring the heavens he apostrophizes that they exemplify virtues that are humanly attainable, that he would

> rather say that you remain
> A world above man's head, to let him see
> How boundless might his soul's horizons be,
> How vast, yet of what clear transparency!
> How it were good to abide there, and breathe free;
> How fair a lot to fill
> Is left to each man still!
>
> (86–92)

Yet even in the course of this most extravagant idealization, an irrepressible skepticism slips through; claims are asserted that insinuate the transparently implausible fictiveness of the idea that the heavens might provide a model for humanity. What the speaker would have us believe is that "there"—that is, in the unsustaining vacancy above us—we shall "breathe free." As Arnold knows full well though—for he tells us so in *Empedocles on Etna*—as we ascend even a mountaintop (to say nothing of ascending to the stars), "[t]he air is thin" (2.213). In fact, in the rarefied fastness of his Apollonian solitude, Empedocles finds not that he can "breathe free" but that in the uplands breathing is constricted:

> the veins swell,
> The temples tighten and throb there—
> Air! Air!
>
> (2.215–17)

And if one gasps for air on the Appollonian heights Empedocles was forced to abandon, then surely we must know that in the heavens where the speaker of "A Summer Night" wishes to abide there can be no air at all, despite all of his wishful assurances that it must be otherwise.

By leavening with doubt the almost strident affirmation of his apostrophe to the heavens, by covertly insinuating that the assertion that the heavens offer precedent and example for what human life could be is contrary to both fact and reason and, perhaps, to desire itself, Arnold, by poem's end, can only leave us to wonder whether "A Summer Night" is really "Human Life" in reverse, whether the overt pessimism of the latter has truly been dispelled. We must now surely suspect that human life, if it is to be carried on at all, must be carried on here on earth, among the Madmen and the Slaves. Indeed, if we would not anesthetize ourselves against the fact, succumb to the Slave's self-blinding and benumbing, we must suspect too that its real site is not simply earth but "the wide ocean of life," where we too must wish to live as voyagers amidst metaphysically engendered adversity. So even this, the most affirming of Arnold's poems, carries within it the seeds of a counternarrative, another account of the overcoming of the longings of consciousness by brute metaphysical fact, the sum and substance of Arnold's poetry of pessimism.

2

Toward Pessimism: *"The Strayed Reveller"* and Other Poems

W‍HILE PESSIMISM IN ITS SCHOPENHAUERIAN RAMIFICATIONS DOES NOT fully emerge in Arnold until the completion in 1848 of "Resignation," a strong disposition to pessimism is already evident in what is one of the earliest, indeed probably *the* earliest, of his significant poems to be published in *"The Strayed Reveller" and Other Poems*, "To a Gipsy Child by the Sea-Shore."[1] Drawing heavily upon the "Immortality Ode" of Wordsworth, Arnold appropriates that poem's Platonic framework only to invert it.[2] Like Wordsworth's "best Philosopher" (110), Arnold's child is a repository of absolute and ultimate truths, innately granted and intuitively known. His knowledge, though, is not of a "God, who is our home" (65), nor of a "Heaven" that "lies about us in our infancy" (66) but of the onto- logical primacy of grief, the certainty of pain, "the vanity of hope" (39).

By this highly self-conscious refusal of influence, Arnold has in this very early poem implicitly declared that he will go his own way, adapting to his own highly idiosyncratic view of things an incident as unpromising as this brief and wordless personal encounter with a child, whose "pitiful wan face and sad dark eyes rested on Mat- thew for some time without change of expression."[3] However insig- nificant and pitiful the gipsy child seems, he is, in fact, the first in a series of exemplary figures, nothing less than an infant Shake- speare, a model to whom the Arnoldian speaker turns for assis- tance in both understanding an inherently pessimistic universe and devising strategies for dealing with its unhappy human conse- quences. Like Arnold's Shakespeare, the gipsy child conveys his pessimistic message, not through language—the fact that Shake- speare is the greatest of all masters of language notwithstanding— but through the evidence of physiognomy. Just as "the pains," the "weakness," the "griefs" Shakespeare expresses "[f]ind their sole speech" (14) not in the wondrousness of Shakespeare's poetry but

54

in the wordless message to be gleaned from "that victorious brow" (14), so too is the evidence of physiognomy paramount in establishing the gipsy child as sage and model. The pleading eyes, the "meditative guise" (3), and above all the "long lines of shadow" sloping down the infant's "pale cheek" that ordinarily only "years, and curious thought, and suffering give" (37–38) are the key elements of proof for the otherwise inexplicable faith that the lonely child has intuitively comprehended the darkest yet most significant of human truths.

It is not just possession of a tragic countenance that entitles these characters to their status of model to whom the speaker in these poems shall questioningly turn for a pattern or rule by which to conduct his own life. For Shakespeare and his infant counterpart have not only intuitively gained this bedrock truth of the essentialness and inescapability of grief, but, having learned this, they have also chosen to persist in life without hope, with sorrow the assured consequence of carrying on. Thus, solely on the evidence of physiognomy, a meditative guise, the Arnoldian speaker feels free to claim that the gipsy child has made a conscious and courageous choice: "Thou hast foreknown the vanity of hope, / Foreseen thy harvest— yet proceed'st to live" (39–40).

How to carry on in the face of the axiomatic certainties of Arnold's pessimism—*how to know and live*—this is undoubtedly the most fundamentally urgent of Arnoldian problems, especially given the fact that Arnold's Empedocles, clearly one of those who knows, chooses otherwise. One major problem, though, is that if Arnold can identify some who could be models, who from the evidence inscribed on their countenances manifestly appear both to know and live, these potential models unfortunately display one built-in limitation on their usefulness that undoes all the good they might do. Even if they could impart their saving knowledge, both remain resolutely silent, though "[w]e ask and ask" ("Shakespeare," 2). Most distressingly, the grounds for this silence may be, not simply the need of the model to preserve his autonomy or integrity by some saving act of concealment, but the more disheartening possibility that the truths he possesses are inherently incommunicable and only acquired by the model himself because he has been granted special innate and intuitive powers denied the rest of us. As the precedent of the "Immortality Ode" suggests, the differences between speaker and model may finally be differences not in degree but in kind, epistemological differences between his transcendent gifts and our narrowly empirical and rational faculties that are so fundamental as to ensure that the example provided us is one that we shall never be able successfully to follow.[4]

Though Arnold's gipsy child is so profoundly estranged from other human contact that he is described as alien even to his "own mother's breast" (12), at first glance he seems to spy a kindred spirit in the speaker, who has also had his moments of gloom and sadness: "With eyes which sought thine eyes thou did converse, / And that soul-searching vision fell on me" (15–16). But any suggestion of real spiritual kinship quickly dissipates, as the disproportionateness in their degrees of knowledge becomes evident: "Glooms that go deep as thine I have not known, / Moods of fantastic sorrow, nothing worth" (17–18). Even in his earliest poem, then, Arnold is ready to attribute to himself those personal shortcomings that typify the Arnoldian persona: he has lived only on the meaningless surface, never at the meaningful depths; his life has been marked by unsteadiness, swings of mood, the eddyings of an unfixed identity that have so far debarred him from becoming truly self-sufficing like the gipsy child. In short, we are given, if only elliptically, all of the basic conditions of the Arnoldian lyric of identity, a speaker who feels he is without fixed identity or true authenticity but then discovers some apparently spiritually viable ideal to emulate, only to conclude that that goal is barred by the untranscendable obstacles of both his own limitations and the inimitability of his model.

Of course, not just the speaker but all humans would seem to be deprived of the opportunity to glean the secret of the gipsy child's bleak metaphysical insight and life-sustaining wisdom. In fact, explicitly excluded from sharing in that vision of the fundamental darkness at the heart of things are two large groups to which presumably most humans belong: those distracted from vision by "longings vain" and those who suffer from a stultifying "weariness, the full-fed soul's annoy," briefly sketched types who seem very much like forerunners of those later all-inclusive categories of Madman and Slave.

Even rarer and finer types, who in their detachment and perhaps in their comprehension of the human predicament resemble the gipsy child, fall similarly short in epistemological endowment. In the middle section of the poem, when Arnold asks, "What mood wears like complexion to thy woe?" he is able to enumerate a surprisingly varied number of those who are sufficiently enlightened and estranged to merit at least comparison with the gipsy child. There is he who "in mountain glens, at noon of day / Sits rapt, and hears the battle break below" (22–23), a figure who bears an obvious likeness to those Culler terms "Strayed Revellers," sympathetically conceived characters like Callicles, the scholar-gipsy, and the strayed reveller himself. But the type Culler labels the "Strayed Reveller" is clearly not the gipsy child's spiritual equal, since Arnold's child has attained detachment not by withdrawal into solitary "mountain glens" but by remaining heroically inviolate while living in the world, his chosen place "not the shelter, but the fray" (24). Then there are the exile, "mindful how the past was glad" (25), and the angel, "in an alien planet born" (26). Angel and exile undoubtedly endure great suffering, but theirs falls far short of the unspecified woe of the gipsy child, perhaps because, while their sufferings have their origins in a space- and time-dependent realm of phenomena, his sorrow derives from innate comprehension of the radical ill ontologically prior to all appearances of time and space.

Finally, there are the stoic wise man—who, finding life wanting, will "in disdainful silence turn away, / Stand mute, self-centred, and dream no more" (31–32)—and "some gray-haired king"(33), who has "[m]used much, loved life a little, loathed it more" (35–36). But the truths of sorrow and suffering they have gained from experience, the gipsy child, in his spiritual superiority and epistemological uniqueness, has innately "foreknown." He is already "a meek anticipant of that sure pain / Whose sureness gray-haired scholars hardly learn" (41–42); yet he seems determined not to withdraw from life as stoic and king do but to proceed "to live," to be in "the fray"—a decision, moreover, taken without illusions, in full cognizance of the "vanity of hope" (39).

With the child, by his innate and intuitive endowments, established as "best philosopher," Arnold returns to his inverted analogy with the "Immortality Ode," following his precursor by extrapolating from the child's present metaphysical enlightenment the promise of his future spiritual triumph. Here, too, it is the passage into the "light of common day" of adulthood that poses the most serious obstacle to recovery of that metaphysically originary truth apprehended in childhood. Yet, paradoxically, growing up implies for Arnold not a dimming of light but a brightening (albeit a specious one) brought about by the first of those puzzling and pointedly fictive supernatural agents who from time to time will inexplicably intrude themselves into his poems:

> The Guide of our dark steps a triple veil
> Betwixt our senses and our sorrows keeps:
> Hath sown with cloudless passages the tale
> Of grief, and eased us with a thousand sleeps.
>
> (49–52)

For all their ostensible supernaturalism, these lines, for the first
time in Arnold's poetry, seem to posit a genuinely philosophic distinction between a realm of phenomenal appearances and an ontologically truer metaphysical reality pessimistically conceived.
According to this curious narrative of the development of human
perception, we have been generously granted this concealing surface of sensory illusion to spare us from the potentially life-negating
effects of a reality that is only "sorrows" and "grief" at its core.
But stripped of its halfhearted mythologizing, this account of things
bears all the marks of the pessimist's division of the world into the
irrelevantly epiphenomenal idea and an unconditioned real that
wills suffering.

Under the auspices of our well-intentioned "Guide," all of us as
adults live within the seeming security of the realm of phenomena,
a surface of saving illusion that makes life bearable by shielding
us from that ontologically truer "tale of grief" played out at life's
incommunicable depths. But that seemingly blanket exemption
from the pains of reality does not apply to the specially chosen gipsy
child. Though adult distractions may temporarily entice him from
the real, he shall never succumb completely to this metaphysically
grounded form of childhood amnesia:

> Ah! not the nectarous poppy lovers use,
> Not daily labour's dull, Lethean spring,
> Oblivion in lost angels can infuse
> Of the soiled glory and the trailing wing.
>
> And though thou glean what strenuous gleaners may,
> In the thronged fields where winning comes by strife;
> And though the just sun gild, as mortals pray,
> Some reaches of thy storm-vexed streams of life;
>
> Though that blank sunshine blind thee; though the cloud
> That severed the world's march and thine be gone;
> Though ease dulls grace, and Wisdom be too proud
> To halve a lodging that was all her own—
>
> Once, ere the day decline, thou shalt discern
> Oh once, ere night, in thy success, thy chain!
> Ere the long evening close, thou shalt return,
> And wear this majesty of grief again.

(53–68)

Those familiar Freudian antidotes to neurotic misery—love and
work the "nectarous poppy lovers use" and "daily labour's dull, Le-

thean spring"—are the means that "[t]he Guide of our dark steps"
employs to lure us away from looking too closely upon life's "tale /
Of grief." Surprisingly Arnold does foresee eventual success
through work for the gipsy child "[i]n the thronged fields where winning comes by strife," success that (even more surprisingly) will
take place under the aegis of the "just sun," presumably the figurative expression of the Victorian faith that a divinely administered
distributive justice will ensure that financial success is dependent
on personal merit.[5] But that piously invoked "just sun" quickly
turns into "blank sunshine" that does not "gild" but "blind," the
forerunner doubtlessly of the "sun's hot eye" of "A Summer Night,"
under which the Slave laboriously produces his "unmeaning taskwork." Here the sun's light is characterized as blinding because,
though only mere appearance and metaphysical falsehood, it still
manages to distract the attention of those who had been in touch
with truth from the darkly noumenal and ontologically real, awareness of which at life's beginning had constituted the gipsy child's
special glory.

It is on the poetic precedent of those Wordsworthian master
tropes of metaphysical enlightenment and the persistence of recollection that the inverting argument of Arnold's own poem ultimately
rests. If the opiates neither of love nor of labor "[o]blivion in lost
angels can infuse / Of the soiled glory and the trailing wing" (with
the heaven-born Wordsworthian children "trailing clouds of glory"
clearly the source for these "lost angels"), why then should knowledge of the essential darkness at the heart of things not also provide
the no less metaphysically enlightened gipsy child with "truths that
wake / To perish never" ("Immortality Ode," 155–56), never to be
wholly obliterated by the quotidian brightness of the world? Thus,
Arnold assures us, his child, too, shall in later life exercise his own
powers of seemingly transcendent recollection of the sorrow of
things, discerning with soul-searing clarity, "Oh once, ere night, in
thy success, thy chain." That the adult gipsy child will have remembered shall be again deduced from the evidence of physiognomy, a
countenance that shall "wear this majesty of grief again." Arnold
thus appropriates the "Immortality Ode"'s Platonized apparatus of
the earthly recollection of a transcendently grounded knowledge,
but only to invert it and propose pessimism as an alternative to his
precursor's optimism. At the same time, by appropriating Wordsworth and ultimately Plato to satisfy the interpretive ends of "To a
Gipsy-Child by the Sea-Shore," Arnold makes it abundantly clear
that he will remain within the traditional philosophic paradigm of
metaphysical explanation, that he needs an Absolute, even if to ex-

plain the prevalence of sorrow in this life requires an Absolute that wills evil. In short, like Schopenhauer, Arnold too would wish to "sneak by."

Shakespeare is obviously better qualified for nomination to sage-hood than the gipsy child. But just as his precocious depths of tragic wisdom and his figurative characterization by the Shakespearean cloud-bordered mountain make the gipsy child something of an infant Shakespeare, so too is Arnold's Shakespeare something of a grown-up gipsy child. From the evidence of physiognomy—at least as that evidence comes to us from portraiture—in the case of Shakespeare we can also deduce the persistence into adulthood of an inwardly constituted and heroically maintained dark vision similar to the "majesty of grief" that the gipsy child will wear again. What is truly surprising about Arnold's Shakespeare is Arnold's portrayal of the greatest of writers as a poet nearly anonymous, one who during his own lifetime "[d]idst tread on earth unguessed at" ("Shakespeare," 11), having carried on the most important and potentially most instructive part of his mental life at an epistemological remove from other men, much as his uncommunicative infant predecessor did.

Culler suggests that Arnold believed Shakespeare lived on earth unguessed at because of the "paucity" of biographical "information" about the most admired of writers available to a worshipful posterity in the 1840s.[6] But biographical questions are quickly subsumed into a more fundamentally Arnoldian perspective in the sonnet, and Shakespeare himself changed from the most eloquently verbal of men to the intractably uncommunicative Arnoldian model. The assertion that "[o]thers abide our question. Thou art free" (1) does not mean, as Culler thinks, "that other poets submit to our inquiry about their personal biography, you do not."[7] What the "We" who "ask and ask" (2) really want is not information about Shakespeare's personal life but some essentially ahistorical insight into that specially intuitive and apparently unsayable metaphysical knowledge granted Shakespeare about the meaning and value of a life that is pain, a knowledge "[o]ut-topping knowledge" (3), implicitly indispensable to all yet restricted to a rare Arnoldian few.

One might always reasonably assume that Shakespeare had already told us all he knew about our painful human predicament in his great tragedies, the most celebrated of all communicative acts. Much of the best commentary on "Shakespeare" has indeed sought to introduce issues of authorship into Arnold's sonnet, with Arnold's Shakespeare looked upon as "the very type of the objective

poet who . . . loses himself in the characters he creates"[8] or as incorporated into a tradition of Romantic criticism "by Coleridge, Haz-
litt, and Carlyle," which attempted "to define a paradoxical
Shakespearean mode of impersonal subjectivity."[9] Yet for Arnold's
purposes, Shakespeare—like the gipsy child—might just as well
have never written plays at all.[10] Indeed, any reminder that Shakespeare wrote plays might actually undermine these purposes, since
we might then want to inquire why those of us who "ask and ask"
could not glean our answers from those great works in which
Shakespeare's genius finds expression. Instead, Arnold implicitly
insists that all the wisdom that Shakespeare has conveyed or will
convey finds its "sole speech" in the unvoiceable and ultimately incommunicable signifiers of portraiture, in the enigmatic suggestive-
ness of a smile and the curve of a brow.

It is primarily through the simile of the cloud-bordered mountain
that Arnold explicates and indeed expands upon this conception of
a Shakespeare possessed of a wisdom we need and desire, but a
wisdom that remains ultimately inaccessible to us, a Shakespeare
who tantalizes and yet implacably "foils" the desperately "searching" speaker and that greater "We" who, as the figure makes clear,
now explicitly emerge as humanity at large:

> For the loftiest hill
> Who to the stars uncrowns his majesty,
> Planting his steadfast footsteps in the sea,
> Making the heaven of heavens his dwelling place,
> Spares but the cloudy border of his base
> To the foiled searching of mortality.
>
> (3–8)

Because these clouds apparently shall never lift, the mountain's
heights, like the Shakespearean inner life they represent, must remain forever beyond the field of vision of "mortality's" searching
gaze, unavailable to humanity in its need, a figurative rendering
that one may be inclined to convert into a doctrine of epistemological limits. That is, what ultimately prevents us from knowing what
goes on in the inaccessible fastness of the Shakespearean inner life
are essential differences between our own restricted mental proc-
esses and the model's virtually transcendent powers of mind that
grant him access to a potentially saving knowledge. Like the gipsy
child, Shakespeare is also a special case, enough like ourselves in
physical appearance to trigger our longings and raise our hopes
that we too can know, but finally so different that his "sole speech"

conveyed only through the inherent silence of his "victorious brow" can neither be communicated to nor articulated by ourselves, the desperate remainder of a suffering humanity.

In adopting a figure that seems, on the face of it, to so frustrate our longings and so dash our hopes, Arnold, surprisingly, does allow us a certain conjectural surmise. Though the logic of the figure of the mountain with its impenetrable border of clouds at the base would appear to deny us any right to speculate about what might go on above the cloud line, Arnold apparently extrapolates from past observation that this, "the loftiest hill," pushes upward to the stars and, by analogy, that Shakespeare carries on his authentic life in the epistemological equivalent of the "heaven of heavens," that hypothetically unconditioned that is figuratively "his dwelling place." As we have already seen, the stars in Arnold are characteristically endowed with anthropomorphized attributes, humanly desirable if perhaps not humanly attainable, so that it is a relatively simple step to ascribe to a Shakespearean inner life—that is, like a mountain summit that makes "the heaven of heavens his dwelling place"—the virtues of the Arnoldian stars and to think of Shakespeare as autonomous and self-dependent ("free" as Arnold had earlier described him) rather than isolated and estranged, the fate of the rest of us in our apartness. Thus shifting from simile to referent in the sonnet's sestet, Arnold—despite all the real biographical testimony to the contrary of his fame among his contemporaries, the praise of Francis Meres, Ben Jonson's tribute, the publication of the Folio—can insist, in accordance with the poem's implicit figurally based argument, that Shakespeare, "[s]elf-school'd, self-scann'd, self honour'd, self-secure / Didst tread on earth unguess'd at" (10–11), leading a life of virtual anonymity, the only way to preserve the good of self-dependence.

But the Shakespearean mountain of Arnold's sonnet is delineated in a way that intimates a second figurative logic, another conceptual direction. For the "loftiest hill" that is Shakespeare is, with careful specificity, described as emerging out of the sea. Like the stars, the sea in the figurative geography of Arnoldian pessimism also often has a highly specialized function: to represent an undifferentiated that for Arnold is the metaphysically real, a cosmic energy inimical to the individuated life of consciousness, the ceaseless strivings of that will mandating that all life is suffering. What I would suggest is that in planting his mountain's "footsteps in the sea," Shakespeare has been endowed by Arnold with a second knowledge over and above that knowledge conducive to self-dependence acquired through that contact with the stars that goes on at the summit of the mountain that is Shakespeare. And the dark knowledge the sea figuratively intimates is the real source of the tragic understanding that we see etched on the Shakespearean brow, an understanding extrapolated from the "pains the immortal spirit must endure" (12), the "weakness which impairs" (13), the "griefs which bow" (13), "pains," "weakness," "griefs" that are without remedy, Shakespeare's figurative connectedness to the sea suggests, because they are inherent in the very nature of things. To be sure, on the Shakespearean "brow" where that suffering is wordlessly articulated—that brow its "sole speech"—Arnold does find evidences registered as well of victory over these "pains," "weakness," and "griefs." But the victory etched on the Shakespearean brow seems not an overcoming and casting-out, a refutation of the poem's dark knowledge, but a purely moral victory, the certainly commendable achievement of not having given in, of having carried on in the face of inevitable defeat.

In this regard, Arnold's Shakespeare is like the gipsy child, that previous model whom Arnold had also credited with achieving a similarly limited mastery over the sorrow at the heart of things, that having "foreknown the vanity of hope," he "yet proceed'st to live." Even if all we might learn from the example of Shakespeare as model is how to know and live, his is still a knowledge and example not ever to be made available to the rest of us who, even as "[w]e ask and ask," must construe his smiling silence as rebuff. That the differences that divide us are not to be overcome, that they are, in some meaningful way, differences in kind, is at least suggested by an interpretively extraneous distinction that Arnold appears to draw between the knowing Shakespeare and the rest of us who must search and be "foil'd." For the Shakespeare who knows has an "immortal spirit," while those others—that is, ourselves—who "ask and ask" are consigned to some implicitly contrastingly lesser status identified by Arnold through the term "mortality." Plainly Arnold's language here has nothing to do with life after death, nor do I think that ascribing to Shakespeare an "immortal spirit" has anything to do with matters as comparatively mundane as the survival of Shakespeare's writings or his fame beyond his lifetime.[11] Rather, by imputing a kind of immortality to Shakespeare and mortality to the rest of us, Arnold would seem essentially to be accentuating what he would like us to understand as the depth of insurmountable difference between the model and those lesser beings who interrogate him. It is a difference that insures that the model's secret remains uncommunicated and incommunicable, his example of self-dependence, of autonomy, of being "free," inherently inimitable by those subject to the limitations of "mortality."

Revealingly, Arnold will use the distinction between mortal and immortal again in a later poem about Arnoldian models and their imitators, "The Scholar-Gipsy."[12] His model there, the scholar-gipsy, is similarly granted an "immortal lot" (157) by virtue of his capacity to maintain an uncompromised fixity of purpose, "one aim, one business, one desire" (152), while the rest of us, "mortal men" (142), are consigned to death from exhaustion by reason of our propensity to change. In this case, too, the extraordinary distinction between the scholar-gipsy's imputed immortality and our apparently grimmer fate as "mortal men" apparently has nothing to do with theological speculation about life after death but seems rather a way of asserting hyperbolically the seemingly absolute depth of difference between the model who knows and those of us who unavailingly seek.

More remarkably, in neither of these poems of untransversable distance between the Arnoldian model and those who would imitate him would their speaker have it otherwise and succeed in his effort to overcome that distance. Even as the speaker of "The Scholar-Gipsy" desperately pursues, he seemingly places the scholar-gipsy's interest ahead of his own, urging the scholar-gipsy to "[f]ly hence, our contact fear" (206), lest we, the poem's pursuing mortals, by overtaking him fatally infect him and thus rob him of the "glad perennial youth" (229) in which, until now, he has enjoyed his immortality. In "Shakespeare" too, despite the obvious anguish Shakespeare's refusal to answer our questions apparently produces in the speaker (and, by inference, in humanity at large), the speaker similarly disregards his own interests and takes the model's side in his efforts to keep us at a distance. To Shakespeare's decision for anonymity and silence—his successful effort to "tread on earth unguess'd at"—so costly and painful to the posterity that reveres his genius, the speaker's response is an emphatically rendered statement of approval, "Better so!" (11). For Shakespeare to have done otherwise, to have entered into contact with the humanity from whom he is now so profoundly estranged, would here presumably, as in "The Scholar-Gipsy," have resulted in the decline of his powers and the loss of that indispensable (though, unfortunately, never-to-be-disseminated) wisdom that made his victory possible—or so this ringing "Better so!" indicates. Thus, in keeping with Arnold's emerging pessimism, the very device he introduces to counter the hopelessness of our situation—the model who has, in some humanly meaningful way, triumphed over our common predicament or at least learned to live in the face of it—is so represented that, in the end, Arnold's proposed strategy of overcoming only worsens the predicament he describes.

Unlike the extraordinarily endowed gipsy child and Shakespeare, Mycerinus, the third of the possible models in *The Strayed Reveller*, is clearly one of us. Like the gipsy child (and I would add Shakespeare), Mycerinus, too, having "foreknown the vanity of hope," still "proceed'st to live." But his wisdom has come not intuitively or innately but from the bitterest experience, and his announced course of action in the face of adversity is one that all of us presumably could follow (if we would). From the episode in Herodotus that supplies the nucleus of the plot for "Mycerinus," Arnold leaves out the important saving explanation by Herodotus: that the gods have issued their shocking sentence of death against Mycerinus so that his good works should not undo their earlier decree that the Egyptian people must suffer 150 years of affliction for misdeeds they committed long before Mycerinus came to the throne. Nor does Arnold follow the suggestion of his source that the retirement of Mycerinus from his public duties to six years of revelry is, in fact, an exercise in folk magic designed to save his own life, a ruse that would turn "night into day" and "make his six years into twelve and so prove the oracle false."[13] What remains, though, is matter enough for the Victorian unbeliever's morality play of denial and defiance into which Arnold recast the anecdote from Herodotus.

Most important is the undeserved sentence of death, after only six years, pronounced by the oracles upon Mycerinus, a decree whose injustice is magnified by contrast with the long life granted his father, his impious predecessor as king.[14] For Arnold, the story of Mycerinus has become an object lesson in the radical disparity between merit and reward that prevails everywhere in the affairs of the universe, a parable whose starkness shows clearly that no power both omnipotent and benevolent can be credited with superintending the destinies of men. Moreover, Mycerinus makes his decision to give himself wholly to pleasure for the brief time allotted him—not, as in the original, to hoodwink the gods by burning the candle at both ends, but as a deliberate, liberating, self-affirming moral act, chosen to enhance rather than reduce his humanity in that pitiless universe that the prophecy discloses.

Rejected in this study in conversion from belief to disbelief are not just the maxims of faith but an entire cosmological paradigm, inherited from the pre-Enlightenment past, a system of macrocosmic-microcosmic correspondences in which the heavens above serve man as a visible emblem of a divinely ordained moral life of duty, of justice, of self-restraint:

> Yet surely, O my people, did I deem
> Man's justice from the all-just Gods was given:
> A light that from some upper fount did beam,
> Some better archetype, whose seat was heaven;
> A light that, shining from the blest abodes,
> Did shadow somewhat of the life of Gods.
>
> (19–24)

But news from the oracle is for Mycerinus incontrovertible proof of the faultiness of his paradigm. Utterly convinced that the sentence imposed by the gods can in no way correspond to what man means by justice, Mycerinus turns away from the geocentric security of his former worldview in search of a new cosmological paradigm that, however comfortless, would truthfully express the moral emptiness at the heart of things.

Apart from his conviction that the universe exhibits no moral design, the metaphysical thinking of Mycerinus is relatively tentative and undogmatic. Injustice and suffering may be the rule of life because of the indifference of the gods, a formulation that probably has its metaphysical grounds in some version of philosophic materialism (whether the atoms in motion of Lucretius or the mathematically determined orbits of mechanistic nineteenth-century astronomy). But this suffering and injustice may just as easily derive from a radically different metaphysical principle: "some Force" (37) that "[s]weeps earth, and heaven, and men, and gods along, / Like the broad volume of the insurgent Nile" (39–40), a cosmic will oblivious to any end or purpose but the self-perpetuation of its own movement, leaving the gods themselves not merely indifferent but irrelevant, vestigial presences stripped of any real authority over man, reduced like him to a role of absolute dependence, "Slaves of a tyrannous necessity" (42). For the first time Arnold here introduces the grounding concept of nineteenth-century philosophic pessimism, suggesting that the ultimate principle at work in the universe is a vast and impersonal will, an ontological unity of undifferentiated flow within which all phenomenal distinctions must finally dissolve.

Once again, though, Arnold's main concern is not really with what is known but with how to live; and under the cruel circumstances the poem discloses, the rational choice would seem to be to pursue pleasure.[15] As Mycerinus explains, the gods have deceived him not

only about the justness of the universe but also into forsaking pleasures that once lost are irrecoverable, joys reserved for "the fiery
prime / Of youth" (9–10), which should be given over to "dances
crowned with flowers, / Love, free to range, and regal banquetings"
(33–34). And in a highly speculative and obviously tentative account
of the origin of the gods (not so very different from that of Blake or
Freud), Mycerinus even intimates that man's mistaken belief in the
"all-just Gods" (20) derives not from his idealism but from his anxieties, his having erroneously projected upon an indifferent cosmos
such notions as justice, duty, and self-restraint out of fear of his
own libidinal impulses. In short, the gods are merely the self-cre-
ated fictions of a too-scrupulous conscience, figments of the superego: "Mere phantoms of man's self-tormenting heart, / Which on the
sweets that woo it dare not feed" (25–26). The adoption of hedonism
may therefore be not just a surrender to license permissible now in
the moral void left by the removal of all transcendent sanctions for
behavior but a breaking free by Mycerinus from mind-forged manacles that may have been the true basis for his self-denying imperatives, the expression of a will essentially Promethean—a will to
resist, to defy those tormenting deities, fictive or otherwise.

Like most statements of romantic Prometheanism, "Mycerinus"
reinforces its arguments by spatially rendering its human-centered
values in terms of sky and earth, heights and depths. Above us are
the heavens, long assumed the seat of the "all-just Gods" (20), pre-
sumptive authors of those edicts that bind and inhibit us, but figures
whom we now recognize for what they are: those sky-gods characterized by Frye as the "the projection of human superstition with
its tendency to deify a mechanical and subhuman order."[16] An enlightened Mycerinus, therefore, can now dismiss as mere effigies
the divinities he had once worshipped as "[n]ot Gods but ghosts, in
frozen apathy" (36). Below the heavens are the groves, functionally
similar to those verdant regions in the poetry of Wallace Stevens
that seem islands of earthly abundance in the void that surrounds
them, appropriate centers within which man can search out authen-
tically human pleasures of which the "dull gods" (65) would deprive
him. Indeed, in the groves (Mycerinus insists, in the most Promethean of his challenges), the gods shall behold a life more godlike than
any they might enjoy in the sky: "Revels more deep, joy keener than
their own" (66).

Yet after setting out the case for hedonism with care and apparent conviction, Arnold himself undeniably calls its adequacy into
question by suggesting that the source of the strength and serenity
Mycerinus displays may not be hedonism after all but a veiled Stoic

inwardness that, despite his tribulations, leaves him "calmed, enno-
bled, comforted, sustained" (111). As irrestible as Arnold's interpo-
lated Stoicism has been to critics of "Mycerinus" made uneasy by
its prevailing moral tone, it is doubtful that a single brief phrase
provides the basis for reconstituting the poem as an exercise in a
doctrinaire Arnoldian Stoicism designed to expose the shortcomings of a palpably inadequate hedonism that Arnold elaborates at
such length only to make its eventual refutation more telling. Why
then should Arnold have introduced into the closing passages of
"Mycerinus" a conjecture so unexpectedly out of keeping with all
that had gone before? The answer, I believe, lies not in the alle-
giance of Arnold to any single overriding dogma but rather in a tentativeness that is one of his most characteristic poetic qualities, a
habit of skepticism that induces him time after time to preserve options, to draw back from certainty. The Stoicism of "Mycerinus" is
just one more example of Arnold's tendency to qualify assent to the
conclusions to which his imaginative logic carries him by some form
of intellectual counterplot woven into the fabric of poem after poem.
We have already seen evidences of this tendency in that wavering
negation, that *aporia*, that suggestively casts doubt on the presumed applicability of the heavens to the lives of men in "A Summer
Night"; we find it as well in the call for a love in a world without love
in "Dover Beach"; and, most of all, in *Empedocles on Etna* in the
interplay between the self-destructive metaphysical arguments of
Empedocles and the mythopoeic counterstatement of Callicles.

The limits of human knowledge are pointedly acknowledged in
"Mycerinus" even in the heat of the hero's own metaphysical speculations. Whether there are or are not gods, whether the universe
operates by principles that are mechanistic or volitional—these are
questions left unresolved, their answers hidden by the impenetrable
barrier of a "circumambient gloom" (53), behind which dwell "powers we cannot see" (51). As he publicly announces his decision to
pursue pleasure in "the silence of the groves and woods" (67), Mycerinus expresses similar uncertainty, pointing vaguely but porten-
tously beyond what has already been said to further considerations
that bear upon that decision in some unspecifiable way: "I will go
forth; though something would I say— / Something—yet what, I
know not" (68–69). But whether the unknown "something" that
stirs Mycerinus would, if articulated, deter him or encourage him is
a question that Arnold's semantically barren terms of presentation
leave simply undecidable.

Perhaps the most serious impediment to certainty for Arnold
stems from the philosophic conundrum of other minds, a problem

posed by the cosmically ordained boundedness of enislement of
each of us individually in "To Marguerite—Continued," and, most
especially, by the epistemological fact of "unmatingness" of which
he complains in "Isolation. To Marguerite." There he tells himself
that, though he may believe himself to be engaged with the world,
the things "[w]hich touch thee are unmating things" (32), a sense
of unbreachable separation arising with every sensation in this our
"life" (35). As a consequence, in our contact with others, while we
may apprehend surfaces, we never sound depths. An especially vexing aspect of the fact that we never genuinely apprehend the reality
that lies behind the appearances of other beings like ourselves are
those cases where Arnold has designated some individual, the gipsy
child or Shakespeare, as a model and yet so devised that model that
we are necessarily debarred from ever knowing him as he really is
and, therefore, from ever really being able to follow his example.

   At first glance, as a model Mycerinus seems exceptionally promising. Among those who meet the primary criterion of the Arnoldian
model, heroically persisting in the face of a knowledge bespeaking
life's unalterable hopelessness, he seems the most accessible and
thus the most easily imitated. His is not an intuitive knowledge,
uniquely his own and shielded from us by an impenetrable detachment and reserve. Unlike the steadfastly unresponsive Shakespeare or the silent gipsy child or the "pensive and tongue-tied"
scholar-gipsy, Mycerinus is willing to address us directly, to spell
out his indictment of the gods and the universe and commend to us
a plan of action that we can both comprehend and follow. He need
only submit the case for pleasure to the test of experience, to prove
that by following pleasure in the face of overwhelming adversity he
has achieved the kind of victory communicated by the expressive
silence of Shakespeare.

   In the final third of "Mycerinus," though, Arnold, shifting from
hypothesis to proof, radically reconstitutes the form of the poem.
What had begun as a monologue by the embittered and defiant king
to the subjects he is forsaking (delivered in a sequence of thirteen
regularly rhymed six-line stanzas, much in the manner of Wordsworth's "Laodamia") abruptly changes at line 79 to a blank-verse
recounting of events within the groves to which he retreats, related
by an impersonal third-person narrator. But in shifting speakers,
Arnold has transformed Mycerinus from the center of consciousness of the poem, reporting upon and interpreting events as well as
his own inner states and feelings, to an object of observation who
can be known to us only externally through the mediating presence
of the narrator. Still, from the narrator's report, it would seem that

as a model Mycerinus has met our test: in the groves, pleasure has apparently sufficed and Mycerinus, in defiance of fate, has achieved joy. But proof of this now derives entirely from life's observable surface, a surface that may just as easily distortingly conceal as express depths, as the narrator finally admits. Arnold does not endow his narrator with omniscience but instead imposes upon him those general limits of perception that clearly preclude any direct knowledge of the mind of another, thereby effectively reducing the promise of Mycerinus as a model whom we can know and emulate.

Paradoxically, though, Arnold has vastly enlarged the speculative freedom of his narrator, permitting him conjectures about the inner life of Mycerinus that clearly run against the grain of observation, imaginative options that both expand the horizons of "Mycerinus" and at the same time exacerbate the reader's epistemological uncertainties. Even as we learn that the face Mycerinus shows the world unquestionably projects a joy that seems to justify his enterprise of pleasure, the narrator appends to this report the skeptic's cautious reservation. That expression of joy, the narrator indicates, may be nothing more than illusion, a disguise adopted by Mycerinus to conceal from others the very different reality of his inner life.

> It may be that sometimes his wondering soul
> From the loud joyful laughter of his lips
> Might shrink half-startled, like a guilty man
> Who wrestles with his dream; as some pale shape
> Gliding half hidden through the dusky stems,
> Would thrust a hand before the lifted bowl,
> Whispering: *A little space, and thou art mine!*
> It may be on that joyless feast his eye
> Dwelt with mere outward seeming; he, within,
> Took measure of his soul, and knew its strength,
> And by that silent knowledge, day by day,
> Was calmed, ennobled, comforted, sustained.

(100–111)

The first of these conjectures has never figured prominently in interpretations of "Mycerinus." Perhaps to preserve the credibility of the narrator in his conjuring of alternative versions of the inner life, Arnold felt obliged to concede that fear of death might have proven too much for Mycerinus, inducing specters so frightful that all other considerations are rendered irrelevant. The second, however, has emerged as a major crux, a conjecture close enough to the preconceptions of so many of Arnold's critics as to be elevated to a statement of intention—"the heart of the poem," according to

Dwight Culler[17]—concealed until now behind a hedonistic facade that Arnold, in a single sentence, dismantles as only "an apparent Epicureanism,"[18] presumably advanced solely for the sake of discrediting it. By this revelation, this crucial turn in the argument, Culler's Mycerinus informs us that he realizes he was "not originally a virtuous person, since he had practiced virtue in the expectation of some reward"[19] but has now learned "that the reward of virtue lies, not in the approval of the gods, but simply in the knowledge of one's own rectitude,"[20] thus establishing himself as "not an Epicurean but a Stoic sage."[21] Surprisingly though, this "silent knowledge" exerts no apparent influence upon the subsequent behavior of the youthful king, since in the lines immediately following this critically pivotal interpolation his revelry continues unabated. So Alan Roper, who also believes that the Stoic hypothesis is "the heart of the poem," goes beyond Culler and, taking into account this obvious discrepancy between speculation and practice, finds the primary judgment the poem makes to be "condemnation, however qualified, of the hapless Pharoah's acts and decisions,"[22] since he has failed to practice the Stoicism Roper finds so obviously normative.

Arnold himself does, of course, invite us to weigh the Stoic option as a principle of interpretation in "Mycerinus." But in the absence of certainty we must assess probabilities, and too many factors militate against the Stoic hypothesis for us to reverse the apparent moral priorities of the poem as a whole and substitute Stoicism for hedonism as the interpretive norm. Perhaps the most damaging evidence against the Stoic hypothesis is that the narrator provides not one but two parallel and equally plausible accounts of how the youthful king actually responded to his predicament. "It may be," the narrator suggests, that if we could peer into the depths of his soul we would find only a man afraid, guiltily recoiling from the spectral presence that darkens the pleasure of the feast with his ominous reminder: "*A little space, and thou art mine*" (106). Only after this does the narrator suggest that if we could look directly into the buried life of Mycerinus we would find—"It may be"—that he had sustained himself in the groves by the Stoic's inner calm and strength. Moreover, after these seemingly balanced speculations, the narrator turns again to that surface of things that perhaps conceals but may just as well express depths. In fact, Arnold's narrator turns again to an apparently imperturbable Mycerinus, whose appearances and actions remain unaltered even after these conjectures are voiced, lending support to the inductive probability that what had sustained him during his self-imposed exile was the very hedonism to which he had originally pledged himself: "It may be;

but not less his brow was smooth, / And his clear laugh fled ringing through the gloom" (114–15).

To resist the laws that ordain his death, as the self-affirming laughter of Mycerinus suggests he does, is not to say, however, that we can alter or circumvent them. There will always remain, impervious to all gestures of Promethean defiance, a circumscribing reality that must inevitably doom to defeat even the most intensely projected of the urgings of desire. Hovering implicitly over the entire poem and conditioning our response to every line is the prophecy expounding the will of the gods, the irreversible sentence of death that both initiated the major action of the poem and yet undermines any hope of its succeeding. Almost from the revellers' first entry into the groves, the narrator will judge the hedonistic enterprise of Mycerinus and his followers, however pleasurable by ordinary human standards, as a "feverish dream of youth" (89), a futile exercise in appearances that in no way affects the metaphysical reality underlying human existence.

In his closing figure, Arnold provides a final statement of the poem's concerns, gathering together all of its major intellectual strains: the hedonism and skepticism and metaphysical pessimism that in one form or another condition the whole presentation of the history of Mycerinus:

> So six long years he revelled, night and day.
> And when the mirth waxed loudest, with dull sound
> Sometimes from the grove's centre echoes came,
> To tell the wondering people of their king;
> In the still night, across the steaming flats,
> Mixed with the murmur of the moving Nile.
>
> (122–27)

In the groves, imaginative center of the poem, desire still unfailingly affirms itself, expressing through the persistence of "mirth" the triumph of pleasure. But as the passage radiates outward, reincorporating into its setting the community Mycerinus had left behind, Arnold again introduces into his increasingly symbolic narrative those epistemological and metaphysical dilemmas that so profoundly qualify the claims to be made for Mycerinus as an example. Whatever he has personally accomplished in warding off, if not death, at least fear, his usefulness as model, a guide to men in their common plight, is severely limited by his inaccessibility to those who live outside the groves. Muted by distance, the mirth of Mycerinus, even as it "waxed loudest," reaches his subjects only as "dull

sound," dying echoes overheard by a "wondering people" separated
from their king, a localized account of what Arnold sees as one of
man's fundamental predicaments—isolation, estrangement, the life
enisled. Indeed, Arnold essentially offers a more developed, more
generalized version of the situation described at the close of "Mycerinus" in "To Marguerite—Continued," with its controlling metaphor of the individual life enisled by a barrier of "echoing straits"
(2) across which flow sounds of consummate loveliness, the apparent expression of the joy of another issuing from far-off glens. But
this joy, like the mirth of Mycerinus, proves unavailing to the distant
listeners who intuitively recognize—with their own presumed
"longing like despair" (13)—that it is a joy beyond reach. Spelled
out in this later poem is what is only suggested in "Mycerinus": the
insuperable distance that separates us from those we would know
is to be accounted for not by geography but by epistemology, by the
very constitution of consciousness itself, the individuating boundedness that mandates that "[w]e mortal millions live *alone*" (4).

With the reappearance in the final line of "the moving Nile" (127),
its "murmur" mingled with echoes of the revels of the grove, Arnold
introduces a second major complication into his assessment of how
far the hedonism chosen by Mycerinus finally may suffice; for Arnold surely need add no accompanying commentary to explicate
what is implied by this closing allusion to the Nile, whose waters
here flow as they have for millennia before Mycerinus and lend to
the poem a sense of time that in its expansiveness approaches the
timeless. It is from this vast and enduring perspective that we are
to reckon the true brevity of pleasure, the fleetingness of that concluding phase of the life of Mycerinus, "the six long years he rev-
elled" (122), measured out to him by Arnold with the bitterest irony.
Implicit as well in this is an element of metaphysical reference that,
in part, is carried over from the earlier, more overtly emblematic
presentation of the Nile in the king's monologue, where it had func-
tioned as a moving image of eternity, the figurative embodiment of
an irresistible cosmic will that "[s]weeps earth, and heaven, and
men, and gods along" (39).

By reviving these earlier associations at so significant a moment
in "Mycerinus," Arnold clearly demonstrates how deeply engrained,
even at this point in his career, was the tendency to conceive metaphysical process in volitional rather than in mechanistic terms, a
conception that was eventually to serve as the foundation for the
fully articulated philosophic pessimism of "Resignation" and the
major poetry that follows it. But there are more direct consequences for "Mycerinus" in Arnold's decision to conclude his poem

with the sounds of the "moving Nile," to close it on a note not of further hedonistic defiance but of metaphysical pathos, a tacit acknowledgement of ultimate unsuccess; for however strenuously Mycerinus has resisted, he has neither cheated the gods nor overcome his predicament. Indeed, colored as this figure is by the metaphysical associations acquired in its earlier appearance, by employing it here Arnold carries that pathos substantially beyond what had been evoked by the original situation of "Mycerinus." Joy is not only brief but illusory, involving only appearances that in themselves are powerless to influence the onward flowing reality that in the end shall subsume all human endeavor.[23]

3

The Poetry of Pessimism: "Resignation" and *Empedocles on Etna*

THE CULMINATION OF ARNOLD'S EMERGING PESSIMISM IN *THE STRAYED Reveller* is, of course, "Resignation," the first and perhaps fullest exposition of metaphysical pessimism in nineteenth-century English poetry. It is a poem that, more than any other poem of its time, expresses that paradigm shift from Romanticism to the post-Romanticism we usually think of as modernity, a change in world-views in which, as Frye puts it, "the noumenal world of Fichte turns into the sinister world-as-will of Schopenhauer."[1] Indeed, "Resignation" gives us the Schopenhauerian paradigm at its bleakest, an unfalteringly comfortless account of human endeavor in a world fatally flawed by the determining agency of the "something that infects" it (278).

The present discussion, with its expressly philosophic orientation, does not even attempt to do justice to the imaginative richness and speculative amplitude of "Resignation," a poem paradoxically noteworthy for never having received the attention that would seem obviously its due.[2] Of necessity, a large number of important topics, familiar and unfamiliar, must be set aside altogether or just barely touched upon in these pages. Not discussed is the Wordsworthian matrix, or, more specifically, "Tintern Abbey," an admittedly formative presence in "Resignation," but less absolutely determining than many critics assert—at least those like U. C. Knoepflemacher and M. G. Sundell, and (to some extent) Stange, who would have us read "Resignation" in purely oppositional terms, essentially as a counterstatement, a reflexive response to a far greater precursor.[3] Not that the parallels between "Tintern Abbey" and Arnold's own poem of revisitation accompanied by a sister do not exist, but many of these parallels may be explained as pure coincidence, deriving from the verifiably real events of Arnold's own life rather than from a program of purposeful reading. Moreover, large and important segments of "Resignation" have no counterpart in "Tintern

Abbey," notably the elaborate quasi-allegory of the strivers, the gipsies, and the poet. Finally, even if we concede the plausibility of
these parallels, they have shown themselves to possess surprisingly
little explanatory value.

Critics who maintain that the philosophy of nature in "Resignation" emerges from a Wordsworthian matrix differ strikingly among
themselves on every key concept in that philosophy, apart from the
obvious fact of its general somberness by comparison with the generally optimistic philosophy of "Tintern Abbey." My own contention
is that the most appropriate and useful matrix for explaining the
admittedly complex philosophy of "Resignation" is an Arnoldian
matrix, that is, that extensive body of writings by Arnold that deal
with the themes and issues in "Resignation" as they are repeatedly
taken up by Arnold elsewhere with no apparent reference to Wordsworth.

The analysis of "Resignation" offered here begins in medias res
with the appearance of the poet, another potential model, but one
whose way of life and implied counsel are in the end resisted. Initially, though, it would seem that the poet provides an apparent
counterexample to that life of passionate striving that for Arnold
verges on obsession and madness. In response to the summons to
live in action and thereby "attain" (1)—voiced not just by the crusader and pilgrim and Goth and Hun of the opening verse-para-
graph but still more enticingly by a father recently dead, who had
cheered on and guided Arnold and his sister on that original excursion long ago—Arnold points to the poet as one who attains without
plunging into action and who, while solitary, maintains a special
form of detachment that he never experiences as loneliness.

What the poet of "Resignation" possesses is a rare capacity for
comprehensiveness and fixity of vision, like that Sophocles of "To a
Friend" who, from the perspective afforded him by his extraordinary elevation of spirit, "saw life steadily and saw it whole" (12).
Granted a similarly figurative "high station" (164), the poet comprehensively surveys his world, understanding—indeed appreciat-
ing—all he surveys, yet remaining distant and detached from those
below, never once wishing to enter into the action that they engage
in but that he shuns. Looking down upon the "ruler" of "some great-
historied land" (154–55), the poet "exults" in the image of power he
beholds but "for no moment's space / Envies the all-regarded place"
(158–59). When "beautiful eyes meet his," "he / Bears to admire"
but "uncravingly" (160–61). And as he "[s]urveys each happy group
which fleets, / Toil ended, through the shining streets" (166–67), he
expresses no wish to share in their observed happiness, never find-

ing in their pleasure or purposefulness reason to repent or abandon his own solitariness.

Unlike the Keatsian poet who "has no identity" but is "continually in for and filling some other Body,"[4] Arnold's poet is pointedly unempathic. Yet the absence of an empathic capability is not just a limiting condition in Arnold's poetics but, he believes, is a general epistemological restriction placed on all those "mortal millions" who are "in the sea of life enisled" ("To Marguerite—Continued," 1) and must "live alone" ("To Marguerite—Continued," 4), or, if "not quite alone," touched only by "unmating things" ("Isolation. To Marguerite," 31–32). Such "unmatingness" would seem in fact to be a general feature of all human perception, debarring us from ever empathically apprehending the true being of the objects and persons around us, mandating that we can never know depths, only surfaces. Other men may yearn that things be otherwise, a yearning invariably undone by the sad facts of the human condition that compel us to live in "[i]solation without end / Prolonged" ("Isolation. To Marguerite," 40–41), but the poet, by a seemingly special dispensation, can unempathically experience the world and still remain undisturbed by longing to have or to become what he beholds. Even while dwelling in separateness, he never suffers from the plight of isolation, never says (Arnold informs us with italicized emphasis) "*I am alone*" (169).

The poet of "Resignation" also possesses a second form of knowledge superior to ordinary human knowledge, a capability of noumenal understanding much like that granted Empedocles upon the "charr'd, blackened, melancholy waste" (2.2) of Etna. There Empedocles—less the poet than the sage in Arnold's loose conjunction—employs his special endowments to see not "wide" but "deep," peering into the crater of Etna to learn fundamental truths of the uttermost bleakness formulated in explicitly metaphysical terms. Like Empedocles, the poet of "Resignation" also seemingly apprehends, if not things-in-themselves in their apparent immediacy, at least that form of phenomenal existence that most closely approximates and perhaps most fully partakes of the purely noumenal. In a pristine nature undisfigured by the activities of men, a nature perceived as an essentially pure flow of duration into which the particularity of events has virtually dissolved, he finds a form of being worthy of his deepest longings, a confluence of sounds where none is individualized or signifying: "The murmur of a thousand years" (188); a field of vision with nothing focused upon so that all instead remains "[a] placid and continuous whole" (190). In this perceived undifferentiatedness, there are—despite the cautiousness of Arnold's language—intimations of an intuition of the metaphysically real, the truly noumenal, either through resemblance and correspondence or possibly even as actual manifestation, an incursion by and showing forth of the noumenal in the phenomenal, visible at least to those possessed of sufficient "lucidity of soul":

> That general life, which does not cease,
> Whose secret is not joy, but peace;
> That life, whose dumb wish is not missed
> If birth proceeds, if things subsist;
> The life of plants, and stones, and rain,
> The life he craves—if not in vain
> Fate gave, what chance shall not control,
> His sad lucidity of soul.
>
> (191–98)

We must bear in mind, though, that however much we might be tempted to ascribe this account of the "general life" to a romantic attachment to nature, we are plainly on the way to the life-imperiling conclusions of *Empedocles on Etna*. To the poet, the "general life"—a life of coming into being and sheer existential subsistence expressed most clearly in the least complex phenomena, "[t]he life of plants, and stones, and rain" (195)—is not just an object of contemplation but of desire, what the poet "craves" and could indeed have and be if his own natural and elemental self might somehow be divested of its complicating and estranging human consciousness. At crucial places in the poetry of Arnold, he displays what can only be called deeply antihumanistic tendencies inevitably implicit in any genuine metaphysical pessimism. These occur almost invariably in conjunction with ontological longings, the wish to overcome metaphysical estrangement from the noumenal (or its phenomenal approximation) in its guise as "the All" (*Empedocles on Etna*, 2.353), "the life of life" (*Empedocles on Etna*, 2.357), or the "general life" ("Resignation," 191). But, Arnold indicates, to achieve this union we must sacrifice all of those attributes and values in which we assume our humanity resides: consciousness, reason, and interest in, concern for, and love of others of our kind. Empedocles himself exemplifies this tendency, and in "the analysis of [Empedocles'] character and motives" in the Yale manuscript, Arnold explains his suicide in just these terms: as the result of his desire "to be reunited with the universe, before by exaggerating his human side he has become utterly estranged from it" (see *Poems*, 155). If the poet of "Resignation" is a far less desperately ambiguous figure than Empedocles, he is nonetheless moved by the same passions, although he does not follow Empedocles in taking them to their logical conclusion: union with the "general life," even at the cost of suppressing "his human side," is what the poet, too, "craves" in "[h]is sad lucidity of soul" (198).

At this climactic moment in a poem that reads very much like a summing-up, a position paper, Arnold's pessimistically based inquiry into metaphysics would seem to have led him to the most profoundly antihumanistic conclusions. The ontologically real, "the general life," turns out to be life stripped to sheer subsistence, an utterly unanthropomorphized ongoingness, existence wholly devoid of all of those human attributes that we customarily suppose give life its meaning and value. Most disturbingly antihumanistic is what the poet teaches from his privileged position: not the characteristically Romantic response, Promethean steadfastness in the face of a reality so plainly inhumane, but submission, the disciplining of our individuated wills to seek union with the ontologically more real "general life" he "craves," even if by the sacrifice of the life of consciousness itself.

Elsewhere, however, it should be noted, in "Human Life" and in "To Marguerite—Continued," Arnold does provide spokesmen who recoil against the pressures and pull of the noumenal, siding with a beleaguered humanity and especially with the deep-seated human need for the "joys," the "friends," the "homes" we would make ours despite the prohibiting will of "unknown Powers" and an unloving "God," severing, estranging, commanding that it be otherwise. In fact, the seemingly privileged position of the poet notwithstanding, the remaining sections of "Resignation" grope toward just such an attitude to the noumenal, standing fast against a reality deemed the enemy of life rather than seeking union with what the poet craves.

In its last eighty lines, "Resignation" takes a sharp conceptual turn, moving from apparent advocacy of these life-negating attitudes to the commending of an ethical practice implicitly more humanistic. At first, the speaker of "Resignation" does seem one of those Arnoldian speakers who look to the sage for guidance. Innately endowed with "natural insight," the poet of "Resignation" is obviously preeminent even among those exemplary few whom "birth hath found, resigned" (27), and therefore an ideal if difficult model to follow. Yet despite admittedly radical epistemological differences between the poet and the ordinary run of humanity whose knowledge derives only from experience, the poet of "Resignation," certainly by comparison with the gipsy child, Shakespeare, and even the scholar-gipsy, is among the most imitable of Arnoldian sages because, though denied "[t]he poet's rapt security" (246), the speaker can acquire through "schooling of the stubborn mind" (26) what the poet knows innately. By putting aside "passionate hopes" (243) and judging "vain beforehand human cares" (232)—in short, by forgoing involvement in the world as the poet does—Fausta, the speaker's potentially wayward sister, can also gain a similar wisdom and thus enjoy the freedom and serenity that come through resignation. Just as the poet is able to look upon the "ruler" at his moment of absolute command and "yet for no moment's space / Envies the all-regarded place" (158–59) and can meet the gaze of "[b]eautiful eyes" but yet "admire uncravingly" (160–61), so too can Fausta forsake these most basic of all human objectives, "love and power," by knowing what they are: "Love transient, power an unreal show" (235–36).

In metaphysical understanding as well, the speaker counsels Fausta to pursue what the poet in his enlightenment craves: "That general life, which does not cease, / Whose secret is not joy, but peace" (191–92). By keeping their distance from "men's business" (250), the speaker even suggests that he and Fausta can narrow the gulf between the phenomenal and the real, move toward ontological reconciliation, and "[d]raw homeward to the general life" (252), living "[l]ike leaves by suns not yet uncurled" (253), and be as if they never were. With this last line, we can recognize how profoundly regressive the impulse behind "Resignation" is, how strongly Arnold resists conventional developmental and adaptive assumptions about human goals and possibilities. Such a regressive impulse was already evident earlier in the contrast that hinges on the word "craves" in the account of the poet, a bit of seemingly casual wordplay in which we actually find libido redirected from its normal sexual channels toward curiously meager, de-eroticized, and (in their generality) implicitly infantile objects. It is not the woman whose eyes meet his the poet "craves"—for he can admire her "uncravingly"—but the most austere, elemental, and impersonal form of being, life utterly devoid of consciousness or feeling, "The life of plants, and stones, and rain" (195). There among these elemental objects, the speaker would have Fausta believe, man's true home is to be found, where life is reduced to absolute rudimentariness and being in the world is like not having been at all.

In all of this we can see the working-out of a logic that inexorably pulls us toward extinction. While never openly advocating suicide like Empedocles, the speaker of "Resignation" nonetheless, in telling Fausta to seek union with the "general life"—which is, after all, "The life of plants, and stones, and rain" (195)—counsels her to pursue a course of self-negation that must surely require the over-coming and elimination of the human consciousness and human de-sire that make her so different and estrange her so profoundly from the wholly elemental. Almost certainly it is advice that can be best accomplished by death. Furthermore, lending some kind of theologi-cal sanction to claims that until now had been made on purely philo-sophic grounds, the speaker invokes one of the strangest of the strange gods of Arnold's poetry. Contemplating the spectacle of earthly existence with the most austere neutrality, this perplexing "He" finds each humanly crowded moment of time not an occasion to judge and perhaps forgive but merely "a quiet watershed / Whence equally the seas of life and death are fed" (259–60). From the perspective of this all-seeing and all-knowing deity, the division between life and death is meaningless, and we may therefore cross that dividing line when we choose without fear of divine condemna-tion and yield to that craving for absorption into the noumenal, even if it entails the eradication by suicide of our estranging conscious-ness. Yet at the point in the poem when life has surrendered its pre-cariously privileged status as a self-evidently intrinsic good and the lure of extinction seems most seductively compelling, the speaker of "Resignation" unexpectedly pulls back from the logic of Emped-ocles, and the argument of "Resignation" takes its last and most critically important turn. In this reversal, this peripety, the speaker in effect draws the line, issues the imperative that invokes against the seemingly irrefutable logic of self-negation the one great com-mand that must govern men, that we must endure and carry on, with or without inducement from or even belief in God. On this mat-ter there can be no debate, no choice, no further appeal. "Enough—we live!" (261) the speaker commands in the simple phrase that reverses the poem's previous drift to self-annihilation.

In the concluding seventeen lines of "Resignation"—those begin-ning "Enough—we live!" (261), the speaker's section rather than the poet's—the poem becomes metaphysically darker yet ethically more positive (at least in the sense of being morally committed) than the preceding portions. Arnold retains the general schematic of pessimism with its metaphysical division between the world as will and the world as idea, but noumenal and phenomenal are subtly but significantly reconstituted. Earlier, in a nature stripped almost entirely of particularity, the poet had discovered a noumenally con-ditioned (or at least resembling) otherness wholly unlike ourselves, but yet a worthy object of human desire since it possesses the "peace" (192) man lacks. What we are presented with here is a metaphysics of immanence, an elemental naturalism in which the true and the good (the ontologically most real and the ethically most normative of values) are perceived to be objectified in nature at its most diffuse and invariant, in the vital ongoingness of "the general life." The "placid and continuous whole" that stretches before the poet is intuitively recognized as example and ideal, the effortless realization of the "repose" so desperately sought through action by the strivers of the opening. In its virtual undifferentiatedness and sheer undirected flowingness, "the general life" seems to exemplify and, indeed, to embody a notion of the will as the ground of being, the ontologically real, that is at the core of Arnold's pessimistic metaphysics. In this metaphysics of immanence, the distinction between noumenal will and phenomenal idea is really an opposition between elemental nature and human consciousness, with "the general life" identified with and in some sense participating in a real at variance with the individuating, particularizing, and estranging consciousness of man.

Quite possibly the poet "craves" the general life because some corresponding elemental core of being in man himself, his own "buried life" or "buried self," calls out to its likeness in nature and would "[d]raw homeward" to true fullness of existence in the real, if only he could shake off the disabling burden of consciousness. These concepts are only sketchily implied by the metaphysics of immanence of "Resignation," but they are clearly and fully expressed and followed out to their logical conclusion in *Empedocles on Etna*. There, of course, Empedocles first places the blame for estrangement from "the All" on an imprisoning human consciousness and its "forms, and modes, and stifling veils" (2.354), and then he asserts the identity of man's "buried life" with the "general life" in his overpowering wish to recover that core of ontological being in himself, to

at last, be true
To our own only true, deep-buried selves,
Being one with which we are one with the whole world.
(2.370–72)[5]

To renounce consciousness and pursue the merger of the buried life in man with its counterpart in nature, the general life, is a course fraught with peril, as we learn from the fate of Empedocles. But it is nonetheless an act faithful to the logic and spirit of a metaphysics of immanence, according to which we may in a single act (like Empedocles') divest ourselves of consciousness, thereby exchanging our metaphysically estranging thought for a metaphysically authentic life, the apparent for the real. Hope so conceived, however, remains deeply antihumanistic and finally must be read as duplicitous. What we are actually tempted by here is not life carried out on some ontologically more real plane but repudiation of our specifically human life, a reaching-out for relief from a human existence felt to be unendurable, by the only sure remedy for such suffering, the release that is extinction.

The poet of "Resignation" never actually attempts to act out these desires as Empedocles does, nor do Fausta and her brother—who, in any case, are kept from pursuing the logic of immanence any further by that restraining imperative and rallying cry, "Enough, we live!" (261). But in this assertion of steadfastness against the pull of the general life, in turning away from what earlier passages had described as a craving for it, the speaker not only establishes his independence of the poet but also shifts the ground of argument in the poem. While still retaining the basic framework of pessimism, the opposition between metaphysical will and phenomenal idea, he no longer represents that opposition as the difference between the individuated human consciousness and nature apprehended as elemental and undifferentiated. Instead, nature and consciousness are treated as essentially alike, conjoined by the common denominator of a shared plight and a common capacity to endure it. Together man and nature comprise the phenomenal, the world of idea, "the general lot" (275). Furthermore, in this revised interpretation, nature most deeply and truly expresses not placidity and peacefulness but a manifest attitude of resistance against the implacable energies of a cosmic will that ordains suffering. Even if the objects of nature do no more than "[s]eem to bear" (270), they remain, nevertheless, a precedent and example for humanity. For us, too, existence is something to be borne, "bearable," though "hardly worth / This pomp of worlds, this pain of birth" (263–64). And it can be borne—that is, we can do as nature does—by remaining as we are now, affirming the need to live and repudiating the craving for the general life that demands the extinction of consciousness.

In place of a metaphysics of immanence predicated on the "general life," Arnold now presents us with a more customary metaphysics of transcendence (that is, a depersonalized Kantian transcendence) predicated on the life-opposing activities of a noumenally grounded "something that infects the world" (278). Beyond time and space, according to this emerging hypothesis, is an essentially volitional reality never known unmediatedly, but whose agency man and nature constantly experience in their ongoing suffering. What binds man and nature most closely together, the basis of their identity in spite of all differences, is their sharing of the common affliction, their pandemic susceptibility to the universal principle that "infects" all phenomenal existence: "The something that infects the world" (278).

The last crucial line of "Resignation" is probably the most profoundly and audaciously pessimistic metaphysical utterance to be found in Arnold. But in its reach toward the noumenally indescribable, it is undoubtedly the most cryptic formulation of Arnoldian metaphysics, so that commentary has been understandably sparse and tentative.[6] Most certainly Arnold does place diverse phenomena—man and nature, all thinking subjects and their objects—under the category "the world," its varied particulars taking their common identity from the infectedness that presumably is suffered by all. But accurately defining or delineating the key metaphysical agent in the equation, "the something that infects," is obviously far more difficult. We should not judge Arnold too harshly for falling back on the elusive and perhaps empty signifier "[t]he something" in his attempts at metaphysical elucidation. Far more rigorous thinkers lapse into similar imprecision when they venture forth into metaphysically unknowable realms that serve as the ground of experience: Locke, for example, who declares the material substance that underlies what we perceive as the material world but that is itself inapprehensible to be an uncertain "supposition of we know not what";[7] even Kant, who must finally forgo his penchant for precision and identify the noumenal by the intentionally unspecific term *Ding an sich*. Still, Arnold does complicate the commentator's difficulties by leaving unclear whether "the something that infects" refers to the cause or the consequence of the operations of the noumenal as they manifest themselves in the world. On the one hand, the critical "something" of the closing line may refer to pure noumenal agency, the unconditioned that exists apart from time and space, beyond the world and yet its determining ground, the origin and generative source of the general infection that besets all phenomena. On the other hand, Arnold's "something" may signify an intrinsic attribute of the phenomenal, present always within each particular, perhaps emerging in the very process of objectification and individuation, instantiated within each phenomenal object at the very moment of its coming into being. In choosing between these two options—in determining whether this "something" is external noumenal cause or intrinsic noumenal property—the first seems more probable, for in assigning a cause for universal suffering or even man's general plight, Arnold most often adverts to some form of external agency. This agency is frequently a personified other-ness: the God who ordains our severance in "To Marguerite—Continued," or the "unknown Powers" (26) to whom we find ourselves "chartered" in "Human Life," or "the Powers that sport with man" (4) in "Destiny," or the "Fate" whose "impenetrable ear" never hears man's prayer in lines that come just before the closing line in "Resignation." So, too, in "Resignation," the most probable and plausible cause of the common suffering—the likely source of the infection that endangers all, the presence designated by the name "something"—is our cosmic antagonist, hostile and su-perior, alien yet intrusive, an otherness outside and beyond that im-pedes and thwarts what we would like to believe is the innate propensity of life toward mildness.

Of course, it is in reconstituting his metaphysics, in shifting from a metaphysics of immanence to one of transcendence, that Arnold seems to come closest to the Schopenhauerian paradigm. In so doing though, Arnold would seem to have made our situation more desperate, since nothing that exists in the world, nothing that can properly be called life, offers any hope of escape from or even ame-lioration of that plight that all life in time must suffer. Yet in a briefly enunciated but profoundly important change of attitude, by adopt-ing a metaphysics of transcendence, Arnold is able to shift the ethi-cal stance of the poem, introducing a note of concern not heard before in "Resignation" and infrequently sounded elsewhere in his poetry.

In "Resignation" we come very close to ending where we began, with a last critical glance at the strivers, those passion-driven men observed once more at their "intemperate prayer" (271) in the clos-ing lines, this time praying "[f]or movement, for an ampler sphere" (273). Just as in the opening lines, we are again told later in the poem that the goals of these strivers are unattainable, their prayers unregarded, by definition deemed incapable of ever piercing "Fate's impenetrable ear" (274). The closing strictures against the life of striving in "Resignation" are directed, however, not at a misplaced faith in the efficacy of action that the strivers cling to—their belief that the good of life is to "attain"—but rather at the moral narrow-ness that the life of action fosters, the obliviousness to all concern for others that the strivers display. In the most meticulously and cautiously crafted of allegations, Arnold charges that, because of the forgetfulness of the common plight induced by our plunge into action, "Not milder is the general lot" (275). By this allegation, he never suggests that entering "action's dizzying eddy" (277), to the neglect of all else, in any way aggravates the suffering of the "general lot," nor conversely does he really intimate that refraining from action, practicing resignation, can ever effect fundamental change in conditions or in some way make the general lot milder. All that can actually be done under the grim metaphysical circumstances of Arnold's world is to show concern for others, a seemingly modest obligation but the basis nonetheless for that primary moral good toward which "Resignation" would finally direct us: compassion, the key virtue in that "Oriental wisdom" Arnold so yearned to attain (*Letters,* 1:89).

In calling for compassion Arnold voices a concern rarely expressed in a poetry that usually has as its governing premise unbreachable isolation, our enislement "in the sea of life," or (as in "Human Life") the denial to us of "[t]he friends to whom we had no natural right" (29) by the "unknown Powers" (26) who rule over us. As a result of the emphasis on isolation as our necessary condition, the personal values promoted by the poetry tend to be largely inward looking and self-concerned. In general, Arnold instructs us to make a virtue of necessity, to insulate ourselves from the cares and needs of others and turn our island into a fortress, or rather into a star where we can acquire and practice detachment, autonomy, and self-dependence.

In "Resignation," though, Arnold does appear to go beyond the life of mere self-concern, criticizing the man of action not only because he engenders disquiet in himself but also because he is so totally absorbed in the intensely private quest that he remains heedless of and unmoved by the suffering that is "the general lot." As an alternative to self-interest, what Arnold commends may not seem like heroic virtue, yet it does bear the distinguishing mark of a true existential humanism: in the face of metaphysical absurdity and an inhospitable universe, the most praiseworthy of moral intentions are those that express concern for others. Of course, the ethic of concern Arnold introduces at the close of "Resignation" may seem inconsequential, even futile, if we assess moral acts by utility rather than intention. But the ethical posture Arnold finally adopts surely invests the practice of resignation with the dignity it lacked earlier in the poem, when it had been viewed as a means to a purely self-interested end, an anxiety-driven way of drawing "homeward to the general life" (252), a life whose utter vacancy might provide us with freedom from pain. Now, in this final version of the concept, resignation requires that we retain our receptivity of consciousness and bear that pain that is recognized to be more certain and inescapable than ever. We are to bear it, Arnold now indicates, because we belong to the earth and are thereby obligated to those others who comprise "the general lot" (275) and must endure the common fate of suffering, even if it should chance that we somehow could gain respite from the suffering ordained for us personally. Once before, in "In Utrumque Paratus," Arnold had spoken out in behalf of the need for man to declare solidarity with the natural order, urging him to maintain a "brother's part" (39) with that "brother-world" that "stirs at thy feet unknown" (38). Now, in the closing lines of "Resignation," by a gesture of compassionateness that suggests that he did at least momentarily attain the "Oriental wisdom" he so yearned for, Arnold in effect reasserts the claims of community not simply as a relationship among men but as one that encompasses all life, and by reasserting that claim he vastly enhances the humanity of his poem without compromising its unflinching metaphysical candor.

Of the major poetic works of Arnold, none would seem, on the face of it, to disclose more starkly its author's disposition toward philosophic pessimism of the kind I have been describing than *Empedocles on Etna*. Its principal action culminates in suicide, the act that, more than any other, would appear most tellingly to express the life-negating tendencies of that form of pessimism (Schopenhauer's own disclaimers notwithstanding); and, furthermore, it is a suicide undertaken on what seem to be closely reasoned metaphysical grounds. As Empedocles himself explains it in his lengthy preamble to his leap into Etna, what makes life so unbearable, what is most devastatingly detrimental to our "human side," to use Arnold's own term in his prose summary of *Empedocles on Etna*, is an implicit opposition between a primary and privileged realm of noumenal reality and a secondary and subordinate realm of phenomenal appearance. In short, I shall argue that Arnold's Empedocles is to be understood as a pessimist *avant la lettre*, having arrived at a metaphysics that in its deep structure does not seem so very different from the Schopenhauerian conflict between the world as will and the world as idea.

To be sure, in the course of the drama, Empedocles proposes reasons other than metaphysical ones why he might wish to commit suicide, and these have attracted by far the largest share of critical attention. To begin with, the historical conditions against which Empedocles so vehemently rails might seem to provide ample grounds for suicidal despair: the intellectual ascendancy of "the sophist-brood" (2.29) and the advent in politics of mass democracy, an "invincible" (2.94) "littleness united" (2.93) that presumably has vanquished the well-intentioned aristocratic elitism that Empedocles himself apparently champions.[8]

No less compelling as a reason for despair are the difficulties Empedocles associates with being a poet. Some of these are also the result of historical forces: for example, the natural antipathy to poetry of an age (very much like Arnold's own) whose strongest tendencies would seem to be pragmatic, skeptical, and leveling. In his youth, when becoming a poet was still a culturally viable possibility, Empedocles, along with his companion Parmenides and their friends "[i]n all the Italian cities" (2.237), could still join the "train" of the apparently divine "Sun-born Virgins! on the road of truth" (2.238–39). Present conditions, however, have clearly become less propitious for the making of poets, with the poet's stance in this new age required to be one of "ceaseless opposition" (2.268) so "[t]hat the world win no mastery over him" (2.270).

But some of the gravest difficulties associated with being a poet would seem to inhere at all times in the very nature of the vocation itself. To be a poet is to serve Apollo, a master who, as Callicles' account of the flaying of Marsyas makes clear, is, "[t]hough young, intolerably severe!" (2.206). What the god, in his severity, requires of those who would be poets is that they live wholly apart from other men in an impossible solitude on the heights, so often a valued dwelling place for the Arnoldian sage, but here characterized as being wholly unconducive to human life, a place where "[t]he air is" so "thin" that "the veins swell / The temples tighten and throb" (2.215–16), leaving the poet as victim capable of doing little more than crying out for "Air! Air!" (2.217). Finding his solitary life in the thin air of the heights unsustainable, the votary of Apollo is forced to fly once more "back to men" (2.220) who "gladly welcome him" (2.221), only to induce with their "chatter" (2.224) "[t]hat other torment" (2.226), an "absence from himself" (2.225) no less threatening to his vocation as poet. Compelled by his association with men to "fly to solitude again" (2.227), he thus finds himself having entered upon a seemingly unending cycle of "oscillations" (2.233) between two patently unbearable situations from which the only escape is the "death" (2.232) that will "[b]ring him" at last to "poise" (2.234).

Further complicating interpretation is the figure of Callicles, who gives us good reason to mistrust any and all of the explanations and justifications Empedocles offers for his despair and, ultimately, his suicide. Even before Empedocles appears, Callicles insists that Empedocles is simply mistaken about historical conditions: "'Tis not the times, 'tis not the sophists vex him" (1.1.150). Indeed, to set the record straight, Callicles tells us, "Gorgias, their chief, speaks nobly of him, / As of his gifted master, and once friend" (1.1.147–48). (Though nothing about a literary text can ever be stated with certainty, we must surely wonder why Callicles would tell us that the Sophists were kindly disposed to Empedocles if the real facts of the case were otherwise.)[9] In fact, Callicles manages to undermine all of Empedocles' bleak ruminations by explaining that the philosopher's view of the world is to be ascribed not to the sage's clear-sighted vision but to some personal pathology, a "root of suffering in himself, / Some secret and unfollowed vein of woe" (1.1.151–52).

On the narrower matter of what it means in general to be a poet, Callicles, both by his life and his work, provides us with a tantalizing counterargument to Empedocles' claim that to be a poet is necessarily grounds for despair. Though a poet himself, Callicles does appear able to negotiate what Empedocles regards as the fatal "oscillations" entailed by that unforgiving vocation, moving with seeming ease between situations that Empedocles judges unbearable, between the "chatter" of men, which Callicles has just left after his last night's revelry with Peisianax—and to which presumably he will return when the events related in the poem are over—and the lonely heights of Etna, where Callicles for most of the drama also dwells in apparent but endurable solitude, if not at the summit, at any rate, at the timberline. Furthermore, through his songs, it is often suggested, Callicles provides a vision of life, of the nature of things, vastly superior to what Empedocles offers. While his unhappy histories of Cadmus and Harmonia, Jove and Typho, and Apollo and Marsyas never gloss over the harsh facts of our existence, we still recognize in those songs—or so the argument of those who side with Callicles goes—a cosmos that suffices, one that is, at least aesthetically, sufficiently harmonious and orderly to preserve the rest of us (if not Empedocles) from the dark logic of Empedocles that leads to his suicide.[10] From the example of Callicles, critics have, in fact, sometimes inferred that the proper contrast to draw in *Empedocles on Etna* is not that between the poet and other, less gifted and hence less fatefully burdened men but that between the poet who, in his vocation, is concerned primarily with the natural, the real, the concrete, and the implicitly life-enhancing and the philosopher, whose bloodless and quarrelsome enterprise seemingly robs life of all its savor.[11] Yet if Callicles, as singer of songs and mythmaking teller of tales, seems to come closer in his aesthetically founded optimism than Empedocles does in his despair to what the poet is, or at least should be, we cannot entirely reject that glimmer of pessimistic possibility raised by those critics of the poem who side with Empedocles. To them, Callicles is able to maintain his optimism because he is still young and naïve, not yet having undertaken that passage from untested innocence to tragic wisdom, from strayed reveller to knowing sage—a passage that Empedocles, according to his recounting of his own history, shows us he has already completed.[12]

The fact that there are so many lines of interpretation—some of them mutually exclusive, divergent rationales and repudiations mingled together within the space of a single text—is certainly reason enough for the sharp interpretive differences, acknowledged perplexities, and even admissions of bafflement that recur so often in the criticism of *Empedocles on Etna*. (Writing over forty years ago, Warren Anderson ended his still-valuable pages on the classical tradition in *Empedocles on Etna* by seconding the conclusion of a "discerning critic" who had stated some forty years before that "'Empedocles on Etna' is what you make of it when you have read the whole poem.")[13] Unsurprisingly, several recent critics of *Empedocles on Etna*, anxious to make postmodern virtue out of this interpretive dissonance and critical puzzlement, have turned to deconstruction and reader-response theory as ways of explaining and justifying the drama's apparent exegetical intractableness.[14]

But I would wish to account for this variability in stated motives and explanations, not by any theory of linguistic indeterminacy (whether Derridean or some other) but in essentially psychological terms. I read *Empedocles on Etna* as overdetermined and conflicted, its multiplicity of competing and sometimes contradictory motives and explanations best explained as defenses against and denials of the darkest but most insistently argued of the poem's dark speculations: the contention that the suicide of Empedocles is metaphysically entailed, that it derives from that truth he has in his wisdom as a philosopher come to about our human predicament as it grows out of the nature of things. If the metaphysical reason for suicide is only one among several, it is nonetheless the one Arnold most pointedly emphasizes. Certainly his prose summary of the argument of the poem bears this out, for there Arnold in his own voice tells us that Empedocles "is a philosopher." This is obviously a term of approval here for Arnold, since this philosopher, the summary tells us, "sees things as they are—the world as it is—God as he is," and "know[s] the mysteries that are communicated to others by fragments, in parables" (*Poems*, 154). Within the text, too, the metaphysical argument is strikingly highlighted, set off and virtually bracketed by the stage direction that introduces it: "A long pause during which EMPEDOCLES remains motionless, plunged in thought" (*Poems*, 198), an authorial directive to some imagined actor plainly meant to invest what he will say afterwards with the character of a revelation. That revelation is of course the long speech laying out the bleakest kind of metaphysics and concluding with Empedocles' leap into the crater of Etna, so that it is to metaphysics rather than to any of the other stated reasons for his unhappiness that Arnold gives the final interpretive say in his drama.

Arnold introduces the turn to metaphysics that follows this pause by resorting to one of his most familiar poetic strategies, an apostrophe to the stars. But unlike "A Summer Night" and "Self-Dependence," this apostrophe is not the usual Arnoldian panegyric in praise of the heavens for its guidance in showing us how a truly human life might be lived. Instead, Empedocles uses the stars as a starting point for an overtly metaphysical essay in the history of ideas that at first glance looks like a historical survey of the basic cosmologies through which humans over time have projected their changing worldviews. He begins with the most traditional of cosmologies and worldviews, the cosmological assumptions in vogue during his earliest years. Then, it was believed, the cosmos had contained a life and vitality like our own and, beyond mere life, displayed evidences of intelligent design, meaningful purpose, and concern for the welfare of earth's human inhabitants:

> You, too, once lived;
> You, too, moved joyfully
> Among august companions,
> In an older world, peopled by Gods,
> In a mightier order,
> The radiant, rejoicing intelligent Sons of Heaven.
>
> (2.282–87)

But now a new, obviously secularized and scientific understanding of the heavens has supplanted this traditional and implicitly religious reading of the stars. The stars, once apprehended as being in some fundamental sense like ourselves—alive, joyful, and intelligent—are now deemed to be utterly distinct from us in their attributes, devoid of any evidences of life, design, purpose, or concern for humanity. The stars of the cold heavens of *Empedocles on Etna*, unlike those of "A Summer Night" and "Self-Dependence," are nothing more than indifferent presences, impelled in their unthinking orbit through the void by an impersonal necessity. The transformation that Empedocles delineates is, of course, a transparent forerunner of what took place in the later stages of a Christian epoch, when the new philosophy called all in doubt and a mathematical and mechanistic Copernican and, later, Newtonian astronomy replaced an earlier cosmology of guiding angelic intelligences and presiding spirits. Empedocles, too, like his later counterparts, has gone from a religiously grounded faith to a scientifically induced disbelief, so it should come as no surprise that Arnold hears in his words the "modern problems," "the doubts" and "the discouragement, of Hamlet and of Faust" (*CPW*, 1:1):

> But now, ye kindle
> Your lonely, cold-shining lights,
> Unwilling lingerers
> In the heavenly wilderness,
> For a younger, ignoble world;
> And renew, by necessity,
> Night after night your courses,
> In echoing, unneared silence
> Above a race you know not—
> Uncaring and undelighted,
> Without friend and without home;
> Weary like us, though not
> Weary with our weariness.
>
> (2.288–300)

Yet having arrived at a view of the stars that is scientifically true and, therefore, one would assume, the last word on the matter, Empedocles immediately reverses himself, declaring what he had just said to be erroneous. In reality, the scientific view is merely another subjective view, a distortion of the true nature of things brought about because the speaker and observer finds himself "dead to life and joy" so that he must "read / In all things my own deadness" (2.321–22). The real truth is that the stars are "alive" (2.303), and not just the stars but all the elements: the air that contains the stars, "the pure dark ether where ye ride / Brilliant above me" (2.304–5); earth and fire, both apparently coalescing in Empedocles account of the "fiery world, / That sapp'st the vitals of this terrible mount / Upon whose charred and quaking crust I stand" (2.305–7), and that also "brimmest with life" (2.308); and finally water, which, with a characteristically Arnoldian touch, is represented by the moon-illuminated sea below Etna, "[t]hat mild and luminous floor of waters lives" (2.315).

Empedocles may seem simply to have given in to nostalgia and reverted to a once-held but now scientifically discredited earlier view of the heavens, but crucial elements from his first words on the

stars are noticeably absent from this third account. Nowhere in the
later version does Empedocles suggest that the order of being in
which the stars, along with all of elemental nature, now participate
is, in any respect, "peopled by Gods" (2.285). Neither does he in any
way now suggest that the stars are "intelligent" (2.287), possessed
of the capability to "know" (2.296) and care for the "race" (2.296)
above whom they shine.[15] The absence of these key indicators suggests that Empedocles has not really reverted to his earlier implicit
anthropomorphism but has rather moved beyond both the religious
and scientific view of things to some third way of seeing, which, I
would argue, making due allowances for the historical context of
Greek philosophy in which these lines are placed, closely approximates the metaphysics of nineteenth-century philosophic pessimism.

In fact, the only one of the attributes that Empedocles initially
ascribed to the stars that really carries over to this final cosmology
is "life." Such a life is, to be sure, vital, pulsating, and (except for
the mind of man) apparently all-pervasive, present not just in the
stars but apparently in all of elemental being, but it is, nonetheless,
a life virtually without further qualities. (This life, Empedocles
maintains, possesses "joy," but it is a "held-in joy" [2.316], never
directly known but merely inferred from the swell of the sea.) What
this life most closely resembles, at least to the reader of Arnold, is
that "general life" about which Arnold had written in "Resignation"—life to be sure, but life at its most minimal, mere pulsation
and duration, "the life of plants, and stones, and rain" ("Resignation," 195), a life, it almost goes without saying, that we can
scarcely imagine humans endowed with consciousness to regard as
a highest good.

In his notes to *Empedocles on Etna*, Kenneth Allott provides this
conception with a philosophic lineage by suggesting that its origin
is "[n]ot superstition in Empedocles but an acceptance of hylozoism. The cosmos is alive."[16] That the cosmos is alive was the view
of several of the pre-Socratics from Thales onwards, though it is
uncertain whether the historical Empedocles in his "implicit materialism" held a view of elemental being that could accurately be
called hylozoism.[17] But beyond antiquity, hylozoism has a further
history, variants of the Greek original emerging in philosophers
ranging from Spinoza, Cudworth, and Leibniz to such a late-nine-
teenth-century evolutionary philosopher as Ernst Haeckel. While
the view that matter is alive need not imply the further claim that
matter contains mind, hylozoism, especially in these later variants,
readily slides into panpsychism, the view that every portion of the

cosmos, including what is usually considered inanimate matter, contains not just life but mind. Thus, for the evolutionary philosopher the term "hylozoism" provides a kind of philosophically sanctioned precedent for the assertion that life and, most especially, human consciousness have evolved along a kind of natural continuum, that something akin to what has finally evolved into the human mind was potentially present in the earliest of material forms.

But the hylozoism of Arnold's Empedocles does not slide into panpsychism. The one portion of the cosmos that does not share in that life found in the elements is mind. Indeed, it is in his treatment in *Empedocles on Etna* of the antithetical relationship between this elemental life and mind, between the ultimately real and consciousness, that we come closest in Arnold's poetry to the pessimistic opposition between will and idea. But Arnold does not really present us with that opposition in its nineteenth-century formulation until he recasts his basic philosophic framework from the essentially materialistic cosmology of the pre-Socratics to something that more closely approximates the epistemology of Kantian idealism, with its basic division of noumena and phenomena. So deeply alive are the elements and so dead does Empedocles feel himself that, almost immediately after recognizing that hylozoistic life in the elements, he expresses an understandable wish to share in that life by uniting with the elements; and he would do so except for the impediment to the kind of vitalistic incorporation he seeks imposed by "mind" (2.345) and "thought" (2.345). If "mind" and "thought" have governed us, if they have been "the master part of us" (2.346), then they shall continue to govern us, or so Empedocles asserts:

> And they will be our lords, as they are now;
> And keep us prisoners of our consciousness,
> And never let us clasp and feel the All
> But through their forms, and modes, and stifling veils.
>
> (2.351–54)

Given the epistemologically restrictive, indeed "stifling," character Empedocles ascribes to these "forms, and modes," the philosophically oriented critic can only assume that Arnold must mean by "forms" something like the Kantian forms of space and time that structure what we apprehend as objects, and by "modes" the Kantian categories by means of which the phenomenal world as we apprehend it is organized and rendered cognitively intelligible. The "All," from the knowledge of which we are hindered by these forms and modes has its Kantian analogue as well in the philosopher's totalizing concept of the unconditioned noumenal, central to Kant's formulation of the thing-in-itself. (Allott, in his note on these lines, states this unequivocally: "The All is the noumenon behind phenomenal appearances. Kant and the unknowability of the thing-in-itself [*Ding-an-sich*] are in the background here" [*Poems*, 201].) In one important respect, though, Arnold goes beyond Kant in the relationship he wishes to see established between the human subject and the thing-in-itself. The philosophy of Kant is a critical philosophy, its epistemology an attempt to impose limits on our metaphysical knowledge. In keeping with the spirit of this critical philosophy, he would have us recognize that the forms and categories condition our knowledge of the phenomenal world—and only the phenomenal world—but do not apply to the thing-in-itself. We would know the thing-in-itself but cannot because knowledge of it lies beyond the cognitive powers of the human understanding. Empedocles, though, does not wish merely to know the noumenal, to apprehend and understand it; he wishes to "feel" and, above all, to "clasp" it, a term that more than any I can think of conveys the intensity of Arnold's ontological longings and the depths of anguish he must sound when that longing is frustrated. And it is frustrated, I should add, not by any contingent conditions, the sufferings imposed by his chosen vocation or even those induced by the historical circumstances under which he must live, but rather by the very nature of things, by the way life at its most fundamental is constituted, by the inherent opposition between the ontologically real and an illusionary consciousness.

It is a mistake, I believe, to equate Empedocles' repudiation of mind and thought with Arnold's advocacy of some greater Romantic good. Arnold does not, for example, mean by this the rejection of some narrow and lesser rational faculty, "the Understanding" (*Verstand*) as opposed to "the Reason" (*Vernunft*), the familiar Romantic distinction originating with Kant that Culler proposes; nor does Arnold limit what is to be cast off, as Walter E. Houghton has it, to "the logical mind" that keeps us "from direct experience of man and nature."[18] What irreversibly imprisons and thereby estranges us from ourselves and from the real is consciousness per se, that which more than any other facet of our being defines us as human. An imprisoning consciousness is what confines our life to a "meadow of calamity" (2.365), an "uncongenial place" (2.366), and it does so because the life we are forced to lead on that meadow and in that place is "this human life" (2.366). Empedocles commits suicide, Arnold tells us in his prose summary, because he believes himself in danger of "exaggerat[ing]" his "human side" and thus becoming "utterly estranged from" "the universe" (*Poems*, 155). The more human we become, the more alienated we shall be from the universe, and from the metaphysical reality it embodies and expresses. However vital and even joyful that life may turn out to be, it is wholly distinct from the life of consciousness, and therefore from the life of humanity to which those who must bear the burden of consciousness find themselves consigned.

Neither should we regard *Empedocles on Etna* as an instance of Romantic Prometheanism (despite the fact that there are echoes of Byron's *Manfred* in Arnold's play). In *Empedocles on Etna*, there is no defiant gesture against the gods or the universe, no jaw clenched in stern resistance or fist shaken at the sky, no railing against a cosmos—or its gods—whose irresistible strength is directed against our human wishes and interests, no striking out boldly even if, in the final reckoning, futilely so as to assert the irrepressible grandeur of the human spirit. Nor is there any hint by word or deed that we are to construe what Empedocles says or does as undertaken in behalf of a long-suffering humanity. In fact, the entire thrust and ultimate aim of this last section of *Empedocles on Etna* convey a will to disparage and cast off our essential humanity, because it is that very humanity that metaphysically thwarts us in our desire to overcome the ontological homelessness we must suffer during life on earth.

Yet if in his final speech Empedocles speaks out not against the cosmos but against our obdurate humanity, how then can we reconcile this apparently self-despising frame of mind with the seemingly incongruous fact, as Houghton long ago pointed out, that Empedocles leaps into Etna "triumphantly"?[19] How can there be triumph in an act that so patently denies and negates the essentially human in himself? The answer almost certainly lies in that third term that Empedocles introduces into his self-analysis in his concluding speech. While "sense" and "thought" might initially have seemed to constitute the whole of our self-estranging (and cosmos-estranging) humanity, Empedocles speaks—admittedly with Arnold's usual vagueness when addressing noumenal matters—of some unestranging other thing, which is neither "sense" nor "thought" but is instead identified only as "our only true, deep-buried selves, / Being one with which we are one with the whole world" (2.371–72).

It is this "true, deep buried sel[f]" that constitutes the real and the true in ourselves, makes us genuinely existent in a metaphysical sense, and links us to that ontologically elemental that is everywhere else in the cosmos but in the consciousness of man. In distinguishing between the customary human life of "sense" and

"thought" and the metaphysically more fundamental life carried on
at the depths of the "buried self," Arnold seems to be making a distinction of the sort he will develop in "The Buried Life": that,
whereas on all those other lines on which we find ourselves in our
normal—and, I would say, phenomenal—existence, what "we say
and do" (65) may be "eloquent" (66) and "well" (66), only on that
line along which the buried life flows can we find what is "true"
(66)—that is, what is ontologically valid. In this conception of an
ontologically real buried life that pervades elemental nature, we
may hear echoes, as Anderson does, of the "general life" (191) of
"Resignation." However, there Arnold seems to cling to the hope
that, by reducing human life to the pure minimalness we find in "the
life of plants, and stones, and rain," we can, while still remaining
alive, possess the "general life" that the poet "craves" (196), though
how this will come about Arnold never satisfactorily explains.[20] But
in *Empedocles on Etna*, Arnold abandons any such allegedly saving fiction and follows the metaphysics of the "general life" and the
"buried self" to its inescapable conclusion by having Empedocles
repudiate our familiarly human life completely by his act of suicide.

In introducing this new and potentially ominous category of the
"buried self" into the speculations of Empedocles, and in designat-
ing that category as all that is ontologically real in ourselves,
Arnold has, in effect, severed all genuine connection between metaphysical reality and the life lived out by the individuated being. By
doing this, he has also implicitly relegated consciousness to the
status of mere epiphenomenon, accident to essence. But Arnold
goes even further, beyond even this poignant estrangement. The
human, as Empedocles here defines it, not only stands apart from
but in opposition to the real as it is present both in the cosmos and
in ourselves; it is a stifling hindrance to self-unity and to cosmic
unity, so that to be one with the self and one with the cosmos necessarily entails dispensing with the epiphenomenal life of consciousness altogether. The great paradox of *Empedocles on Etna* is that
to bring the vital and pulsating in ourselves—the life in ourselves—
into unity with the vital and pulsating in the universe—the life in
the universe—we must eliminate all traces of human consciousness, perform that act by which, according to our usual understanding of things, life ends completely. In this respect, Arnold as
pessimist goes beyond even Schopenhauer as pessimist: for where
Schopenhauer backs away from that final commendation of suicide
that the logic of pessimism would seem inescapably to dictate, Arnold, speaking through Empedocles, urges us to carry that logic to
its dire conclusion, to rid ourselves of the suffering inherent in the

98   A LONGING LIKE DESPAIR

opposition between will and idea by the one means that is truly efficacious, suicide.

Of course, by introducing these metaphysical concepts, Arnold
only worsens Empedocles' plight, gives him grounds for despair
from which there can be no appeal nor evasion. In these cosmic circumstances, absolute and unalterable as they are, it is difficult to
find any justification for that sense of triumph that Empedocles undeniably voices when he leaps into Etna. But I would suggest that,
here as elsewhere in Arnold, the presence to consciousness of what
is acutely painful and obviously undesired calls forth psychological
defenses designed to allay the anxiety that such thinking produces.
In this case, the defense raised to ameliorate the true harshness of
the solution by suicide in *Empedocles on Etna* is regression, a
strategy that would render less fearsome the otherwise intolerable
by associating it with the vanished pleasures of some earlier stage
of life.

Regression may simply be a remembrance of "past times, / Their
soul of unworn youth, their breath of greatness" (2.383–84), a linking of the recent historical past with Empedocles' own personal
past, a nostalgic looking back upon the good days of a youth that
"fell on a different world / From that on which his exiled age is
thrown" (2.262–63). Yet even if he could recapture what he felt in
his "prosperous days" (2.261), Empedocles would at most attain
what he terms a "refuge" (2.383), shelter and protection perhaps
from a spiritually corrosive present but scarcely a lasting sanctuary
from which to ward off permanently the outcome he most fears, his
final and irreversible estrangement from the reality with which he
would be reunited. Perhaps the main reason why Empedocles can
hope for no more than a temporary stay against this apparent fate
is the strange and seemingly predestined future that he imagines
for himself: his belief that he shall undergo a series of deaths and
reincarnations (a notion Arnold clearly borrowed from the philosophy of the historical Empedocles), with each subsequent life posing
"more peril for us than the last" (2.378). For Arnold's gloomy Empedocles, reincarnation means not an opportunity for redemption,
a second chance in which to remedy his present human failings, but
the necessary and inevitable exacerbating of these failings unless
he can leave life immediately and entirely. His greatest fear is that,
during these repeated reincarnations, the senses—or, as is more
likely, the "imperious lonely thinking-power" (2.376)—will grow
ever more dominant and strengthen its hold over him, until finally
any hope of sharing in the life and joy of the whole while still on
earth will be lost, and, consequently, he "shall sink in the impossi-

ble strife, / And be astray for ever" (2.389–90). To avert that fate, Empedocles knows he must choose death now, while his "soul" (2.412) still "glows" (2.412) with the lingering residue of youthful feeling that yet remains to him. By choosing death at this perhaps last propitious moment, he can apparently forestall the devastating prospect of future reincarnations in which feeling and vitality can only further decline; by committing suicide he shall, in effect, get himself off the wheel.

In regressively resorting to memories of a youth in which he experienced "fullness of life and power of feeling" (2.258), Arnold is able to provide Empedocles with a defense against anxiety that lends a coloration of the known, the familiar, the implicitly pleasurable, to what otherwise, it would seem, can never be truly desired, the death Empedocles has chosen, that which only can be feared. Still, it seems impossible that, for all the "fullness of life and power of feeling" Empedocles had experienced in youth and that he would bring to bear on this present moment of understandable dread, he really did, even at that time, "clasp and feel the All." It is this that is Empedocles' great and ultimate goal and the one from which he is kept by epistemologically imposed barriers that would seem to inhere in the very nature of human cognition, the life of the individuated consciousness with its "forms, and modes, and stifling veils." To achieve that goal, one would have to eliminate the life of consciousness altogether, presumably through that death in which no remnant of the individuated life any longer remains. Once again we face the inherently fearsome, the inescapable source of inevitable anxiety, an anxiety that can perhaps be warded off by the psyche's defenses, but this time only through a still deeper form of regression, a looking backwards to a time before individuation occurred.

In that passage in which Empedocles first announces his decision to commit suicide, one line conveys with exceptional clarity both the anxiety raised by that prospect and the defenses summoned forth against that anxiety to make the unthinkable doable. He calls on the elements, his "willing ministers" (2.26) and "helpers" (2.27), to "[r]eceive me, hide me, quench me, take me home" (2.36). In that wish to be both received and hidden, we hear the longing to be a part of, to belong to, the elemental other (with the regressively infantile character of these feelings surely to be assumed) and, at the same time, the ontological insecurity that fosters such longing. But even more telling is the phrase "quench me," for it tells us that Empedocles does realistically understand the true nature of the future that he has chosen, a death he knows to be extinction, a quenching of the "spark of man's consciousness" (2.30) and of a "soul" (2.412) that at the moment of death still "glows" (2.412)—presumably for the last time by its own autonomous powers—to "meet" (2.412) the roaring "sea of fire" (2.411) that is the core of Etna. Yet despite the fact that being received by Etna requires the cessation of consciousness, its extinction, the site of that cessation and extinction is still what is wished for, still "home."

By leaping into Etna, Empedocles thus hopes to recapture not the lost time of youth but a time more primal, more originary, before the estrangements of individuation set in. What he apparently believes he will gain by this act is reunion with that from which he is now most devastatingly estranged, reunion with the "parent element" (2.347). In death he will "gladly share the fruitful stir / Down in our mother earth's miraculous womb" (2.339–40) and return once more to that place that seemingly looms as the principal good in Empedocles' final rationale for suicide, the place that is "home." There, prior to that first individuating separation, he somehow intuitively knows, we had security; we had love. If Empedocles can psychologically transform in his own mind's eye the outcome he most fears, extinction in death, into what he most deeply desires, a return to the maternal womb, then it is easy to see why he would leap into Etna "triumphantly."

Arnold's Empedocles is, of course, a fictional character, but his desire to return to the "parent element," to "gladly share the fruitful stir / Down in our mother earth's miraculous womb," is not so very different from the longings the speaker of "To Marguerite—Continued" expresses. For that speaker, too (and in his voice one can reasonably hear the tones of the poetic voice of Arnold himself), there is a longing to return to a time before the individuated life began and severance from the whole occurred, a regressive yearning for what we can never really know with certainty actually existed but yet what we "surely" "feel" "once" was a moment in what can be nothing else than our infantile history when "we were / Parts of a single continent" (15–16). But that longing Arnold knows even before he utters it is unfulfillable: it is "a longing like despair" (13), he tells us in a prefatory disclaimer uttered just before annunciating what that unattainable object of desire is. And I would suggest that the regressively formulated longing for reunion with the elements woven into the declaration of intent to commit suicide in *Empedocles on Etna* is of the same nature, a longing like despair, a yearning for what the speaker, even before he articulates it, knows at some most basic level to be unattainable, perhaps to have never been. It is a defense summoned forth by Empedocles to allay the anxiety understandably raised by the desperateness of the terrible course he has embarked upon as a consequence of the severe truth about the nature of things at which he as a philosopher has arrived. That is, the truth for Empedocles is that the only relief there can be from the metaphysical circumstances that ordain only suffering for those who must bear the burden of consciousness is to cast off consciousness altogether, a goal to be achieved only by ending life itself.

We can little doubt that the single most important event in *Empedocles on Etna* is the suicide of Empedocles; and, it almost necessarily follows, the single most important question about the drama—perhaps the single most important question about Arnold the poet that the critic of Arnold must answer—is, Why did Empedocles commit suicide? Did Arnold the poet hold so dark a "vision of the tragic and alienated condition of man" (to borrow Culler's phrase) that, under the cover of the inherent dialogism of drama, he finally could covertly recommend suicide as the only truly efficacious solution to the hardships of human life? It is almost certain, I believe, that at some ultimate level—I would say at some metaphysical level—the Empedocles who was Arnold's philosopher, on that "charred, blackened, melancholy waste" (2.2) where the real nature of things was disclosed to him, where he saw the truth in all of its greatness and severity, came to the conclusion that the conditions of life disclosed by that truth were unbearable; and that the only sure source of relief from a life so unbearable was suicide. This is the conclusion to which the philosophic logic of the work leads Empedocles, and, I would add, this is the conclusion to which Arnold understands his own philosophic predilections must lead as well. It is Arnold, after all, who puts the terrible words in Empedocles' mouth, and it is Arnold who vouches for their trustworthiness by saying of Empedocles in the prose summary, "He is a philosopher," apparently meaning by this that "[h]e sees things as they are—the world as it is—God as he is: in their stern simplicity" (*Poems*, 154). And seeing truly, the philosopher acts as he must.

But one cannot pursue such logic without the gravest trepidation and without sometimes giving way to the wish that things were otherwise; and so incorporated into the stern manifest argument of the drama are countervailing elements, defenses and denials, some of them introduced by Empedocles himself, and some by that alternative figure of possible authority Arnold provides us with in Callicles. One may, as Empedocles does, mask the terrible prospect of death through regression, identifying death with some lost good, with feelings known to us in youth or even in infancy. The marshaling of such defenses, of course, really changes nothing since Empedocles still keeps to the suicidal course he has chosen, but they at least lessen the frightfulness of death, ameliorate its harshness, its own seeming unbearableness, even when Empedocles chooses death as an antidote to the unbearableness of human existence. Empedocles also, to some degree, masks any purely metaphysical rationale for his suicide by suggesting other causes for his suicidal unhappiness: historical circumstances have changed for the worse; his vocation as a poet makes impossible demands on Empedocles the man. These are grounds for unhappiness certainly, but they are local and therefore contingent grounds, capable of being rectified by a change in circumstances or a change of occupation. Only the metaphysical argument laid out at the very end of the drama lends to Empedocles' suicide what he implies it has in the prose summary, a philosophically necessary character, offering those who come after him and also see "things as they are—the world as it is"—the most starkly enticing of precedents for dealing with the unalterably bleak conditions of human existence.

The songs of Callicles, too, provide another implicitly contrary vision and thus a way of averting those fearsome ramifications that apparently follow from that "truth of truths" that Empedocles arrives at through his philosophic clear-sightedness. Without ever moderating or falsifying the distressful nature of the events described in the stories of Cadmus and Harmonia, Jove and Typho, and (most especially) Apollo and Marsyas, Callicles (in contrast to Empedocles, or so we are frequently told) renders our perception of them bearable, and perhaps even pleasurable, by the transformative and even life-enhancing powers of myth and art. In addition, Callicles presents us with the most serious of all challenges to the reasonings of Empedocles, declaring the philosopher's arguments to be demonstrably false, distortions of the real facts induced by something akin to derangement, "some root of suffering in himself" (1.1.151).

It is surely not surprising that Arnold would so multiply alternative rationales for (and even repudiations of) the Empedoclean solution, since acquiescence in the primary reasoning of Empedocles—the reasoning that Empedocles himself appears not just to contemplate but to act upon—may simply carry us to conclusions too horrible to contemplate. Yet none of this should obscure the fact that Arnold chose to write his most expansively reflective and philosophic work about the suicide of a philosopher whose philosophy, at least from the evidence of the prose summary, Arnold clearly admired, and we must only wonder why he would have so chosen if his basic purpose was only to discount or discredit that philosophy. But if he did not choose to discount or discredit that philosophy, we must then go on to ask what was it in the philosophy of Empedocles that led Arnold to write as he did about the life and death of Empedocles.

We must bear in mind that, even before Arnold had completed his drama, those discussing it had tended to minimize the relevance of the philosophy of the historical Empedocles to the ideas expressed in *Empedocles on Etna*. In 1849, Arnold's friend J. C. Shairp set the tone for much of what was to come, by telling Clough that "Matt" "was working at an 'Empedocles'—which seemed to be not so much about the man who leapt in the crater—but his name and outward circumstances are used for the drapery of his own thoughts."[21] Among the major modern critics of Matt's "Empedocles," no names loom larger than Culler and Houghton. Culler introduces his own chapter on *Empedocles on Etna* by approvingly quoting Shairp; Houghton begins his highly influential essay in much the same spirit, assuring us that Arnold's Empedocles is not the "Sicilian philosopher who lived in the fifth century B.C. No one can read the existing Fragments, or what is known of his life and times and imagine that Arnold was trying to recreate the man or his thought or his environment."[22] But I would argue, to the contrary, that what Arnold understood to be the life (at least his life at the point of his supposed death by suicide) and times of Empedocles are precisely what he was trying to re-create in writing his play about a Greek philosopher whose once flourishing reputation had declined as the result of an increasingly hostile political and intellectual environment. I would also argue that more important still in attracting Arnold to Empedocles was his thought. It was his philosophy and not merely the manner of his death that led Arnold to choose Empedocles as the protagonist of this major work in preference to the other major candidate Arnold considered for the role, Lucretius, a philosopher who, like Empedocles, had also, at least according to philosophic lore, committed suicide.

First and foremost, of all the philosophers of antiquity, it is Empedocles, with his "profound pessimism about our world" and "bleak metaphysics" (the terms used by Brad Inwood, Empedocles' most recent translator and an authoritative modern commentator), whose philosophy would appear to come the closest to the core premises of that nineteenth-century philosophic pessimism we find in both Schopenhauer and Arnold.[23] Admittedly, in nineteenth-century pessimism metaphysical agency is monistically conceived, with the sole metaphysical reality being a cosmic will whose blind strivings are antithetical to our human needs, desires, and interests, thereby inducing suffering as the law of life. Empedocles, however, conceives of metaphysical agency dualistically, with two disparate and profoundly opposed cosmic forces, love and strife—one essentially benign, the other essentially malign—alternately ruling over things. But during the course of human existence, strife is all that matters. During that time "our world belongs to strife," as Inwood puts it, belongs to what Empedocles, as fierce in his denunciations of this primal metaphysical agency as any nineteenth-century pessimist, calls "mad strife," "baneful strife," "destructive strife." It is "strife" whose "hostility" results in "all being borne apart separately"; it is "strife" that inflicts a suffering that seems virtually ubiquitous on the "wretched and unhappy race of mortals."[24]

What made Empedocles intriguing to Arnold, though, was not just that he could be thought of as a philosophic forerunner, a writer who postulates his own "something that infects the world." Beyond that—and of obvious interest to the Arnold who wrote *Empedocles on Etna*—are the views of the historical Empedocles on the questions of death and immortality. The historical Empedocles clearly believed in reincarnation, and in this Arnold's Empedocles follows his original—appending to that belief, however, the further proviso that successive reincarnations will only make a bad matter worse by further strengthening the deleterious hold that sense and thought have over us now, during our current life in the world. But reincarnation for both the historical Empedocles and Arnold's Empedocles "does not entail the immortality of the soul."[25] Like all compounds, human beings must perish because "sooner or later the mixture which constitutes them must dissolve."[26]

Thus, there is an additional stage of immortality beyond reincarnation, and it is "the ultimate end of our personal existence in cosmic dissolution," "a blessed and happy event"[27] for Empedocles, since it means release from a world about which he was so profoundly pessimistic and a return to the unmixed elemental. It is this sequence of stages that Arnold's Empedocles foresees as his future in what is to come after death, and if he purposely short-circuits the process and chooses to enter directly and "triumphantly" (to use Houghton's term) into the final stage, the "blessed and happy event" of the extinction of his "personal existence in cosmic dissolution," Arnold's Empedocles clearly still does nothing that is inconsistent with the philosophy of the historical figure upon whom Arnold based his fictional creation. But Arnold actually goes a step beyond anything that is stated explicitly in the writings of the philosopher. If the ending of one's "personal existence in cosmic dissolution" is an apparent good for Empedocles, then it would seem to follow that the most effective way of achieving this desired good is always close at hand. We can always cast off our "wretched and unhappy lot" through suicide. The historical Empedocles, however, never calls for this drastic remedy in so many words, but the text of the philosopher that Arnold thinks of as Empedocles would appear to have been constructed for Arnold from deeds as well as words. The suicide that Empedocles is supposed to have chosen thus becomes, in Arnold's drama, the philosopher's final statement of philosophic instruction for dealing with a life determined by the governance over us of "baneful strife."

Lucretius, too, according to legend, was supposed to have committed suicide, but he had allegedly done so because his wife had given him a love potion (or so we are told in the account given us by Suetonius and popularized most notably by Tennyson) and not because suicide was a logical corollary to his basic philosophy. To be sure, one can find ample reason for contemplating suicide in the indifferent universe postulated by Lucretius, where events are determined by the random movements of atoms in the void, and where, while there are gods who oversee the doings of humanity, they are gods unconcerned with our welfare. But even in a world of such unconcern, genuine happiness is still possible for humans by adhering to the tenets of an Epicurean philosophy. Death for Lucretius is also unquestionably an extinction that is inescapable and is not to be feared; still, there is no good reason for us to choose it prior to the time when nature ordains it since happiness is always potentially available in this life to those who seek it out. But in the dire philosophic vision of Empedocles, matters are very different: at least for the duration of our world and our life, the universe and the humanity within it are ruled over by strife, whose purpose (even if not its conscious intention) is, in effect, the separating of all that has been mixed, thereby producing misery for all who fall under strife's destructive dominion. Thus, in turning not to Lucretius but to the darker vision and darker example of Empedocles, an example compounded both from his writings and his reputed biography, Arnold was able, at least tentatively—that is, hedged about with all sorts of defenses and denials—to recommend a course of action that he could never support when speaking in his own voice but that follows evidently from a pessimistic philosophy like the one that in any number of poems he had clearly come to espouse. He is able to say, at least ventriloquistically through the possibly authoritative voice of one who "perceives still the truth of truth" (*Poems*, 154), that death is preferable to life and an option, a way out, that can and should be exercised when one chooses.

4

Arnold in Love

NOWHERE ARE THE PAINFUL CONSEQUENCES OF METAPHYSICAL PESSIMISM more evident than in our sexual desiring and, by extension, our romantic love. Indeed, it is in the genitals—according to Schopenhauer, "the real *focus* of the will" (*WWR*, 1:330)—that we find the closest of analogues to the noumenal will as he describes it: an irresistible force whose blind urgings take absolute hold of our individuated being, overwhelming the endeavors of the comparatively feeble phenomenal reason to pursue those ostensibly higher interests most in keeping with our human dignity. The sexual impulse is, Schopenhauer tells us, the "most distinctly expressed type" (*WWR*, 2:514) of "the will-to-live"; and since that will inevitably engenders suffering, sexual desire itself "[o]f its nature . . . is pain." The "metaphysics of sexual love" (to borrow the title of a celebrated chapter in *The World as Will and Representation*) is just that: metaphysics masquerading as love, the expression of an impersonal noumenal agency that in bringing lovers together seeks no further goal than its own continuance. And to further this end, that agency fosters the "*delusion*" (*WWR*, 2:538) in those compelled to work its will that they have freely chosen, coming together out of some deep-rooted personal affinity in order to undertake the spiritual commitment of romantic love.

Unsurprisingly, a major corollary to this indictment of the sexual impulse is a corresponding indictment of women that has few parallels in vehemence. Women, the sex at large, are to be understood as primary carriers of our metaphysical infectedness, agents of "the will-to-live," their lives biologically and psychologically programmed to fulfill basically genital, procreative, and hence implicitly noumenal imperatives. In the notorious diatribe "On Women" in *Parerga and Parilopomena*, Schopenhauer presents his most vitriolically misogynistic explanation of the metaphysically determined female character: "At bottom," he writes there, "women exist solely for the propagation of race" and thus possess "a very meager and limited faculty of reason." Utterly uninterested in intellectual pleasures and pursuits and devoid of all moral capacity, guilty, apparently by nature, of "falseness, faithlessness, treachery, ingratitude, and so on," women are, Schopenhauer concludes in the most brutal of summary judgments, "the sex that takes second place," "the Number Two of the human race."[1]

Because Schopenhauer's antipathy to sex and his intense misogyny are represented as the logical products of his metaphysical premises, men can obtain relief from the sufferings inflicted by the noumenal will by resisting the enticements of the women to whom they are drawn by the pleasurable urgings of the sexual impulse. Such resistance is, in fact, at the heart of Schopenhauer's program for human salvation, the famous "denial-of-the-will to live" that manifests itself in "the transition from virtue to asceticism" (*WWR*, 1:380). Predictably, ascetic practice is a specifically masculine practice, a renunciation of sex that obviously requires the avoidance of women: "His body, healthy and strong, expresses the sexual impulse through the genitals, but he denies the will, and gives the lie to the body; he desires no sexual satisfaction on any condition. Voluntary and complete chastity is the first step in asceticism's denial of the will to live" (*WWR*, 1:380).

A deep mistrust of and aversion to sexual desire (with an accompanying antipathy to women) may be seen as nothing more than a philosophically logical corollary to a metaphysical pessimism volitionally conceived. But it is difficult to believe that one would maintain such views, let alone vent them with the apparent rage and contempt Schopenhauer displays, unless the attitudes underlying these opinions have been deeply rooted in one's life experiences. In the instance of Schopenhauer, as virtually all of those who write on these matters agree, there clearly seems a close connection between the philosopher's professed aversion to sex with its concomitant misogyny and the events of his own life. Having grown up in "an unusually loveless domestic atmosphere,"[2] Schopenhauer at seventeen had to deal with the death of his father, "almost certainly a suicide."[3] At twenty-six, he was thrown out of his mother's house "for good,"[4] never to see her again, apparently because of a quarrel over a younger lover she had taken into her home after her husband's death. It should come as no surprise, given even this sparse account of the family background, that Schopenhauer remained a lifelong bachelor, a solitary, "subsisting on a thin and intermittent sexual diet of shallow, casual relationships," mainly with "prostitutes" and "servant girls" according to the account of Brian Magee, an important and not unsympathetic commentator.[5] Nor should it

come as any surprise either, given this family history, that Schopenhauer's philosophy itself, his metaphysical pessimism, is frequently
seen to have essentially derived from these unhappy events, his
view of the universe best understood through psychological and
even psychoanalytical explanations.

In most respects, no two lives would seem to differ more than those
of Arthur Schopenhauer and Matthew Arnold. Unlike Schopenhauer, Arnold came of age in a large and (we may safely conclude)
essentially caring family, one in which, as far as the evidence we
have permits us to judge, his mother and father were devoted to one
another and to their children. It must be added that the father's emi-
nence and influence, and perhaps even his moral earnestness, were
a sometimes distracting, even threateningly inhibiting presence in
his son's literary and intellectual endeavors, a matter that has understandably been a significant consideration for many of those
who write on the younger Arnold. Nonetheless, we still have no reason to doubt Thomas Arnold's love and concern for his gifted, if
sometimes mildly rebellious and vexing child. Furthermore, in
marked contrast to Schopenhauer, Matthew Arnold did marry, a
marriage of thirty-six years that by every indication was also loving
and successful, marred only by the deaths of three of his six children—tragedies that would seem, however, to have strengthened
the bonds between husband and wife.
   Arnold's upbringing and marriage, his family history broadly considered, would seem to point to a life that should have been well-
adjusted and happy. Still, the fact remains that there is in many
ways a radical disjunction between the broad biographical outline
and the written record. In the years between his beginning college
and his settling into marriage, he not only produced his most cheer-
lessly pessimistic poems but also displayed in the poems and letters
an aversion to sex—Arnold would, after all, as the culminating
event in his famous sequence of love poems, have the passionate
woman he claimed to love so ardently be translated into "my sister"
("A Farewell," 77)—as well as an antipathy to women: "I hate the
word" he told Clough (in that famous letter written when Arnold
was on his way to "the Hotel Bellevue for the sake of the blue eyes
of one of its inmates" (Letters, 1:119). If Arnold is less shrill than
Schopenhauer in expressing that aversion and antipathy, I believe
the case can still be made that, at times at least, similar feelings are
present in Arnold in ways that are not truly different in kind from
what we find in Schopenhauer. Moreover, even within this broad
and basically benign biographical outline of loving parents and a

happy marriage, we are able to identify troubling details that convey a sense of the life that was in the mid-nineteenth century's hothouse of sexual postponement, denial, and repression and its attendant guilt, anxiety, and neurosis that Peter Gay describes so well in *The Bourgeois Experience*. (Since I will draw heavily from Freud in the pages to come, it should be noted that Gay has also shown, both in his social histories of the nineteenth century and in his biography of Freud, that it was from the same bourgeois world of postponement, repression, and anxiety that Freud took the data for what he would regard as universally valid psychoanalytic theories of the mind's functioning and its disturbances, so that, even historically considered, these theories possess a certain amount of explanatory possibility.)

One of those troubling biographical details strikingly conveys a sense of the historical moment in which Arnold and his family lived. In 1953 the distinguished Victorian scholar Kathleen Tillotson published in *Notes and Queries* a passage from a letter by Harriet Mozley, John Henry Newman's sister, to another sister, Jemima, that Tillotson rightly believed sheds considerable light on the mysterious breaking-off of the engagement between Arnold's sister Jane and George Cotton, a teacher at Rugby School, as well as on the premature death from a heart attack only a year later of Thomas Arnold: "We have heard private accounts of Dr. A[s] death, . . . He had just broken off a match of his daughters on acct. (solely) of the gentlemans mother being of intoxicating habit and they attribute this attack much to what he went thro'. I th[ough]t what then ought the poor daughter to suffer."[6] From the tone of this passage, I do not think we can construe Dr. Arnold's seemingly callous behavior as simply the standard practice of an age very different from our own, a historical past, not merely remote but inaccessible, a world irrecoverably gone and thankfully well lost. Mrs. Mozley responds just as we do, with compassion for a daughter whose sufferings seem totally unwarranted and with unqualified anger at the impossibly rigid father, the terrible price he paid for his actions notwithstanding. The responsibility for the sufferings of both father and daughter, Mrs. Mozley unequivocally tells her sister, is "solely" his.

Only months after Tillotson's note appeared, Norman Wymer, then completing his biography of Thomas Arnold, offered a rejoinder to the really rather amazing and heretofore unknown accusation of paternal cruelty brought against Thomas Arnold by Mrs. Mozley's letter. While conceding that the father's angina had been "brought on by his daughter's broken engagement," Wymer reported that in the archival material he had examined he found "nothing to support the belief that Arnold himself was relieved to think that Jane would not be marrying the son of one too fond of drink," but rather he "appeared to have a high opinion of Cotton and to have regretted the rift."[7] Tillotson then closed the exchange with the simple but seemingly compelling rejoinder that "although Wymer's archives do not appear to confirm Mrs. Mozley's letter, they do not appear to contradict it."[8] Neither Tillotson's evidence nor arguments, however, changed Wymer's views; and in his biography of Thomas Arnold published in the following year, Wymer made no mention whatsoever of Mrs. Mozley nor the drunken mother, contending instead that it was Cotton who was solely responsible for the sad chain of events, having decided that, "though he was fond of her, he was not in love with Jane Arnold," and therefore chose to break the engagement "only a month before the wedding."[9]

In one crucial regard, Wymer's explanation of this episode—its apparent evasiveness notwithstanding—would seem to have prevailed. In 1969, Kenneth Allott published what was to become the standard edition of the poems and therefore the source for most readers of Arnold of whatever background information they have about them. In his notes to "Resignation," Arnold's poem to Jane, Allott cited and followed Wymer's biography exclusively, never once mentioning Tillotson's note or the story it told. All we learn from the notes about this strange episode is that "George Cotton (then assistant-master of Rugby) broke off the engagement in early May" of 1842, and that this and Jane's ensuing depression were the "predisposing causes" of Dr. Arnold's collapse and fatal heart attack. To be sure, Honan, in his 1981 biography, revived the charge that Dr. Arnold had been angered by learning about the drunkenness of Cotton's mother, augmenting the earlier account with the intriguing bit of information that "Jane tried to defend" her fiancé against "her father's fury," thereby creating a "situation," Honan gingerly concludes, that "produced enough strain and tension perhaps to contribute to Dr. Arnold's final illness."[10] Somewhat surprisingly, those who have written most recently on Arnold's life have made no mention of Cotton's drunken mother: in his account of the engagement Hamilton closely follows Wymer,[11] and neither Murray nor Lang allude at all to the engagement and the unhappy consequences that followed from it—a surprising omission by Lang, since he elsewhere suggests that Jane's later engagement to W. E. Forster inflicted "a grievous psychic wound"[12] on Matthew Arnold.

The hair-raising narrative of these events provided by Tillotson's note as augmented by Honan—a father's insistence that his daughter end her engagement for the most morally narrow-minded and seemingly irrelevant of reasons, Jane's apparent resistance to her father's wishes, the fatal heart attack of the father that followed—is plainly of interest not just to the biographer. After all, Tillotson herself suggests, for obvious reasons, that these matters are "surely a part of the background of Arnold's poem 'Resignation: To Fausta,' with its recollection of their father as leader of walks on the fells."[13] That suggestion, however, has never really been taken up by those who have written on the poem (including myself in an earlier essay), perhaps because the poem itself seems too psychologically intractable, sending out very mixed signals about the family triangle that appears to form its never-quite-articulated psychological core.[14] If the account of the broken engagement and Thomas Arnold's death provided by Tillotson and Honan is accurate, it would not be much of a stretch to conjecture that, a year after Thomas Arnold's death, Jane might have judged herself in some measure culpable of causing it by her willfulness in opposing his wishes—a judgment in which, from the evidence of the poem, Matthew Arnold might plausibly have concurred. In that case, there would seem to be something truly disturbing, perhaps even cruel, about a poem that has as its dramatic starting point the chiding of a sister who would seem to be accused of a further recalcitrance that could conceivably be construed as disrespect by her reluctance to complete a walk plainly intended to memorialize their father dead only a year, a death for which Jane may have felt herself responsible and for which she may have been thought by her brother to bear some indirect responsibility.

From one vantage point, the one closest to its manifest narrative surface, "Resignation" is a poem in which Arnold, to a remarkable degree, identifies with the father, demanding of Jane a passivity and submissiveness that can easily be seen as urging her to a self-correction of her earlier catastrophic willfulness. But such an explanation, looked at in isolation, tends to obscure the poem's obviously deep ambivalences and overdeterminedness. For from another vantage point, that of the poem's philosophic debate, it is Jane who, as silent spokesperson for the goal-oriented strivers, identifies most with the father, who is remembered from that earlier excursion as making "clear the goal to every eye" (46), while the speaker, in his philosophic allegiances, emerges as the truly rebellious child, preaching repetition, withdrawal, incorporation into the near-vacancy of the "general life," the course commended by an "Oriental wisdom" that stands in striking opposition to the father's teaching of striving forward, teaching tacitly enacted in his remembered leadership of his children's "motley bands." Finally, if we may take into account as a psychological context for "Resignation" not only the recently broken engagement but also Lang's speculation that Jane's second engagement caused her brother a "grievous psychic wound" (*Letters*, 1:lvii)—one Lang surely implies is rooted not just in the fact of Jane's later engagement but in Matthew's earlier and undoubtedly too intense feelings for his sister—we may decide that the element in "Resignation" that probably provides us with the greatest access to the poem's psychological conflictedness, its longings and their denials, is its speaker's strictures against love. In urging his female listener to seek a plainly regressive detachment from the activities of life, to "[d]raw homeward to the general life," the speaker of "Resignation" instructs her to recognize not only "power an unreal show" (236) but also "love transient" (236). These warnings against attachment to the things of the world can certainly be accommodated to the poem's generally Stoic cast of mind, but still the personal circumstances under which the poem was written render the judgment "love transient" an especially unfeeling one when read as advice to a sister who only a year earlier had perhaps unsuccessfully fought against the command that she break her engagement. Taking the complications of the poem's overdeterminedness still further, we may also speculate that the discrediting of love might at the same time have served Arnold himself as a self-censoring barrier against his own uneasy feelings toward a sister he loved too much.

The events recounted by Mrs. Mozley and their implicit coloring of the narrative of "Resignation" are not the only reasons to attribute to Arnold a troubled sexuality and an aversion both to women and to love at the time he was most dedicated to being a poet. In his highly sympathetic biography of Arnold, Honan tells us that, on the basis of "hard evidence," he is forced to the conclusion about Arnold "that as a young man he did not like women."[15] Arnold's most recent biographer, Ian Hamilton, also treats issues of women and love as a problem for Arnold. Oxford in the 1840s, Hamilton tells us, was "a kind of priesthood," the fellows "not permitted to be married," and the colleges therefore "seething with several varieties of sexual indecisiveness," so that we might reasonably expect to find that "quite often a crisis of belief was in reality a crisis of frustration."[16] Turning more specifically to Arnold himself, Hamilton conjectures that prior to his affair with Marguerite he had "no close relationships with women" as far as we know, and in his letters he "was either to be chucklingly vulgar about sex, or to represent it as a threat, an undermining of the high-toned intellectual life."[17]

Even more revealing as an indicator of Arnold's troubled sexuality than his chuckling vulgarity and aspersions upon women in the letters are the puzzling crosses scattered through Arnold's pocket diary in the 1840s. As Lang persuasively argues, these seemingly random and scattered markings, inserted without comment by Arnold in his diary on innumerable occasions from 1845 to 1847, probably serve the same function as the asterisks found in Clough's *Journals* from roughly the same years. As these have been interpreted by Anthony Kenny, Clough's editor, they provide a record of the occasions when the journal-keeper had given in to what Clough (who did comment on his own markings) terms a "wretched habit," his own "worst sin," plainly a reference to masturbation, the self-condemned vice in which both poets evidently engaged. Placed in historical context, the guilt both men obviously felt can be seen as a manifestation of what Gay has called the "panic over masturbation"[18] in the nineteenth century, a form of torment that became virtually obsessive among medical practitioners and the public alike. But even by the standard of that guilt-ridden age, the diary entries and record keeping by Arnold and Clough seem something extreme, sexual anxiety raised to a fever pitch by two young men in their mid-twenties shielded from the company of eligible women by professional restrictions, cultural inhibitions, and their own apparent timidity, and perhaps something still deeper and darker, an anxiety that in the case of Arnold seems almost certainly to find confirmation in the poetry. Nor are the subsequent facts of Arnold's happy marriage and a presumably successful sex life that produced six children necessarily inconsistent with the implied neurotic fear and anxiety that we find expressed by the poet in his twenties, those years when Arnold apparently felt most strongly what Lang calls "the coercions of the postpubertal, premarital libido."[19] In fact, the two extended case histories with which Gay begins *The Tender Passion* (the second volume of *The Bourgeois Experience*) are precisely of this nature, accounts of the reflections and dreams of Otto Beneke and Walter Bagehot compiled from their diaries and letters. These reflections and dreams reveal the deepest and, on occasion, most immobilizing of sexually generated anxieties and neuroses, which, nevertheless, would seem eventually to have been largely cured by happy marriages and loving wives.[20] From the observations of others and the tenderness of the letters to his wife, Flu, that have been passed on to us, Arnold too, like Bagehot and Beneke, very probably had the sexual anxieties of his bachelor years allayed by a happy marriage and a loving wife. But this is a study of Arnold the poet and of poems written largely before he had passed through the apparent sexual crisis manifested in the poems, letters, and diaries written during the years before marriage.

Certainly Arnold the poet, though critical of women and mistrustful of love, treats the topics of women and love with far less asperity than did Schopenhauer the philosopher. Indeed, in his love poems Arnold represents himself as a lover, a man who desires love, seeks love, and even believes, on occasion, he is in love. Yet his is a love poetry like no other,[21] the love poetry of a poet of pessimism, constituted by concepts and attitudes that almost inevitably attach themselves to a metaphysically grounded pessimism. Arnold also demystifies romantic love, displays a tacit antipathy to the sexual impulse, and, at times, a disturbing hostility to the women who seemingly loved him in return, often justifying his views in these matters by appealing to the very nature of things.

One early poem clearly about love between the sexes is that strange, disjointed, lifelessly abstract allegory of romantic (and Romantic) temptation,[22] "The New Sirens," a poem acknowledged by Arnold himself to be "exactly a mumble" (*Letters*, 1:138). For all its murkiness, what we do plainly find there is the representative situation of most of Arnold's love poetry, a diffident Arnoldian speaker who refuses the love to which others succumb, in this case those youths who, charged with remaining at their stations as "[w]atchers for a purer fire" (140), instead abandon their posts and yield to the enticements of the sirens. Yet at poem's end, we hear none of the accusations we might have anticipated: charges of dereliction of duty, of forsaking a higher good for the baser end that in the traditional Circean scenario transforms men into beasts. Morality largely gives way to psychology, to dissatisfaction with the profoundly flawed nature of the sexual impulse that tempts us. The pose that the speaker seems ultimately to adopt is, in fact, one of postcoital reflectiveness and regret—though, strangely enough, the speaker's own postcoital disappointment is apparently arrived at without his ever having experienced the antecedent pleasure. "Is this all?" he asks,

> this balanced measure?
> Could life run no happier way?
> Joyous, at the height of pleasure,
> Passive at the nadir of dismay?

(199–202)

The "balanced measure" longed for here should not be confused with the virtue of moderation, a rationally pursued Aristotelian

mean between excess and deficiency. What Arnold apparently desires is that curiously inert condition he fervently seeks again and
again in his poetry: poise, equilibrium, calm, a condition essentially
defined by lack, by what he does not have or cannot or would not
be. Yielding to the entreaties of the New Sirens—that is, entering
into the sexual life—would be to submit to change, to the psychologically feared condition of eddying, here defined by the explicitly sexual rhythm of "[m]ad delight and frozen calms" (196). In "The New
Sirens," Arnold states that preference common in his poetry for a
diminished pulse, for a stasis and quiescence without content. Furthermore, to reinforce his case against the sexual impulse, Arnold
adopts a no less characteristic strategy, an act of self-projection to
some vantage point from which one can judge and condemn the passionate life. We are to look "adown life's latter days" (210) to an
imagined old age, "when change itself is over, / When the slow tide
sets one way" (219–20) (certainly an odd sexual foreboding for the
poet in his early twenties), thereby projecting himself into a felt consciousness of vanished desire, into an unpleasure of absence that
seems reason enough to choose never to enter into a sexual life that
in the end so devastatingly fails us.

But beyond its denunciation of sexuality per se, "The New Sirens" is also the first and probably the most strident of all those
poems by Arnold that express hostility to women and the sexuality
of women. In devising this cautionary tale for the modern male—
telling him, in effect, that the more things change the more they are
the same, that the New Sirens are no different than the sirens of
old—Arnold makes clear the responsibility of women in general for
those dangerous liaisons and fatal attractions to which men, the superior sex, have always been drawn. Originally the New Sirens also
dwelt where Arnold's sage customarily dwells, in the uplands where
they were to be "[w]atchers for a purer fire" (140), assigned, like
the male poets, to an apparent apprenticeship to sagehood that neither male nor female ultimately completes. The differing reasons
for the failures of female and male are in themselves instructive.
Because of some inner deficiency, the New Sirens are simply unable
to endure the long wait required of them: "drooped in expectation"
(141) and "wearied in desire" (142), they abandon their stations
and descend from the heights to seek ease and slumber "[i]n some
windless valley farther down" (146). The men, on the other hand,
fail because women entice them from their duties, a scenario of
male transgression ultimately attributed to the vices of women that
date back to the Fall.

Once down from the mountains, the New Sirens begin life anew in regions that often prove the natural habitat of women in Arnold, an everyday world among "the seats of men" (150), whether it be the simple village to which Margaret in "The Forsaken Merman" finally returns or the empty splendors of Marc's court that Iseult of Ireland chooses in "Tristram and Iseult." It is from this site that the sirens' song emanates, proclaiming and celebrating the value of what Arnold deems to be the specious goods, material and sensual, of ordinary human existence. In fact, the "turbid inspiration" (151) for their song is drawn from what Arnold, in a phrase of obvious symbolic signification, disparagingly terms "some transient earthly sun" (152), that sun that so often in Arnold's poetry signifies involvement in or commitment to ordinary and everyday social existence, a sun much like that under whose "hot eye" (38) the Slave of "A Summer Night" "year after year" (42) toils at "some unmeaning taskwork" (40).

But geographically the New Sirens (for obvious reasons) appear to belong most significantly not to the temperate, sunlit valley but to the sea, the symbolic locale of entrapment, the setting in which the Arnoldian Madman gives vent to his passion. As the poet's dream of foreboding makes abundantly clear, the New Sirens are unmistakably the progeny of the sirens of old; in fact, their destructive beckonings are the same as those of the sea-maidens, "[w]ho on shores and sea-washed places / Scoop the shelves and fret the storms" (11–12). But being women, the sirens, both new and old, are never figuratively granted the heroic dignity of mariners who, like the Madman of "A Summer Night," courageously voyage out on "the sea of life." Women, instead, hug the shoreline, "wending" only to "reefs and narrows" (10), living out their own storm of passion as agents of shipwreck.

Of course, the New Sirens of this later day would have themselves regarded as nineteenth-century women, de-eroticized and idealized, not defined, as the male perspective of that Homeric legend suggests they should be, by a sexual nature intrinsically destructive of the civilizing aims of men. Displaying none of the "uncouthness / Of that primal age" (49–50) and manifesting nothing like that "heart of stone" (55) that their counterparts from an earlier age possessed—or so they claim—these modern sirens would have those whom they have invited to be their lovers regard their love as "romantic," the term Arnold employs in his prose paraphrase. While their love includes the sexual, they would have us believe that feelings of affection can and shall continue beyond the performance of the physical act of sexual love itself. But Arnold's aim is to undo the pretensions to spirituality of women and the illusions of love

these foster, to expose women and love as distractions from the real
duties and purposes of life that men must fulfill. In love, there is
only the sexual, that terrible and often fatal passion to which the
spiritually inclined male from time to time inevitably falls victim but
to which women, driven by overpowering libidinal drives, seem irretrievably consigned.

In insisting that love must be either "lawfully attractive" (the
New Sirens' self-justifying phrase in the prose paraphrase) or un-
lawfully sexual (the to-be-rejected-out-of-hand reality of the poem
itself), Arnold gives voice to that allegedly perennial and irreconcil-
able conflict between the tender and the sensual that Freud believed to be rooted in childhood ambivalence toward the mother.
Such conflict can exact enormous psychic costs: Freud himself identifying it as the basic cause of male "psychical impotence."[23] Thus,
to reduce risk in a situation of conflict between the tender and the
sensual, when a call to romantic love conceals erotic temptation,
Arnold advocates a policy of strict sexual avoidance (not unlike the
"voluntary chastity" recommended by Schopenhauer). Only by such
denial, by tacitly choosing self-imposed impotence, can we hope to
ward off the psychic discomfiture that Arnold, in the concluding
portion of "The New Sirens," seems to believe is the inevitable af-
termath of sexual gratification: a consciousness of loss experienced
as unpleasure, whether the "ennui and lassitude" that follow cli-
max or the decline in potency brought on by aging.

Moreover, a concern with defects in the sexual function, so
threatening that they lead the speaker to prefer inhibition to gratification, doubtlessly results not just from fear of the sexual act but
from fear of the sexual object, fear of becoming subjugated to the
sexual powers of women, who in the course of the poem plainly undergo that debasement that Freud finds universal in the sphere of
love. Indeed, by the speaker's lurid dream of women who, wearing
the New Siren's "forms" (10), "fret the storms" (12) and destruc-
tively draw the ships that are "that way tending" (13) shoreward
with "beckoning hands" (16), Arnold makes it only too clear, even
at the poem's beginning, that the New Sirens, despite protestations
of difference, are in aim one with "the fierce sensual lovers of antiquity" (*Poems*, 49). The tender solicitations of these modern women,
their call for a love that matches the male need for idealization,
merely mask the most voracious of appetites, their desire for pres-
ent-day trophies that shall add to the "whitening-bone-mounds"
(55) piled high by their predecessors in the speaker's dark dream-
fantasy of victimage and castration.

At the very close of his poem, Arnold divests the New Sirens of any fatal attractiveness, leaves them disempowered by the day's early light. In its revealing brightness, the New Sirens are clearly not divinities; they possess neither the gift of a supernatural malevolence that controls wind and wave to achieve the destruction of men nor the transcendent spirituality they wished to ascribe to themselves by virtue of the idealizing fantasies men create in moments of tender affectionateness. Instead, in the morning's light, the New Sirens are recognized for what they are, "unsplendid, discrowned creatures" (249), with "Souls as little godlike" (250) as those of the men who worshipped and made love to the New Sirens. Yet a revelation of ungodlikeness that another poet might regard as proof of a common humanity and a reason for renewal of love based on reciprocity is for Arnold a new cause for condemnation. With daybreak there is to be no saving aubade, no reaffirming declaration of a love that carries over beyond the night's passion. Instead, at dawn, Arnold tells us in a disconcertingly callous passage, when "[s]cores of true love knots are breaking" (261), all lovers' vows are cancelled at "divorce which it proclaims" (262). Claiming to speak not only for himself, the one who resisted and abstained, but also for those who on the night just passed had professed and enjoyed love, Arnold's speaker predicts and ordains for the women of the poem the failure of beauty and its compelling power, the departure of those who had loved them, the end of the happiness possessed only hours earlier: "Cold in that unlovely dawning, / Loveless, rayless, joyless you shall stand!" (265–66). All in all—not just in its inhibitedness but even, more disturbingly, in its anger—"The New Sirens" seems the most inauspicious of beginnings for a poetry about love, a subject Arnold returns to a few years later, bringing with him the same inhibitedness and anger, even after having been captivated by the "[s]weet notes" ("Parting," 24) of his own New Siren at Thun.

In a letter to Clough from Switzerland in 1848, Arnold announced his intention to "linger one day at the Hotel Bellevue" in Thun "for the sake of the blue eyes of one of its inmates,"[24] a woman for whom he apparently cared enough to return to Thun in 1849 to carry on a brief, troubled, and ultimately unsuccessful love affair that for many critics serves as the basis for the Marguerite poems. What I hope to show in the pages that follow is that the romance with Marguerite, whether real or imagined—and the letter to Clough implies it was real—poetically played itself out in conformity with those hostility-ridden anxieties already in place in "The New Sirens."

Even the letter to Clough indicates this: only a few paragraphs

after jauntily announcing his romantic intentions, Arnold launches
into the most harshly derogatory statement about women in his
writings. Commenting on a waning interest in the poet Béranger, in
whose Epicureanism Arnold detects "something fade," Arnold describes himself as strangely consoled for his loss of pleasure in an
author once admired: "In the reste, I am glad to be tired of an author: one link in the immense series of cognescenda et inadagenda
dispatched." Then in a startling turn in focus, he points to relations
with women as another instance that falls under this general principle: "More particularly is this my attitude in regard to (I hate the
word) women. We know beforehand all they can teach us: yet we
are obliged to learn it directly from them" (*Letters*, 1:120). Elliptical
and cryptic as this proposition is (though surely more comprehensi-
ble to his longtime companion Clough than to us), one can certainly
glean from it a deep distrust of and distaste for his own sexual
needs and desires, a necessary evil that drives the young Arnold
away from the company of men and into an involvement with
women that he would otherwise forgo if not for those physical urges
that he knows "beforehand" to be valueless and transitory. So even
as he journeys to the woman who is apparently Marguerite, Arnold
already reveals an antipathy to sex and a hostility to women that
surely must threaten to undermine the love he will shortly profess.

"A Memory Picture" is the one poem in the series that Arnold called
Switzerland that deals with the first phase of the Marguerite affair.
To be sure, this day of "tender Leave-taking" (the words of the
poem's original title) seems full of hope, concluding in a lingering
kiss and a promise by Marguerite of fidelity: "Some day next year,
I shall be / Entering heedless, kissed by thee" (19–20). But here, as
elsewhere in the love poetry of Arnold, surfaces prove depressingly
deceiving. What the intensity of the gaze that his "light" friends rid-
icule most truly expresses is not a lovesick tenderness, as they
think, but an urgent need fostered by doubt and mistrust to affix to
the tablets of memory the portrait of the beloved, whom the speaker
knows he must lose, despite all her vows of fidelity. Even as she
pledges herself anew, Arnold can read in her gesture the futility of
that pledge, however sincerely given, the certainty of unfaithful-
ness, woman's way: "Many a broken promise then / Was new
made—to break again" (37–38). Then, in what shall prove to be a
characteristic strategy of the love poetry, he essentially absolves
Marguerite of responsibility for that breaking of vows he foresees
as a future certainty, shifting blame from the individuals involved
to the workings of some impersonal and external agency, some fault

residing in the very nature of things—in this case, time "whose current strong / Leaves us fixed to nothing long" (57–58).

Yet here, as elsewhere in the "Marguerite" poems, one can certainly detect compensatory elements, psychological gains that accrue from the failure of love, a reduction in libidinally posed dangers, a circumventing of the threat that an enduring union with Marguerite (or perhaps with any woman) would seem to carry for Arnold. Even while his friends bemusedly assume that his long farewell gaze during his tender leave-taking is sustained by an essentially erotic intent, he himself tells his reader that what that intentness signifies is not a wish to possess the libidinal object but something more akin to the concentration required by portraiture, an implicit preference for "the dim remembrance" (62) of Marguerite over "the clear impression" (61) of the living woman that stands before him. This preference we may conjecturally ascribe to risks that the "clear impression" entails, not only the risk of losing the living Marguerite, who is the source of that impression, but the risk posed by success in love as well. For the first time in a poem in which he professes love—but certainly not the last—Arnold in "A Memory Picture" will make the case for the substitute gratification, urging the deflection of the libido from its ostensible object and the rechanneling of its energies toward ends about which he feels more secure, in this case "a memory picture" he senses will produce less anxiety than the real woman from whom he departs.[25]

When he returns a year later, though, Marguerite's vows of fidelity at that first parting have, surprisingly, held true: "My Marguerite smiles upon the strand, / Unaltered with the year" (3–4). In fact, of the Marguerite poems, only "Meeting" significantly affirms the possibility of a love that endures, though it is an affirmation made in an extremely odd and inimitably Arnoldian fashion. Just when success seems assured, when the poet "spring[s] to make my choice" (1), one of the strange gods that intermittently appear in Arnold's poetry offers words of counsel, ostensibly kindly intended but delivered in "tones of ire" that mark them as an angry command to the lovers to desist, to "[b]e counseled and retire" (12). Over forty years ago Paull Baum suggested that, mingled with "God's tremendous voice," we may hear "the paternal tones of Dr. Arnold's memory."[26] If a critic as cautious and conservative as Baum could discern a father's tones here, it should not seem unreasonable for a reader of the twenty-first century to carry his supposition a step further and hear in that "God's tremendous voice" and in those "tones of ire" the introjected father in general, the commanding voice of the superego intervening in the speaker's life at a moment of blatant sexual transgression. But Arnold's response to the "guiding Powers who join and part" (13) is not to comply with their command but to request exemption from laws that seem designed to cover just such cases as his; they are to "warn some more ambitious heart, / And let the peaceful be!" (15–16).

In his rejoinder, the speaker defends himself by representing himself not as innocent or chaste, and hence blameless of the charge that apparently arouses God's ire, but as "peaceful," the professedly saving virtue that Arnold claims for both lovers, but which—given the sexually compromising circumstances in which God finds them—would seem a virtue essentially beside the point. Moreover, in pleading for that exemption, the vice of which he declares the lovers innocent seems no less beside the point: not lust or licentiousness but a curiously irrelevant ambitiousness. At first glance, this may seem a strategy of desperation, an attempt to placate the God who would have them break off the embrace they seem on the verge of enjoying, but by means that would allow him to remain with Marguerite—though under the subtly altered conditions of a love represented not as passion but as an implicitly asexual peacefulness.

In "Resignation," a psychologically significant contrast between ambition and peacefulness had already been put forward by Arnold. There the ambitious are the single-minded, goal-oriented strivers, pilgrim and crusader, Goth and Hun, those whose declared motto is *"To die be given us, or attain!"* and to whom the incorrigibly restless Fausta shows troubling affinities. The problem of the "ambitious" in "Resignation" is not that they pursue misguided goals, choosing material over spiritual goods, but that in their ambition they subjugate themselves to the "passions, and the state / Of struggle these necessitate" (24–25). And as an alternative to a life of such disquietude Arnold points to those "[w]hom an unblamed serenity / Hath freed from passions" (23–24), an oddly assorted group made up of the poet, the gipsies, and apparently the speaker himself, those linked by an innate or acquired propensity to peacefulness.

During most of "Resignation," passion is a vaguely generic concept that usually manifests itself in restlessness, reluctance to do over or look back, a trait shared by the fanatic strivers of the opening and the stubborn Fausta herself. But late in the poem Arnold differentiates between two types of passion: "love and power" (235) (categories much like Freud's twin drives of libido and aggression). To become one of the untroubled "peaceful," Fausta (as I have noted) must eschew the pursuit of power (here seen as the wish to have things her own way) and avoid the temptation of love, knowing "[l]ove transient, power an unreal show" (236). Like the poet who can look upon "the ruler" of "some great-historied land" (54) without envy and who, when "[b]eautiful eyes meet his" (160), "[b]ears to admire uncravingly" (161), she is to live dispassionately, pursuing neither love nor power, not just to be spared disquietude but to gain access to a more ontologically desirable mode of being. She is to "[d]raw homeward to the general life" (252), that minimally subsisting life "of plants, and stones, and rain," a life "[w]hose secret is not joy, but peace" (191–92). If the peace recommended to Fausta can return her to her ultimate home in the metaphysically real, we might reasonably feel free to ask, why then, by the same logic, should not the similar and presumably metaphysically sanctioned peace the speaker of "Meeting" claims for himself and Marguerite not win them a similarly metaphysically sanctioned dispensation, on the grounds that their lives are in harmony with the workings of the ontologically real? Of course, it goes without saying that to be numbered among the "peaceful" one must live minimally, specifically avoiding in this case the only one of the passions that would seem really applicable to the situation of the lovers: that of love—the reason why, after all, the poem's God has, in the first place, counseled them to retire from the embrace toward which the speaker springs.

Though by urging upon his sister a commitment to resignation that apparently implicitly asks her to remain chaste, indeed celibate, the speaker of "Resignation" may seem unkind, unbrotherly, and even prudish—especially in light of her recently broken engagement—at least he involves himself in no manifestly personal contradiction. But if Arnold still conceives of the "peaceful" in "Meeting" as he had in "Resignation"—that is, to be one of the "peaceful," one must disavow love—then the fact that it is his lover who he assures an angry God is one of the peaceful (and thus one of those who has disavowed love) clearly involves Arnold in a troubling contradiction. He would enjoy the love he "spring[s] to" and all that term sensually implies and yet is willing to placate an angry God by a de-eroticizing formulation that would exchange the "bliss" so palpably "at hand" for the lower-keyed and lesser good of mere peace, lest God leave him nothing at all.

Even more to the point, in "A Farewell," Arnold again singles out peacefulness as the preeminent good of his romantic relationship with Marguerite. Though all is apparently over between them, Arnold insists that they still retain their "true affinities of soul," that "the bent of both our hearts / Was to be gentle, tranquil, true" (47–

48), though, unhappily, on earth they could not "satiate" (87) their "thirst for peace" (88). Then, astonishingly, he holds out the comforting prospect (and cold comfort it must be) that he and the woman with whom he still shares "true affinities of soul" will be reunited in that life whose way is peace, the life hereafter. Only there and then can the lovers achieve that asexual communion that the peaceful who share "affinities" most truly desire, the spiritual proximity without physical contact of the heavenly bodies in parallel orbits. There in a relationship of closeness without sensuality, he will be granted the right to call Marguerite by that title by which apparently he has always secretly desired to call her, "My Sister" (78)—a goal, one suspects, present even in "Meeting," whose speaker would also enlist the woman who seems ready to return his kisses into the ranks of the unimpassionedly peaceful.

That Arnold would change a lover into a sister tells us more about the psychological predisposition he brought with him to Thun than about what actually transpired during his stay with Marguerite. With almost exemplary conciseness, the ordering of events and feelings in "Meeting" supplies a perfect paradigm of what is psychologically most fundamental to Arnold's love poetry: the terrible moment when desire seems virtually to turn into its most feared and fearsome antagonist and we apprehend "longing" as "despair." Even as the speaker springs toward the loved object, an action directed toward consummation and release, countercurrents of unpleasure are set in motion, a note of warning sounded and internal strategies of disentanglement and retreat initiated, a sequence that resembles that classic pattern Freud formulated under the term "signal anxiety."

Having described anxiety in his earlier writings as untransformed libido, the unpleasure that emerges as apprehensiveness when libido "is aroused but not satisfied,"[27] Freud in 1925 reversed himself, concluding, "It was anxiety which produced repression, and not, as I formerly believed, repression which produced anxiety."[28] It was a reversal of truly momentous consequence, the basis of almost all subsequent developments in Anglo-American psychoanalysis. As a leading historian of psychoanalysis, Nathan G. Hale, Jr., unequivocally states:

> By reformulating psychoanalysis in terms of the central experience of anxiety, Freud opened the way to all that was to come in fundamental alterations of analytic theory—the primal anxiety of the existentialists, the anxiety aroused competitive capitalism of Karen Horney, the anxiety created by insufficient and inauthentic love of Eric Fromm, the ego psychology of Anna Freud and Heinz Hartmann.[29]

With this revised formulation, anxiety is no longer the unpleasurable discharge of dammed-up and seemingly unexpendable libidi-
nous energy but a response to the world, a way of coping with the
gravest of psychic difficulties. As Freud would now explain it, anxiety (of all kinds) is simply the reaction to a traumatic situation in
which the ego finds itself "helpless in the face of an accumulation
of excitation, whether of internal or external origin, which cannot
be dealt with."[30] It was not a voiding but a signal, a signal to the ego
of danger, against which the ego, to rescue itself, must mobilize its
defenses, often a neurotic flight from or a neurotic transformation
of the source of danger. Here, as virtually everywhere else in Freud,
an internally originating anxiety and its reactive mechanisms of defense are strongly tied to reminiscence. Occasions of anxiety in
adult life are usually not self-contained responses to a clear and
present danger but a reoccurrence of "affective states" that "have
been incorporated in the mind as precipitates of primaeval traumatic experiences."[31] Predictably, too, such "primaeval traumatic
experiences" are likely to arise during our earliest relations with
our mother—on occasions "of missing someone who is longed for"
(136; a condition that Freud breaks down even more finely into loss
of the loved object and fear of the loss of the loved object's love). It
is here, Freud speculates, that we shall find "the key to an understanding of anxiety and to a reconciliation of the contradictions that
beset it" (137).

In "Meeting," what surely triggers the signal of anxiety, and thus
provides the logic of adhesion for events and responses that follow
one another for no discernible reason, is clearly the woman to
whom the speaker springs, apparently to close with in an erotic embrace that would seal their love. Since, contrary to expectation,
Marguerite has remained faithful, "unaltered with the year," we
may reasonably suspect that behind the figure who has waited for
him looms dimly but oppressively an earlier, remembered presence,
presumably maternal, whose love he feared he would lose, perhaps
as punishment for desires like those he feels now for Marguerite.
And it is most likely out of fear that a love so tainted might succeed
that there arises the never-quite-articulated anxiety that is the
probable cause of the poem's abrupt transition from an apparently
untroubled evocation of love triumphant to a desperate attempt to
stay the wrath of a God angered by it. To retain the loved object, the
speaker must render her libidinally neutral, divest her of qualities
that are the source of danger but also of her desirability by turning
passion into a peacefulness acceptable to Arnold's puritanically
wrathful divinity.

For the first two-thirds of "Parting," Arnold presents us with two obviously opposed and apparently mutually exclusive objects of gratification, Marguerite and nature. At first, Arnold manages to suspend judgment, allowing the divided energies of the will to flow along parallel and unconverging tracks, celebrating Marguerite and his Alpine surroundings with equal ardor, momentarily holding in abeyance the need to choose. Only after he actually chooses, reaching toward Marguerite for the embrace and the kiss that would seal their union, does the paradigmatic love-denying scenario begin to unfold. On the very verge of sexual success, he recognizes in the soon-to-be-attained object a source of danger that engenders an instinctual anxiety that, in its turn, warns the ego to mobilize its protective defenses—in this case, a fear-driven, headlong flight into a nature psychologically identical with the maternal object of infantile regression. Unlike "Meeting," where Arnold never really justifies his retreat from gratification, in "Parting" he offers one allegedly compelling reason for turning away from love and fleeing to nature. In a passage justly described even by some of Arnold's staunchest admirers as "priggish," he places the blame squarely on Marguerite herself for whatever fears he has of losing the loved object or losing the object's love:[32]

> In the void air, towards thee
> My stretched arms are cast;
> But a sea rolls between us—
> Our different past!
>
> To the lips, ah! of others
> Those lips have been pressed,
> And others, ere I was,
> Were strained to that breast.
>
> (63–70)

Though he had earlier praised her for "[t]he unconquered joy in which her spirit dwells" (40), only when his appeal for a kiss seems about to be granted, and she stands close enough so that his "arms reach to clasp" (161) her, does the fact of her wayward past become a problem sufficiently disturbing to immobilize the speaker as lover, turning the "void air" that yields so readily to his outstretched arms into the impassable and self-imposed barrier of the estranging sea. Only in this moment of recoiling from physical intimacy does the speaker finally and decisively make his choice, fleeing from the sexual into a nature conceived of as a haven of purity, a sanctuary where he can become a child once more under the unfolding protectedness of an undisguisedly maternal presence.

In his great essay, "The Most Prevalent Form of Degradation in
Erotic Life," Freud seems to describe just such a conflict between
sexuality and purity as that which leads Arnold's speaker to renounce gratification in "Parting." For Freud, the psychic impotence
from which his disablingly conflicted patients suffer is rooted, predictably, in the incestuous entanglements of early life, disruptive
disturbances that arise in infancy itself, when the awakened longings of infantile sexuality come into conflict with the already existing tender affections. To prevent this now-repressed incestuous
conflict with its attendant guilt and discomfort from breaking out
again in adult life, most men, even in marriage (Freud finds) seek
to keep the tender and sensual basically separate, by

> *lowering* the sexual object in their own estimation, while reserving for
> the incestuous object and those who represent it the overestimation nor
> mally reserved for the sexual object. As soon as the sexual object fulfills
> the condition of being degraded, sensual feeling can have free play, con
> siderable sexual capacity and a high degree of pleasure can be devel
> oped.[33]

In choosing Marguerite, then, Arnold would seem to have resolved any potential erotic conflict between the sensual and the
tender, as Freud says most men do, by selecting "a sexual object"
who "fulfills the condition of being degraded." At the moment of
sexual success, however, the speaker in fact collapses into impotence (though some readers may view his conduct as commendable
restraint), inhibiting gratification by the impassable psychological
barrier he constructs from that fact of female degradation indispensable to his own sensual fulfillment, "[o]ur different pasts" (66).
Following the lead provided by Freud, I would suggest that the reason for that short-circuiting of desire that seems suspiciously like
impotence in "Parting" is the inability of the speaker to rid himself
of those feelings of tender affection for Marguerite that recur
throughout the sequence, feelings apparently incompatible with the
sensually gratifying role for which she has been chosen. What Arnold contradictorily asks of Marguerite, a woman known to have a
past, to have been degraded, are just those gifts the ego, guided by
an idealizing tenderness, most esteems: her constancy, her sympathy, her love.

Furthermore, as Freud maintains, when one makes an object
choice in adult life based on both sensuality and tenderness, the

"object selected" is, in some deeper sense, "only a surrogate" for "some lost original"[34]—the mother upon whom, in infancy, we had bestowed tenderly affectionate feelings that we found similarly threatened by sensual desires experienced as debasing. In "Parting," the deep connection—indeed the implied surrogate relationship—between the woman loved by the speaker in adult life and the mother loved in infancy is made especially evident by the rapidity with which the speaker turns from the rejected Marguerite, fatally tainted by past improprieties, to a nature now represented almost wholly as a projection of maternal purity.

Initially Marguerite is only a disembodied voice, a pure musicality eminently susceptible to the kind of idealizing tenderness that would render her company a desirable alternative to the austere and impersonal solitude of the mountains. Just from the tones of her voice (which may not even be speaking English—"pauvre enfant—allons, sortons, dinons" are the only words of the apparent original of Marguerite ever reported by Arnold),[35] the speaker can glean remembrances of the secure and familiar, can hear enough of the sounds of home to wonder whether "some wet bird-haunted English lawn" has "[l]ent it the music of its trees at dawn" (19–20). Mingled with these disembodied tones are intimations of an originary purity, sounds that so resemble the natural music of the pristine stream at its mountain birthplace that the speaker can only ask: "Or was it from some sun-flecked mountain-brook / That the sweet voice its upland clearness took?" (21–22). Not until Marguerite visibly stands before him as a fully embodied object of masculine desire does the initial fantasy give way. No longer is she a maiden of the uplands, the music of whose voice raises memories of a familiar and trustworthy rural Englishness; she is a woman with a past who belongs (to carry on the Arnoldian figures) to the cities of the plain.[36] Only when he actually reaches out to touch her does he set in motion that sensualizing process that renders Marguerite patently unsuitable for the role in which he has just imagined her, as the object of his tender affection, as the woman he loves. The "[s]weet lips" he has implored to "bend nearer" (41) are suddenly perceived as a source of pollution, or so the stirrings of anxiety warn, a carrier of a sexually transmitted contamination, acquired doubtlessly by Marguerite from her earlier lovers but perhaps inherent in the debasement that accompanies any sexual contact.

Furthermore, just at this point of flight from the woman he professedly loves, the nature Arnold's speaker chooses in preference to Marguerite also undergoes a profound transformation. The Alpine landscape becomes radically psychologized by this anxiety-impelled decision, regressively transformed into a manifestly maternal presence:

> Blow ye winds! lift me with you!
> I come to the wild.
> Fold closely, O Nature!
> Thine arms round thy child.
>
> (75–78)

Arnold will use nature for clearly regressive ends in his poetry of the next several years, praising Wordsworth for having "laid us as we lay at birth / On the cool flowery lap of earth" ("Memorial Verses," 48–49) and the idyllically restorative Kensington Gardens for reminding Arnold that "in my helpless cradle I / Was breathed on by the rural Pan" ("Lines Written in Kensington Gardens," 23–24). But only in "Parting" does the Arnoldian speaker expressly look to nature for a maternal enfolding, one presumably free of the sexually generated taint that has fatally contaminated the love of Marguerite.

Yet in the very next stanzas Arnold abruptly shifts from the recesses of infantile memory to the more neutral ground of metaphysical speculation. The Alpine surroundings, which anthropomorphically represented the mother as nurse and comforter, a presence that could "calm me, restore me; And dry up my tears" (83–84), become instead a vehicle for thinking about the metaphysically originary, "the stir of the forces / Whence issued the world" (89–90). This turn to metaphysics, as we might have expected, is carried out in accordance with those vitalistic and volitional presuppositions we have seen elsewhere in the poetry, with the metaphysical principle conceived of as the pulsing and flowing, the elemental and minimal. Pure "stir" and issuance, ongoingness and originary power, those "forces" Arnold locates on the "high mountain-platforms" seem finally but another version of that "general life" that the poet of "Resignation" "craves," "That life, whose dumb wish is not missed / If birth proceeds, if things subsist" (193–94), another instance of the metaphysical will in its benignly immanent form, unestranged and unestranging, if only we would shed our complicating humanness and revert to our elemental and uncomplicated buried life.

Arnold's association of the maternal and the metaphysical can hardly be accidental. We must surely suspect that the metaphysical principle within ourselves—the ontological reality Arnold terms the "buried life" in his metaphysics of immanence, the means by which we establish our own ontological contact with the general life—also is linked to and perhaps is psychologically a derivative of that primal, tender affection that can be directed only to the mother during our earliest relations with her. Toward her we then briefly felt—or wish to believe we felt—a not-as-yet eroticized desire we could safely direct to the loved object, without fear of running the risk of tainting her or ourselves by the contaminating effects of sensuality. (Freud himself maintains that "[o]f these two currents affection is the older," but then he rather ambiguously adds: "From the very beginning elements from the sexual instincts are taken up into it—component parts of the erotic interest—which are more or less clearly visible in childhood and are invariably discovered by the neurotic in psychoanalysis.")[37]

Feelings just such as these—our primal, allegedly untainted affections toward the mother, now overwhelmed and presumably lost amidst the confusion of our sensually governed libidinal energies—are, I would suggest, what Arnold wishfully hopes we can recover by metaphysically drawing "homeward to the general life" ("Resignation," 252). Derivatives of such feelings are what probably impel the poet of "Resignation"—"Who bears to admire uncravingly" (161) the "[b]eautiful eyes" (160) of a face in the crowd—to crave instead existence at its most minimal, "The life of plants, and stones, and rain" (195). We may also plausibly conjecture that those vaguely delineated feelings that are reawakened in Empedocles at the end of his long closing monologue (the point of his suicide) can probably also be best understood as psychological derivatives of these first, maternally directed affections. Carefully differentiating such feelings from thought and sense, Empedocles discovers within himself a third thing, a tertium quid, joyously intense and yet still uncontaminated, free from the "bondage of the flesh" (2.374), an unextinguished "glow" at the irreducible core of his inner life that is the continuing expression of an originary and ontologically real being, "our own, only true, deep-buried selves, / Being one with which we are one with the whole world" (2.371–72). Most ominously, it is a self he would preserve at all costs, even by sacrificing through suicide a humanly indispensable yet ontologically estranged thought and sense.

"Isolation. To Marguerite" records the final disintegration of Arnold's love affair with Marguerite and, more shockingly, the dismaying inference that he has drawn from its unhappy outcome: that he never has been, never will be, and never can be loved in return by the woman he would choose. Proceeding tentatively by a series of suggestive but ultimately flawed analogies, Arnold by trial and error finally carries us to the great and fundamental revelation of the "Marguerite" poems: the universality of his own predicament, his entrapment in an isolation he will soon figuratively render as enislement in the most moving of his attempts to capture the anguish of our human condition.

In the wake of love's failure, the speaker assumes he will again become the person he was prior to love, a man innately superior to other men and therefore able to live as a being apart. Though simple timidity or, perhaps, some deeper libidinal constraint may be the real reason for his solitariness, Arnold's speaker, nonetheless, would make virtue of necessity and pursue a "remote and sphered course" (16) far above other mortals who must live in "[t]he place where passions reign" (17). Despite his ill-conceived lapse into love and desire, the speaker knows his natural habitation is among the stars, Arnold's customary site of autonomy and self-dependence.

But in "A Summer Night" and "Self-Dependence," the poems that most fully elaborate this conceit, a life like the stars, however deeply yearned for, seems humanly unattainable. Unlike the earthbound poet who envies their imperturbability, the stars of "Self-Dependence" are free of distraction because they are content to dwell in loneliness, never demanding that "the things without them / Yield them love, amusement, sympathy" (19–20). Similarly, in "A Summer Night," Arnold acknowledges that he never can finally ascribe to the stars that which is most basic to the human heart, never say to the heavens "that your mild deeps retain / A tinge, it may be, of their silent pain / Who have longed deeply once, and longed in vain" (85–87). So even as the speaker would declare his heart a star in "Isolation. To Marguerite," he tacitly acknowledges the implicit inaptness of the analogy. His heart, as he knows only too well, is a "lonely heart," riven by vain longings that the stars in the perfection of their self-dependent autonomy never feel.

If the heart feels loneliness and longs for sympathy with some other like itself, it is because it is a living organ and nothing like the stars, inanimate, matter in motion, mindless and soulless components of a mathematically governed, wholly mechanistic celestial order. As a truly elucidating analogy, the heart thus requires that which is both heavenly and vital, contradictory attributes that only come together in the classical fictions of mythology. For this purpose, Arnold chooses Luna, a divinity who lives in the sky, and who, though chaste by nature, has in one crucial episode so powerfully felt the pull of desire that, to pursue her love for Endymion, she too has left her own "remote and sphered course" for the soiling earth, "the place where passions reign."

While Luna may have deviated from her ordained chasteness on only this one occasion, still, erotic longing, Arnold indicates, already plainly carries with it the consciousness of debasement that Freud tells us is universal in the sphere of love. In a passage that wonderfully encapsulates the inextricable intermingling of desire and debasement, Arnold calls our attention to

> the conscious thrill of shame
> Which Luna felt, that summer night,
> Flash through her pure immortal frame.
>
> (19–21)

That even Luna, the very pattern of chastity, should experience love as shame seems further confirmation of Arnold's no doubt psychologically compelled conviction that the sense of degradation he has found invariably conjoined to the sexual impulse is neither accidental nor merely contingent and thus avoidable or remediable, but it is something intrinsic, desire's necessary correlative.

However, the analogy between Luna and the human heart quickly shows itself profoundly flawed. The ontologically chaste Luna has engaged in but one aberrant episode of love, otherwise remaining much like the stars, undesiring and self-dependent, never demanding "that the things without them / Yield them love, amusement, sympathy" ("Self-Dependence," 19–20). But for the speaker, desire invariably frustrated has been the law of life, a law cruelly imposed by those mocking Arnoldian divinities, "The Powers that sport with man" ("Destiny," 4), who, having "hurled him on the Field of Life" (7), leave him there in perpetual unhappiness, "An aimless unallayed desire" (8). In noting his fundamental unlikeness to Luna, the speaker, in effect, concedes that in the matter of the passions he is not really superior to other men. The "remote and sphered course" he arrogated to himself, rightly understood, is a mere figment of anxiety and its attendant defenses. His true home is not the heavens, among the stars and the gods, but the earth, "the place where passions reign." Because, like other men, he has repeatedly known desire, he has "long had place to prove / This truth" ("Isolation. To Marguerite, 28–29)—a truth utterly unknown to Luna when she undertakes her quest for Endymion—"How vain a thing is mortal love" (26). Moreover, he knows it to be vain not because he is innately superior to the passionate many but because he shares the common plight to which, from this point forward, he will give the name "isolation," the title and true subject of Arnold's poem.

Unbreachable isolation as a basic condition of the speaker's existence—that "Thou hast been, shalt be, art alone" (30)—would seem, at first glance, to be a conclusion derived from the cumulative evidence of bitter experience, love repeatedly offered but unreturned, persuading us "How vain a thing is mortal love" (26). But a few lines earlier, the speaker had supplied us with a more cogent reason than simply unrequited love for believing that the proposition "Thou hast been, shalt be, art alone" expresses an axiomatic fact of the inner life, a universally necessary truth that no stroke of future good fortune can ever disconfirm or invalidate, not even love's requital (which Arnold apparently did experience two years later with his marriage to Frances Wightman).

In that almost casual reference to the "thrill of shame" that Luna finds attached to her feelings of love, Arnold alerts us to the most psychologically compelling of reasons why love must fail and unbreachable isolation must be our fate. Love has failed not simply because of the failings of the woman loved, her callousness or restless infidelity, but because he himself (or so the voice of anxiety signals) is deeply complicit in and perhaps primarily responsible for his loss, having offered the object of his regard a love somehow tainted and unworthy. Strictly speaking, that mingled sense of shame and desire is not truly innate, nor does the isolation he speaks of have a truly necessary character. But so early in our psychological history do shame and desire come together, at that unremembered juncture when a purely tender regard for the mother is compromised and seemingly sullied by the erotic designs of infantile sexuality, that shame and debasement must ever after seem an intrinsic and indelible feature of love for another, thereby making rejection by that other (or our own drawing back) the inevitable and self-engendered outcome of our appeal for love. It is this self-imposed barrier to erotic fulfillment already in place in earliest infancy, I would argue, that induces in Arnold the conviction that he shall never succeed when he reaches out to another in love and that, therefore, he is to be locked in "isolation without end / Prolonged" (40–41), a condition apprehended as innate, inherent, and permanent, one that holds true not only for himself but all others too. The extension of what has been to what shall be is plainly pivotal, the point in the poem at which accusations of blame disappear and Arnold moves toward those universally applicable speculations, according to which all are to be pitied.

Tentative as always, Arnold does initially draw back from the im-

plications of the absoluteness of this judgment, hedging his bet by
qualifying his claim that "[t]hou hast been, shall be, art alone," conceding that the "lonely heart" may be "not quite alone" (31). Still,
even as he adds this seemingly mitigating qualification, Arnold is at
the same time quick to inform the heart (and his readers) of how
modest that qualification is. In fact, the epistemological conditions
under which we live—the apprehension of objects outside ourselves
as external and separate—carry with them, in every act of perception, a pervasive consciousness of our profound and dismaying estrangement from those objects in whose being we long to
sympathetically participate. So, to the words of apparent comfort
he offers the heart—"Or if not quite alone"—Arnold is obliged to
attach a disclaimer of evident despair:

> yet they
> Which touch thee are unmating things—
> Oceans and clouds and night and day;
> Lorn autumns and triumphant springs;
> And life, and others' joy and pain,
> And love, if love, of happier men.
>
> (31–36)

This is the most fully elaborated exposition of one of the key concepts in Arnold's pessimistic epistemology, what I earlier termed
"unmatingness." Epistemologically, Arnold is not really concerned
with the conundrum of other minds in the usual philosophic sense.
In perception we obviously do apprehend self-subsisting objects
that exist in the world, but we do so, Arnold complains, "unmat-
ingly," observing only surfaces, never sounding or penetrating to
the depths of the other, whether that other is "oceans" or "clouds"
or "life" or "love." It is not entirely clear whether the grounds of
"unmatingness" reside in the nature of the objects themselves, their
enclosing impenetrableness, or in a deficiency in the empathic powers of the observing consciousness. But it is manifestly evident—to
Arnold's sorrow—that we can never know and certainly never participate in the real and inner nature of the persons and things that
make up our world.

In all, this notion of "unmatingness" and of the isolation that follows from it does not seem very different from the account of isolation we find in Freud. For Freud, isolation as a mechanism of
defense resists a threatened psychological danger, primarily by
leaving the traumatatizing experience "deprived of its affect,"[38] rendering it remote, disconnected from us, through a process very

much like amnesia. In "Isolation. To Marguerite" as well, the object who is the cause of the traumatic experience is isolated in much the same way, her person plainly divested of the affect that should accrue to it. But in this case Arnold deploys the mechanism of isolation still more broadly, leaving the perceived particulars of the world at large as devoid of affect as Marguerite herself. While a strategy designed to ward off present danger by isolating oneself from all perceived objects and events runs the risk of solipsistically causing the speaker grave psychological harm, immobilizing him against real involvement with the world, it undoubtedly also yields offsetting benefits, benefits akin to that gain from illness that (according to Freud) latently motivates all our attempts at repression and, indeed, neurotic behavior generally. If an epistemologically determined consciousness of isolation adheres to all impressions, any future attempt at love will be—on virtually a priori grounds—foredoomed, rendered futile and pointless by the nature of things. Thus if the speaker, so convinced, refuses to seek the love of Marguerite again, or that of some other woman (undoubtedly another surrogate for the lost original), then the strategy of isolation will have worked; he will have realized the gain from illness by being spared repetition of the anxiety and pain occasioned by his just concluded and traumatically unsuccessful attempt at love.

There is a further reversal still to come. Having insulated himself against future temptation by his realization of the "unmatingness" inherent in things, Arnold seems to qualify some generally encompassing conclusion yet again, intimating that such isolation may not, in fact, hold true in every case. The appearance of love that touches him only as one of many "unmating things" may have a meaningful existence for others, since all around him are men who claim to be and appear to be in love and, more important, who seem to be loved in return and, therefore, appear happy. Still, even as Arnold offers that concession he negates it, propounding a distinction between appearance and reality that reasserts "unmatingness" as the essential truth of things. "Happier men," Arnold tells his heart,

> at least,
> Have dreamed two human hearts might blend
> In one, and were through faith released
> From isolation without end
> Prolonged; nor knew, although not less
> Alone than thou, their loneliness.

> (37–42)

In his poetry, Arnold does occasionally present us with a second-ary realm of human existence in which consciousness can imagine its wishes fulfilled, but he does so in such a way that its transparent unreality, its status as mere wish-fulfilling dream, is clearly evident. In the cool grove, Mycerinus and his followers seem to enjoy their revels, achieve gratification, be happy, but even as they live out the "feverish time of youth" (89) in "one dream" (89), the truly real con-tinues unregarded on its destructive course and, like the waters of the "moving Nile" (127), "[s]weeps earth, and heaven, and men, and gods along" (39) in its metaphysical inexorableness. And similarly, only in a nonexistent "land of dreams" can the speaker of "Dover Beach," his groundless imaginings triggered by the Arnoldian cata-lyst of the moonlit sea, contemplate a world that includes "joy" and "love" and "light" and "certitude" and "peace" and "help for pain" (33–34), even as a wishful possibility.

Clearly at this point the speaker can no longer claim the superior-ity of the specially endowed, the being apart who plies a "remote and sphered course," striving toward the hubris of a starlike self-dependence that needs no other. By poem's end he knows himself to be just one among many, an earthbound inhabitant of "the place where passions reign," the "darkling plain" now recognized as the common and inescapable home of all humans without exception. His only superiority is that of the undeluded for whom wisdom is sorrow, who grimly understand that universal estrangement is the necessary consequence of the order of things. In this regard, Ar-nold's spokesman would seem to have become something of a sage, tragically knowing like Shakespeare or Sophocles. However, he has become a sage not because he has gained or been granted some starlike or mountaintop vantage point from which to comprehen-sively survey the lesser life below him, but because introspection has taught him he is at one with that life, linked by the bond of a common plight.

Unfortunately, while true enlightenment discloses to him that he must suffer the common plight, at the same time it precludes his benefiting from the psychologically saving illusion available to other "[h]appier men." Though estranged from all things at the truest level of being, those who have allowed themselves to dream have somehow overcome that estrangement, having miraculously through "faith" gained imaginative release from that consciousness of "isolation without end / Prolonged" (40–41) fundamental to human knowledge itself. For the dreamers though, "matingness" is present as an empirically conceivable possibility, and conceivable within the happiest of all wish-fulfillment scenarios, that in which "two human hearts might blend / In one," in what certainly seems an adult re-creation of that fantasy of infantile unity remembered or imagined as our first and truest happiness. But to the speaker, such flights of fancy and miracle-fostering dreams are automatically ruled out precisely because they raise the possibility of overcoming estrangement and arousing desire with its "thrill of shame" once again. No doubt a highly commendable wish to live in truth, free from illusion—a purportedly intrinsic good—figures prominently in this decision to accept estrangement and loneliness as his irrevocable destiny. Other motives though, more covert and self-protective, must surely enter into that decision as well. To avert the greater evil of a feared loss of love, Arnold's speaker (one is certainly given cause to speculate) chooses—or is psychologically compelled to choose—the lesser evil of a metaphysically determined isolation for which no individual is to be held accountable. He would thus seek refuge in a comfortless but safely estranging reality from libidinal energies that would, unhindered, turn outward toward some loved object for gratification. Moreover, it is a reality in which all men participate, at some ultimately meaningful level, so that even those who appear happy, looking as though they have sought and perhaps found love, are, at that more meaningful level, the speaker ruefully yet reassuringly tells his heart, "not less / Alone than thou."[39]

By the exclamatory "Yes!" that begins "To Marguerite—Continued," Arnold emphatically instructs us that we are to read this poem as a reiteration of the final point in "Isolation. To Marguerite," a figurative working out of the stern conclusion to its diffusely abstract predecessor. We are all islands and in essence the same, alone and isolated. Empirically observed individual differences and idiosyncrasies are to be disregarded for the sake of the figure's more valid metaphysically determined and universal truth, one from which there can be no exemption, not even the transitory reprieve of a happiness based on the evanescent immateriality of dreams.

In selecting the island as his master trope for the isolated individual, Arnold actually darkens and deepens the characteristic bleakness of his poetry of pessimism. Elsewhere, bleakly enough, he had likened human existence to a ship sailing "life's incognisable sea" ("Human Life," 8), a figure that certainly conveys our isolation, since we are like ships that pass in the night, sighting and hailing one another but never making significant or abiding contact. But as ships we at least experience an energy and movement that are effectively precluded by the figure of the island. As islands, we are fixed forever in place (immobilized to use a term that perhaps captures Arnold's sense of our neurotic inadequacy), and we are totally surrounded by a containing environment apprehended as an absolutely inimical otherness from which there can be no release.

In his usually authoritative notes, Kenneth Allott takes a significantly less grim view of the implications of this figure. By judiciously employing a richly overdetermined language whose softer connotations may ameliorate the harshness of what that language read literally seems to maintain, Arnold—according to Allott—hints at an eventual metaphysical release from present existential despair. A keyword for Allott in this covert and cryptic counterargument is "enclasping" (5), which he tells us "suggests an embrace rather than imprisonment and, in conjunction with 'shoreless' (l. 3), may imply that the individual also knows that he belongs to a General Life which seems to him boundless (i.e., without apparent beginning or end)."[40]

But while Arnold, in "Resignation," does treat the general life as a good, most of his philosophically oriented poems protest the destruction of all we humanly value by an antithetically conceived metaphysical reality. "To Marguerite—Continued" clearly belongs in this second category: the sea's flow feels "enclasping" only because we find ourselves constrained at every point by an otherness in no way like ourselves, not a general life toward which we are invited to "draw homeward to" but an alien element whose taste of salt indicates its unsustainingness. The "bounds" of the "sea" that "enclasps" us seem "endless," not because in its sublimity it sends forth intimations of a transcendental timelessness that spreads beyond the time-bound limits of the individuated consciousness, but rather because we can discover no breaches in that circumscribing otherness that envelops us, no humanly negotiable channels through which we might make contact with those longed-for others who also inhabit the phenomenal.

One reason the speaker's response to that separation is so anguished is the extraordinarily high valuation he places on the inward being of the individuated life. In a passage whose extraordinary lyric intensity invests it with an almost ontologically transforming potency, Arnold virtually sanctifies the inner life by depicting the island, in a sort of quasi-theophany, as a place little less than divine:

> But when the moon their hollows lights,
> And they are swept by balms of spring,

And in their glens on starry nights,
The nightingales divinely sing;
And lovely notes from shore to shore,
Across the sounds and channels pour—.

(7–12)

Here again the moon and the stars serve their familiar Arnoldian function as a catalyst to hope, conjuring up waking dreams in which wishes are fulfilled, desires realized. But unlike "Dover Beach" and "The Forsaken Merman," the moon and stars in "To Marguerite—Continued" do not shine down upon some body of water nor turn it into a promise-filled "moonlit sea" whose transformed appearance leads us to hope that a seemingly alien reality and the life of consciousness can in some humanly valued way be connected. Here they shine on the land, on glens and hollows that lie at its very center. And as if summoned forth by the moon and stars that shine upon it, that vital center sends out its own seemingly sacralized utterance through the "divine" singing of the "nightingales" who dwell there—an expression, we are tempted to surmise, that conveys not communicative intent but a sense of ontological plenitude, much like that expressed by Keats's nightingale singing "of summer in full-throated ease" ("Ode to a Nightingale," 10). Arnold thus seems to reverse customary arrangements, investing land and life and consciousness with an ontological primacy usually reserved for the sea and the not-ourselves it usually represents.

But if these songs express no real communicative intent, they nonetheless evoke in the listeners the wish to communicate, to make contact with the "marges" of the other islands, to know the being of another person as it truly is. The "estranging sea" turns out to be no more than barely severing "straits," so narrow, in fact, that "lovely notes" are conveyed across them, alerting us to the presence nearby of others like ourselves and, even more, to their desirability. But even as we learn of the proximity of those we might love, we know ourselves to be permanently estranged from them. Once again Arnold hints at an apparently saving knowledge only to negate it. Even as we hear that seemingly divinely saving utterance, we find associatively linked to it, in what seems the same act of perception, the nullifying fact of insuperability, that the watery barrier separating us from those other islands whose "marges" we would "meet" shall never be overcome.

So mixed a message predictably evokes a correspondingly mixed psychological reaction, a reaction marvelously encapsulated in one of the most hauntingly revelatory phrases in all of Arnold's poetry.

In those special moments, when "lovely notes, from shore to shore, /
Across the sounds and channels pour" (11–12) and we are most
acutely conscious of the apparent worth of those from whom we are
estranged, desire becomes so intertwined with a contradictory consciousness of the unattainability of the object desired that all distinction between these feelings of desire and its frustration
becomes blurred. It is then that we respond to the tantalizingly divi-
nized notes of that music with what Arnold, speaking from the very
nadir of despondency, calls "a longing like despair" (13). Indeed, at
the critical point at which we apprehend these two separate and
conflicting states of consciousness in virtual simultaneity, despair
seems actually to displace the pleasurable expectations that had
provoked it; and desire as a clearly demarcated state (perhaps one
physiologically attended by sexual arousal) essentially disappears.

With this iteration of a "longing like despair," we seem once
again to have manifestly represented that traumatic condition
Freud calls "signal anxiety." In hearing those "lovely notes," the
outward expression of the beautiful inner nature of one with whom
we would be united, we are reminded of that lost original, the sheltering and nurturing mother, loving and beloved, whose feared loss
once evoked the deepest anxiety. Correspondingly, desire for a
loved object in later life and the fear of loss that necessarily accompanies such desire almost automatically summon forth an overwhelming anxiety like that occasioned by the most traumatically
fearful of primal events. But anxiety is also a signal, mustering our
psychic defenses against the danger that imminently threatens.

In this instance, the mechanism of defense is clearly regression—a defense, Freud notes, more injurious to the instinct involved than even repression.[41] The turn to regression is expressly
displayed by the speaker's ostensible recollection of a time when
we felt ourselves "[p]arts of a single continent" (16). (I have said
"ostensible" because Arnold, with characteristic tentativeness, tells
us that what is remembered "surely" took place "once" and yet we
only "feel" [15] that it happened.) In that ostensibly recollected par-
adisal epoch we dwelt in "once," we felt not alienation but a sense
of belonging to—indeed, of being incorporated within—that first
special object whose love nurtured and sheltered us. Then there
were no apparent divisions, no clearly demarcated ego boundaries;
all was like ourselves; we felt "[p]arts of a single continent" (16).
Arnold's turn to regression seems basically consistent with the general psychological conditions expressed by the allegory of enislement in "To Marguerite—Continued," for "the use of regression as
a mechanism of defense" has as its "precondition," according to the

fundamental precepts of psychoanalysis, "a peculiar weakness of the ego organization."[42] Regression comes about because, while the ego is "strong enough to enforce its protests against the instincts at a very early date," it is still "too weak to fight out this conflict by more mature methods."[43] "To Marguerite—Continued" portrays exactly that: the workings of an ego already "strong enough to enforce its protests against the instincts," suppressing them so thoroughly within the ego's enisled boundaries that they can never truly pursue their object but must instead expend their energies on little more than helpless clamor. But at this level of organization, the bounded ego still does not conceive of itself as fully enough developed to be considered starlike, autonomous, and self-dependent. Rather, it looks upon its self-contained condition, its "endless" boundedness, as constraint and even imprisonment against which the instincts must hopelessly struggle, finding relief only in remembrances of a lost continent of infantile unity.[44]

Having earlier identified the waters that surround us as a noumenal signifier with the "General Life," Allott surprisingly claims that "[t]he 'single continent' " is also a noumenal signifier, "the One or the All from which men are divorced in their individual lives," adding that " 'once' = before birth."[45] In *Empedocles on Etna*, Arnold does use the term "the All" in a Kantian sense as a noumenal signifier, as the ultimately real from which we are kept apart by "the forms, and modes, and stifling veils" (2.354) of "mind" (2.345) and "thought" (2.345). (Indeed, so strikingly Kantian is Arnold's use of the term there that in his notes to *Empedocles on Etna*, Allott defines the "All" as "the noumenon behind phenomenal appearances.")[46] And to overcome estrangement from the All, Empedocles flings himself into Etna to achieve that union that will come only with his atemporal and depersonalized life after death.

But the "single continent" of which we feel we were once part in "To Marguerite—Continued" was plainly compounded from the stuff of earth, just as the islands we have since become are compounded of earth. Looking to the poem's apparent metaphysical design, we make no great leap if we draw the further inference that Arnold's vanished continent should figuratively represent exactly what the islands in metaphysical terms represent, phenomenal existence conceived as antithetical to the sea as noumenal signifier. Where the islands, however, stand for our fragmented and painfully isolated phenomenal existence now, the "single continent" would seem to represent phenomenal existence prior to psychological individuation, the life that once was, a secure and familiar wholeness in which, enveloped by love, we knew no longing. So encompassing

was that recollected continent that we can only conclude that it was
a time when we knew no sea of elemental otherness, an alien noumenal that now holds us apart. In that long-ago, longed-for time, we
might indeed well have believed that the truly real, the ontologically
privileged and genuinely originary, was what was in essence most
like ourselves—we who have now come to understand ourselves to
be the merely phenomenal, accidental and derivative.

That precarious faith that we were once parts of a single continent is given whatever modicum of credence it may have by the belief that, though as islands we live surrounded by water as far as
the eye can travel, we know ourselves to be of the same substance
as that larger body of earth that presumably lies under and sup-
ports the sea; and, by the same geological logic, we still remain
firmly attached to that unperceivable bottom, a lost Atlantis perhaps, but yet a continent whose reemergence and restoration we
yearningly hope will eventually take place. In an earlier sonnet,
"Written in Butler's Sermons," Arnold had also devised an allegory
of islands, presumably because that figure lent itself to an analogous construal.[47] In regarding "Affections, Instincts, Principles, and
Powers, / Impulse and Reason, Freedom and Control" (1–2) as independent mental entities, rationalists like Bishop Butler merely contribute to "unravelling God's harmonious whole" (3). In fact, Arnold
explains, these faculties, seemingly separate from each other, are
indeed like islands, but coral islands, each organically intercon-
nected to the others and all of them the vital outgrowth of a common
generative and unifying source. Thus the islands that are the mind's
faculties rest on similarly unobservable "foundations" (6) that reside "[d]eep and broad, where none may see" (5). There

> man's one nature, queen-like sits alone,
> Centred in a majestic unity;
> And rays her powers, like sister-islands seen
> Linking their coral arms under the sea.
>
> (7–10)

Using the sonnet on Butler's sermons as a figurative precedent,
we may safely conclude that that "once" when we felt ourselves
"[p]arts of a single continent" does not refer to life "before birth"
as Allott thinks; it refers to a time after life on earth began but before the differentiation of the ego really occurred and we lived almost wholly in the security of an all-enveloping maternal presence.
Nostalgia for that earliest relationship is contaminated, though, by
recollections of a not-much-later time when tender affection for the

loved object would be suffused by impermissible eroticized feelings that the mature ego knows must be held in check. That the tender and the sensual here as well are fatally intertwined is made only too evident by the filling-out of the oedipal configuration that follows Arnold's lament for that yearned for but now irrecoverably lost "once." What gives this configuration its distinctively oedipal character—what leads us to suspect that the speaker's ostensibly tender memories are conditioned and tainted by unannunciated sensual motives—is the sudden intrusion of the angriest of Arnoldian gods into this seemingly benign scenario of remembrance of a primary identification with the mother, a god whose sole function is clearly to sever and prohibit. Having permanently disjoined the participants in that initial union, he would now bar any later meeting of "marges," presumably with some other now undisguisedly libidinal object who serves as surrogate for that lost original. The deity who so violently bursts into Arnold's reminiscence and regret as "A God, a God" seems clearly the now introjected father of the oedipal configuration placed before us in his most familiar and inhibiting cultural guise.[48]

This overdetermined mingling of the philosophic and psychological carries forward into the great closing stanza of the poem as well. Though Arnold seems to answer the heartfelt questions of the first lines with a grim and authoritative finality, the poem actually ends in inconclusiveness, desire covertly reasserting itself against the seemingly categorically irreversible terms of prohibiting closure that the exclamatory tones of the final stanza suggest:

> Who ordered, that their longing's fire
> Should be, as soon as kindled, cool?
> Who renders vain their deep desire?
> A God, a God their severance ruled!
> And bade betwixt their shores to be
> The unplumbed, salt, estranging sea.
>
> (19–24)

The sudden appearance of this cruelly uncaring God, whose ordinances we must obey, however unwillingly, simply reinforces what we should have suspected was the case all along: that some omnipotent external agency (metaphysically understood as pessimism's antithetical noumenal cause) is responsible for the isolation in which, to our sorrow, we are now and probably forever fixed. Try as hard as we may to reach out to those we love, external barriers installed by the deity who "bade" our severance insure that there shall be no more connectedness, that "our marges" will not "meet again" (18). Yet we can only wonder why that decree of severance is necessary, since the "longing" whose "fire" is "as soon as kindled, cooled" scarcely seems of sufficient potency to impel us across those malevolently ordained straits to "longing's" goal. Here, as elsewhere in the "Marguerite" poems, Arnold complicates the question of blame, cautiously intimating that what fatally inhibits gratification is some preexisting defect in the workings of desire itself. Latently underlying Arnold's unhappy account of ungratified longing is once again the familiar nullifying scenario of signal anxiety: the engendering at the point of arousal, at the kindling of "our longing's fire," of a concurrent and "cooling" consciousness of apprehensiveness and unpleasure. Ever watchful to ward off the concomitant suffering that memory tells us gratification would induce, anxiety, by its signal of imminent danger, instantaneously mobilizes those counteracting defenses that reverse the stirrings of arousal, cooling them and thereby restoring them to the habitual inertness—detumescence, perhaps, to be physiologically more precise—in which alone safety resides.

In the poem's closing line, though, Arnold surprisingly qualifies his seemingly unconditional metaphysical judgment, allowing the problematicness and indeterminacy that so often infilitrate his pessimism to insinuate themselves. Of the three modifiers that characterize the sea—and, by extension, the all-controlling noumenal otherness for which it stands—the last two simply reinforce our sense of how wholly alien and inimical that element is for those "enisled" within it. If the sea is "salt" to our human taste, then it can neither nourish nor sustain a human nature, which is, in essence, centered in the "hollows" and therefore requires for sustenance, it must necessarily follow, the purity of fresh, inland waters. In addition, by calling the sea "estranging," Arnold surely implies not only that as phenomenal accident to noumenal essence we are forced to live out our lives in a sort of ontological homelessness but also that, even within the framework of purely human relationships, noumenal agency seems to interpose its clearly hurtful will. The effect of this estranging noumenal cause is that we are granted none of the consolations that might derive from a collective, communal solidarity nor, most hurtfully, any of the pleasure or comfort or even "help for pain" that could be obtained from success in love with some single individual—Marguerite, for example—a bridging of straits that would enable us to fulfill that most poignant of Arnoldian wishes, that we "be true to one another." Moreover, by using the participial form "estranging," Arnold seems to suggest that the cause of our

suffering is not some cataclysmically overwhelming event, a severing flood at the dawn of time, but that even now some active and
intentionally malevolent principle still works to maintain our "isolation without end / Prolonged."

However, with the other one of these three terms—
"unplumbed"—Arnold offers at least a modestly skeptical opening
to the possibility that, metaphysically, things are not as they seem,
that judgments must be provisional and closure withheld. At first
glance, the figure may seem only to exacerbate hopelessness, to remind us that, as far into the depths as we have reached, we have
found only otherness as our containing environment. But the fact
that the sea is still "unplumbed"—just as in "Human Life" it is "incognisable"—does not mean that it is ultimately bottomless.
Whether we shall at some future time sound bottom or, reformulat-
ing that question according to the poem's implied metaphysical categories, whether we shall then find that the not-ourselves is actually
undergirded by the submerged remnants of that continent to which
in a better time we once wholly belonged—an originary and sustaining power in essence like ourselves but greater—this is a perplexity that inevitably follows from Arnold's decision to call the
"sea" "unplumbed," a skeptically framed intimation of uncertainty
that present knowledge leaves epistemologically unanswerable.
While such a cautiously posed formulation can scarcely be construed as a light in the darkness and a basis for hope, it does at
least preclude absoluteness, that closure in utter despair toward
which "To Marguerite—Continued" seems, almost in all other
ways, so inexorably to move.

Nowhere is Arnold a more tepid and fastidious wooer than in "A
Farewell." In his eagerness to have love over and done with, and in
his relief when it is concluded, he offers a bewildering array of reasons why their love cannot and should not go forward, reasons predictably traceable to just such anxieties as we have observed in the
earlier "Marguerite" poems. Here, though, so powerfully inhibiting
are the anxieties produced by the prospect of sexual involvement,
so completely is desire diverted from its chosen object, that the only
condition under which love is deemed acceptable is when he and
Marguerite shall truly come together in the life hereafter—not as
sexual partners, of course, but in a relationship like that of brother
and sister, drawn to one another by a sympathy both enduring and
chaste.[49]

This last of the Marguerite poems, "A Farewell," begins (like others) with a renewal of love that seems filled with promise. Even

after a year's absence, Marguerite appears unwavering in her love, eager as her lover to embrace once more:

> I came! I saw thee rise!—the blood
> Poured flushing to thy languid cheek.
> Locked in each other's arms we stood,
> In tears, with hearts too full to speak.
>
> (9–12)

Symbolically enhancing that sense of promise is the poem's initial setting, a lakeside path that looks out upon waters "[w]here sweet the unbroken moonbeams lay" (3), that Arnoldian landscape whose glimmering waters almost invariably function as a catalyst to hope and often hope of success in love. By the concluding lines, though, love having failed, the stars assume a more conventionally austere Arnoldian aspect, as the lovers themselves are actually translated into stars that retain a modicum of sympathy for one another, but a "sympathy august and pure" (70), thus cleansed of any need or wish to touch or embrace. In that life hereafter, the lovers, as stars, shall feel their "unquiet pulses cease" (82) and satiate that "thirst for peace" (84), whose satisfaction will allow them to attain the poem's final and most significant good: an eternity of asexual but "neighbouring" proximity, pursuing forever parallel courses that never converge.

Initially, the fault for love's failure appears to have been Marguerite's, she having lapsed shortly after her lover's arrival into a languor to which she seems only too prone:

> Days flew; ah, soon I could discern
> A trouble in thine altered air!
> Thy hand lay languidly in mine,
> Thy cheek was grave, thy speech grew rare.
>
> (13–16)

But almost immediately, the speaker surprisingly absolves Marguerite of any real blame, declaring that, in some enigmatically fundamental way, the real problem is his own unsuitability to serve as the male object of a woman's love:

> I blame thee not!—This heart, I know,
> To be long loved was never framed;
> For something in its depths doth glow
> Too strange, too restless, too untamed.

And women—things that live and move
Mined by the fever in the soul—
They seek to find in those they love
Stern strength, and promise of control.

They ask not kindness, gentle ways—
These they themselves have tried and known;
They ask a soul which never sways
With the blind gusts that shake their own.

I too have felt the load I bore
In a too strong emotion's sway;
I too have wished, no woman more,
This starting, feverish heart away.

I too have longed for trenchant force,
And will like a dividing spear;
Have praised the keen, unscrupulous course,
Which knows no doubt, which feels no fear.

(17–36)

What is most disconcerting in all this is the superior virility he
unhesitatingly ascribes to his imaginatively projected rivals for
Marguerite's affection, men he assumes she would prefer even now,
while he and she are avowedly still lovers. Of course, since women
are "mined by" the profoundly unstabilizing flux and fever of the
female soul, they quite naturally "seek to find in those they love /
Stern strength, and promise of control," seemingly epitomizing
masculine virtues that the speaker unhappily realizes are not his.
Indeed, only a few lines later he endows his presumptively successful rivals with an even more explicitly phallicized masculine identity, with "will like a dividing spear," an attribute the speaker both
lacks and has "longed for." In the face of such potent rivals, he can
only choose to submit, to surrender the field to those foreordained
victors upon whom Marguerite would, even at this point, bestow her
favors.

Arnold's speaker is not without passion, but it is a passion that
lacks the masculine singleness of purpose women "seek to find in
those they love," a phallic "will like a dividing spear." But the
speaker's difficulties run deeper than merely lacking what other
men possess, the indispensable basis of that manliness for which
women love them. His is a different kind of passion, diffuse, perhaps
even "eddying" (to use one of Arnold's most frequent terms of self-
condemnation), a way of feeling that he now tells us is in essence

the same as the passion innate in women, "things that live and move / Mined by the fever in the soul." Their failings are his failings, and he has "wished, no woman more, / This starting, feverish heart away." Oddly enough, though, as the poem moves toward its surprising conclusion, we learn that neither the spearlike dividing male will nor the feverish and mining passions indigenous to women are to be valued. For even as he and Marguerite part, the speaker tells her that they also are linked by a more fundamental and valued attribute than their fevered passion, a proclivity to tenderness undisclosed to the world and possibly, at the present moment, to themselves also that insures love's continuance beyond this temporary farewell. That shared proclivity is even now known though to that strange divinity who seemingly presides over the Marguerite poems, in this case a surprisingly benevolent "He, who sees us through and through" (46) and "knows that the bent of both our hearts / Was to be gentle, tranquil, true" (47–48).

With the unanticipated appearance of this overseeing deity, we may understandably feel that in the last of the Marguerite poems we have returned to the oedipal crisis of the first. But where the speaker of the first poem had tried to assuage the "ire" of God by asking that He "let the peaceful be," here the God "Who sees us through and through" has no need of "ire," since He knows that erotic motives that everywhere else debase the affections were never truly foremost in their love. Having never really transgressed, they deserve no admonishment. The more likely outcome of this now strangely de-eroticized relationship is that the "Eternal Father" will "smile" (61) approvingly at the lovers in a life hereafter when their souls have at last become "[a]s good, as generous, as they are" (64), because while on earth they have heeded His instructions to set aside their sensual designs and chose instead to " 'Be counselled, and retire' " ("Meeting," 12).

Even stranger than this wisely chosen, seemingly temporary separation as the end of the affair is that fantasized heavenly immortality through which the speaker tells us that he and Marguerite shall finally realize the love of which they were always capable. Their inherently constitutional gentleness was—no doubt at some ontologically pure level of being—always truer than the passions that seemingly had governed their earthly lives, but not until "one day ... life past" (53) shall they be apprised of the truth of their natures, "see ourselves, and learn at last / Our true affinities of soul" (55–56). On the few other occasions in the poetry where Arnold posits a life after death, a vague supposition in "Resignation" and "The Buried Life," but more fully hypothesized in *Empedocles on Etna*, the

direction in which one moves to attain immortality is clearly downward to the depths of darkness, where, with the extinction of consciousness, one is able to subsist forever in an elemental and
impersonal immortality, indistinguishable from "[t]he life of plants,
and stones, and rain" ("Resignation," 196). But, in "A Farewell,"
the lovers do retain their discretely individuated human consciousness, though one purged of earthly impurities, since they have been
literally translated into stars, Arnold's basic image for a life of consciousness in which one accepts an inescapable solitariness in exchange for the greater good of calm.

One reason Arnold wants his lovers to become stars is the bleakness and even brutality of earthly conditions as they are depicted
in "A Farewell." Just as in "Human Life," in "A Farewell," too, we
must live as disappointed voyagers, consigned to

> wear out life, alas!
> Distracted as a homeless wind,
> In beating where we must not pass,
> In seeking what we shall not find.

(49–52)

In "A Farewell," though we are not simply ships that pass in the
night, there is in fact contact with others, but contact that is conflict, conflict akin to the clash of "ignorant armies" in "Dover
Beach." On our "wild earth of hate and fear," in the "raving world"
of "earthly jars," there is only clamor and strife, cowering fear as
we are continually beset by savage aggression—or so the speaker
repugnantly describes the world from the safe haven of his imagined starlike existence.

It should come as no surprise then that an Arnoldian speaker,
faced with such conflict, would be willing to live chastely and austerely as a star, despite all the seeming costs (isolation and the an-
esthetization of feeling being the most obvious) incurred by such a
transformation. When the speaker of "A Farewell" and Marguerite
shall ascend to their starlike vantage point, they shall look not out-
wards, to attain a comprehensively Sophoclean perspective on
human existence, but down and in for an introspective revelation of
"our being's whole" (54). They shall see and know themselves as
"He, who sees us through and through" (46), sees and knows them
and recognize at last their fundamental likeness, their "true affinities of soul" (56), and only after that moment of self-understanding
shall they truly be bound to one another in love.

While they will be brought closer to each other in their lives after

death than they were when their "ways were unlike here" (73), the
lovers of "A Farewell" will still be granted, at most, a heavenly
proximity allowing them to do no more than ply "more neighbouring
courses" (74), fixed forever in separate and separating orbits as
neighbors who "greet across infinity" (76). On reflection, the situation in the heavens, especially for lovers, does not seem a noticeable
improvement over the situation of those doomed to live as ships that
pass in the night, nor even that of the desperate millions who find
themselves "on the sea of life enisled," divided from those they long
for by "echoing straits." In only one important respect do the dis-
tanced lovers of "A Farewell" differ from their mortal counterparts:
the greetings from Marguerite that are transmitted "across infinity," unlike the "echoing songs" of the nightingales heard on the
other side of the straits, do not provoke those libidinally prompted
and unfulfillable desires that in this sequence of love poems invariably carry in their wake anxiety, that "longing like despair" that for
Arnold is attendant upon every episode of love.

Through this imaginative metamorphosis that turns the lovers
into stars, Arnold, in a miracle of magical projection, has apparently managed to spare them that pain invariably conjoined to love
"[o]n this wild earth of hate and fear." Unfortunately, the cost of
that gain has been the need to divest themselves of every libidinal
impulse and interest that had governed their relationship upon
earth and, still more, to forfeit even the most modest of human satis-
factions that love provides, "The thousand sweet, still joys of such /
As hand in hand face earthly life" (71–72), since even these require
a measure of physical contact. He is willing to have them make so
great a sacrifice, the poet explains, so that they may gratify the sole
aim allowed them in the life hereafter—what Arnold, in a chillingly
antihumanistic passage, calls "The thirst for peace a raving world /
Would never let us satiate here." Arnold thus paradoxically concludes his famous sequence of love poems with what is surely the
most strangely placed triumph of Thanatos over Eros in the literature of love, yet a perfectly appropriate Schopenhauerian resolution
to the problems endemic in all romantic attachment.

But the concluding lines of "A Farewell" offer one still more remarkable illustration of just how drastically the libidinal impulses
are to be repressed. Though only days earlier the lovers were
"locked in each other's arms," now, with Marguerite's reversion to
languor indicating that love has already begun its inevitable turn
downward, the speaker can only look forward to addressing her in
the renewed love of their afterlife by the most unlikely term of endearment one could imagine calling the woman one loves. He shall

then be able to address her as "My sister!" (78). This title, however, shall be deservedly hers only in that best of times, when, "life past" and all passion spent, conditions will be established ideally conducive to a love based wholly on tenderness and not at all on sensuality. Then they shall feel a true but profoundly attenuated sympathy for one another, "A sympathy august and pure" (70), with "pure" clearly the crucially operative term here.

We must understand that there will be more than ample compensation for the elimination of sexual desire from the life hereafter. In accordance with some Arnoldian principle of the conservation of energy, the libidinal energy wastefully directed in this life to purely sexual objects will be expended in that afterlife in performing the "quiet work" customarily assigned the stars in Arnold's poetry. The lovers shall be allowed to help "maintain" the peace they have been made part of, "The hush among the shining stars" (79). But even more revealingly, they shall assist in performing the most significant of the duties assigned the heavens in the figurative "world-making" of Arnold's poetry: a responsibility to preserve "[t]he calm upon the moonlit sea" (80).

With this image we have come full circle to that familiar image of moonlight on water with which the poem began, the description of Thunsee, "the lake / Where sweet the unbroken moonbeams lay" and beside which the speaker rode on his way to his passionately anticipated rendezvous with Marguerite. In both cases, these almost identical images carry out roughly the same characteristically Arnoldian function, serving as a wish-fulfilling catalyst to hope, an imaginative gate of entry to a "land of dreams." Over the course of the poem, though—and presumably over the course of this episode of love also—the nature of the wishes to be fulfilled has changed from a libidinally impelled desire for a distinctively sexual gratification to a dream of peace that is the antithesis and effective undoing of that more pleasurable but doubtlessly more disturbing sexual wish. Despite all disclaimers, that reassuring vision of the afterlife with which "A Farewell" closes—a vision ostensibly of love but of love purified—is in fact a vision clearly directed against love, at least earthly and human love as Arnold has experienced it (perhaps even at some point with Marguerite). It is a love beset by anxiety, that profoundly human love in which the sensual and the tender are inextricably and therefore disturbingly mixed.

"The Buried Life" bears an "obvious relation" "to the Marguerite series,"[50] serving many readers as a kind of final philosophic coda to it. Again we find Arnold in love, and in love with a woman whose

playfulness calls to mind an earlier Marguerite with the "arch smile
that tells / The unconquered joy in which her spirit dwells" ("A
Parting," 39–40). Though all of the "Marguerite" poems proper
begin in vows of love, usually sealed by an embrace, each one traces
an eventual retreat from passion and, in most cases, a final and predestined collapse of love. Only in "The Buried Life" does romantic
desire seem to intensify as the speaker in his wooing tries to wean
Marguerite from the guardedness of their mere banter, the way relations between the sexes are normally carried on, he chides her, in
a conventional and callous world. Instead, he would have her enter
into a true and serious communion of souls, one that has already
been initiated by the lovers' silently peering into one another's eyes
and by their holding hands—perhaps as a modest beginning to the
physical relationship that would seal that communion of souls. But
these introductory remarks on love are quickly swamped by the
long, abstract, and, for the most part, impersonal meditation on the
buried life that takes up the remaining seven-eighths of the poem.
In this light, "The Buried Life" has understandably been catego-
rized as just another exercise in the vagaries of the Arnoldian philosophy, indeed an exercise more confused and confusing than
most.[51]

   Predictably, the major interpretive crux in discussions of "The
Buried Life" is the idea of the buried life itself, an inherently enigmatic notion made still more enigmatic by Arnold's figurative ren-
derings of it. Understandably, no critical consensus has as yet
emerged, even among the best of commentators on Arnold's poetry.
Culler, for example, offers a fundamentally social explanation, describing the individual's buried life as "the river of his best self,"[52]
a notion appropriated from *Culture and Anarchy*. Yet how that unregarded river, which seems to do nothing more than flow between
birth and death, is supposed to issue in the sorts of moral and political accomplishments (like the creation of the State) that in the
prose of Arnold is what the best self achieves, is never really explained by Culler. Then there is the basically psychological account
by Honan, who takes the buried life to be the "individual's deepest
identity,"[53] as that term was conventionally understood in the Erik-
sonian moment in which Honan wrote, though what the behavioral
ramifications are of this supposedly psychological concept is never
specified. Finally, there is the biological definition proposed by
Langbaum, which explains the buried life as the means by which
man is "in spite of himself carried to the fulfillment of his biological
destiny and genuine self,"[54] but how the lives we pursue on our
other lines could ever lie outside our "biological destiny" is simi-

larly left unexplained. Of the major critics, only Stange treats the buried life as an essentially philosophic concept, maintaining in his discussion of "The Buried Life" that "Arnold's interest in the nature of the self is, in the strictest sense, ontological."[55]

Seconding Stange, I would only add that—if we are to have both a buried life that is man's "genuine self" (56) and, contrastingly, other seemingly inauthentic lines on which he ordinarily lives—we must introduce a dualism of the real and the apparent into any such ontological account, a dualism we have already found basic to Arnold's Schopenhauerian and thus pessimistic metaphysics. Here, too, we have the noumenally real as the ground of all else and, antithetically, the purely phenomenal, which though metaphysically understood as mere appearance is nonetheless the realm in which we conduct the business of ordinary human life. Moreover, just as in "Resignation," with its account of the general life in nature the poet "craves," in "The Buried Life," too, Arnold intimates that the noumenal may somehow be immanent, indwellingly present if unperceived in a world otherwise seemingly constituted wholly by the phenomenal.

In "The Buried Life," it is not in nature, however, that the immanently noumenal is to be found but in the self, in an indefinite "something in this breast" (6) (the indefinite pronoun "something" being among Arnold's most common signifiers for the metaphysically real). But that "something" remains "indiscernible" and "unregarded" while we expend our lives in "the hot race" (91) run daily in the phenomenal and illusory world. Most remarkably, though, in "The Buried Life" Arnold tantalizingly intimates that the agency by which the depths of the buried life might be sounded, the means by which that possibly noumenally grounded "lost pulse of feeling" (85) might be stirred to motion, is the most unlikely of noumenal catalysts, human love, since almost everywhere else in Arnold love is deemed antithetical to the metaphysically real and destined for inevitable frustration and defeat by its unrelenting cosmic antagonist. But in "The Buried Life" it is only "[w]hen a beloved hand is laid in ours" (78) or "[w]hen our world-deafened ear / Is by the tones of a loved voice caressed" (82–83) that the buried life reveals itself, at that instant disclosing its ultimate responsibility for and control over our individual human existence. Only then, when it is touched by love, does the buried life become a discernible object of knowledge, enabling us, by apprehending the real, to live in truth. Conversely, by the same logic, we might also infer that if love can put us in touch with the noumenal, then the noumenal, in some obscure and inexpressible way, must possess attributes identical with or at least corresponding to that preeminent human value, love.

But the logic of such an inference notwithstanding, in the end, Arnold retreats from any such argument and conclusion. What the love-engendered and apparently noumenally empowering "bolt" that is "shot back somewhere in our breast" (84) finally discloses is an ontologically true that has nothing whatsoever to do with the good as we conceive it—a metaphysical reality whose attributes are in no way convertible into humanly valued principles or practices and that certainly in no way produce or enhance love. So, in one of Arnold's most disheartening aporias, that closing scene of metaphysical disclosure in "The Buried Life" leaves us with nothing more than another portrayal of human life that craves, as its crowning attainment, incorporation into life at its most austerely minimal, the contentless flow of the purely subsisting, a noumenally real devoid of all the value-enhancing accidents of phenomenal existence.

To see how and why Arnold produces such an outcome, I shall return to the poem's beginning and undertake that more detailed analysis that his deeply conflicted text requires. Here, too, just as in so many of the "Marguerite" poems, we find Arnold entering into a meditation on metaphysics from the unlikely setting of an apparent tryst, with the speaker alone with the woman he loves, urging her to suspend their "light war of mocking words" (1), the homage they pay to ways of the world that should be irrelevant to them. Now, he tells her, is the moment to give up play and begin the serious business of authentic love, a moment auspiciously suited to taking his hand, looking into his eyes, and speaking words (if words are necessary) whose subject can only be their love for each other. But from such promising starting points in the love poetry of Arnold, desire is quickly deflected to an object sexually less threatening, to nature or to an afterlife as brother and sister or to the bloodless abstraction of the buried life, diversions of energy presumably instigated by the sexual anxieties that underlie such substitutive object choices in the poetry of Arnold.

Though a socially conditioned inauthenticity contaminates even this dialogue between lovers, in "The Buried Life" Arnold moves quickly away from any speculation on the social conditions (or the perhaps still more pertinent psychological conditions) that render their love inauthentic and turns instead, as we have noted, to the familiar and perhaps safer ground of Arnoldian metaphysics. We are alienated both from others and from ourselves, not as the consequence of some socially or psychologically determined individual choice, but as the externally imposed outcome of the workings of some inexplicable metaphysical causality. To explain why even lovers cannot live or speak in accordance with what is best and truest in their nature, Arnold reverts to terms he customarily employs to signify some form of metaphysical agency at work in the affairs of humanity. The lovers live and speak inauthentically because such a persistence in falsity has "been deep-ordained," decreed by that mysterious *deus absconditus,* whom Arnold in other poems usually calls "God" or the "Powers" but who in "The Buried Life" is simply "Fate" (30).

On most occasions, the metaphysical agency that bounds, enchains, or controls us evokes indignation and hostility in the Arnoldian speaker whose characteristic posture is one of protest against its denial of the "joys," the "friends," the "homes" that we desire and deserve. Yet here the buried life we must obey is unexpectedly looked upon as an unequivocal good, beside which all other human pursuits are dismissed as "distractions" from what should be our sole aim: that is, following, even if unknowingly, the river of the buried life. To be sure, at very special moments "what we say and do / Is eloquent, is well" (65–66), but Arnold judges even the seemingly most praiseworthy speech or deed as finally wanting by the ontological standard that alone measures the worth of one's words and acts, that " 'tis not true!" (66).

After having stipulated this austerely minimal concept of metaphysical truth as that alone which is to merit our unqualified approval in "The Buried Life," at poem's end Arnold rather surprisingly reverts to the poem's preliminary discourse on love, asserting that when all else fails to make the buried life known to us, we may establish contact with it—indeed, make the buried life a real object of human knowledge—through what appear to be the metaphysically transformational powers with which the love between a man and woman is somehow endowed:

> Only—but this is rare—
> When a beloved hand is laid in ours,
> When, jaded with the rush and glare
> Of the interminable hours,
> Our eyes can in another's eyes read clear,
> When our world-deafened ear
> Is by the tones of a loved voice caressed—
> A bolt is shot back somewhere in our breast,
> And a lost pulse of feeling stirs again.
> The eye sinks inward, and the heart lies plain,
> And what we mean, we say, and what we would, we know.
>
> (77–87)

By these surprisingly efficacious means of transmission—the touch of "a beloved hand," "[o]ur eyes" reading clearly in the eyes of the loved other, or the "tones of a loved voice" caressing "our world-deafened ear"—that mutual, sensually imbued love apparently unleashes a resuscitating bolt that "stirs a lost pulse of feeling," and this, in turn, seems to render visible to the "eye" that gazes inward (not, it should be noted, out to the beloved other) to see plainly "the heart" in which the buried life presumably resides. Furthermore, as an unanticipated benefit of that process, the noumenally grounded buried life not only comes into plain sight but also registers its effects upon the phenomenal world by lending our acts and words of love that truth absent from them at the poem's beginning.

We thus seem to have arrived at the happy ending to that plot of love with which the poem began but from which it seemingly diverged during its long and rambling middle. Because "the heart lies plain," the lovers should now be ready and able to renew their dialogue of love with the sincerity and seriousness—the truth—it earlier lacked. But "truth" is a double-edged term here, having one meaning within the context of the poem's metaphysics and another within the context of its discourse on language. Metaphysically conceived, truth is that which corresponds to or participates in the unrepresentable noumenally real, which in the discourse of Kantian and post-Kantian idealism is that ultimately real without attributes, the thing-in-itself, that lies outside the forms and categories of the human understanding and thus can apparently never be a phenomenally intelligible object of knowledge. Moreover, in its effects, as Arnold describes them, the noumenally real shows no concern for those values or purposes humankind cherishes. On the other hand, truth in language in "The Buried Life" is determined by a criterion of sincerity, by the correspondence of our psychological intentions with our words and deeds. For a declaration of love to be "true," inward feeling must somehow match the words that are uttered. But clearly, as we look to the effects of that miraculously revelatory moment when the buried life becomes visible to the inward eye—when "the heart," the apparent site of the buried life, "lies plain"—the consequence of that revelation would seem to have everything to do with metaphysics and nothing whatsoever to do with human relationships in the world we inhabit, especially that erotically motivated relationship between the sexes that we exalt as love:

> A man becomes aware of his life's flow,
> And hears its winding murmur; and he sees
> The meadows where it glides, the sun, the breeze.

And there arrives a lull in the hot race
Wherein he doth for ever chase
That flying and elusive shadow, rest.
An air of coolness plays upon his face,
And an unwonted calm pervades his breast,
And then he thinks he knows
The hills where his life rose,
And the sea where it goes.

(87–98)

Instead of a libidinally charged fulfillment in love, our rare, love-engendered manifestation of the buried life gains us only the peace of "rest," "a lull in the hot race," a perhaps premonitory acquaintance with what may be the end of our endeavors, attainment of "[t]hat flying and elusive shadow, rest."

What we will apparently do, then, after this showing forth of the buried life in ourselves is to withdraw into passivity, retreat from what we customarily think of as life into the sheltering stasis of an "unwonted calm" much like that which Arnold speaks of in "Resignation" as the "unblamed serenity" that is the final fruit of our deliverance from passion. Paradoxically, though, the premonitory attainment of such "calm" in "The Buried Life" is attributed to the presumably excitatory power of the impassioned speech and gaze and touch of love. Furthermore, not only what we do but what we know as a consequence of this special revelation is also conceived of in essentially negative terms. By that act of metaphysical cognition in which "[a] man becomes aware of his life's flow," he learns that there is an ontologically elemental and determining core of being in ourselves that participates in the "general life," the metaphysically real that underlies all else. But conversely, he also must recognize that "the buried life," the ontologically real, has nothing to do with those goods, pleasures, and values that come to us through our experiential consciousness of the world and ourselves. As he becomes "aware of" that which is axiomatically assumed to be the most fundamental, the most true, the most real, he becomes aware as well that, in its austere and contentless purity, "the flow of the "buried life" extends beyond the mere temporally determined boundaries of life on earth. Unlike those other lines that we normally move along in our life of consciousness, "the buried life" is continuous with life as it was before birth—before the isolating process of psychological individuation, with its complicating and alienating division into subject and object, had been set in motion. Moreover, it is also continuous with life as it shall finally be, continuous with that barely representable life of pure being that apparently lies beyond death, or so that subsuming image of the undifferentiated sea—toward which the river of the individual life flows to reach its final goal of dissolution—strongly suggests.

At the conclusion to "The Buried Life," it seems safe to say, the perhaps anticipated happy ending, in which the lovers surrender their individual identities in a sensual blending together in one another's arms, is plainly nowhere in evidence. Despite the expectations raised in the final verse paragraphs by the look, the voice, the touch of the beloved, and despite intimations that her tenderness will place love on a new foundation of truthfulness, such a happy ending is displaced by a longed-for moment of metaphysical consummation, union with the cosmic whole to be achieved by surrendering our individual identity to a sexually less threatening but, in all other ways, less satisfying object. In the very last line of "The Buried Life," with its remarkably rendered foretaste of immortality in the quiet and invitingly undifferentiated waters of "the sea where" our life "goes," we are offered another fantasized version of the Empedoclean solution, extinction of consciousness as an antidote to contamination by life, in this case a contamination woven into the poem through the subtext of the threatening presence of a likely lover.[56]

Of course, in "The Buried Life," unlike *Empedocles on Etna*, Arnold seems perfectly willing to postpone that metaphysical consummation until the appointed hour of natural death. Moreover, to soften the chillingly austere outcome the poem seems finally to look to, he clearly attempts to insulate what seems particularly inhumane in the conception of the buried life from censure by placing within an appealingly pastoral setting the poem's ultimate metaphysical good, the essentially contentless flow of the merely subsisting. In fact, he surrounds the river of life with the greenery of "meadows" and ascribes to the region through which it flows the most temperate of climates, one radically unlike that found in Arnold's more customary poems of our climate, the stifling heat of "the sun's hot eye" ("A Summer Night," 38) under which "most men" (37) languidly give over "[t]heir lives to some unmeaning taskwork" (40). In "The Buried Life," too, we futilely expend our energy and power in life's "hot race." But in the country of the buried life, the sun shines less harshly, and its warmth is further tempered by "breezes" that accompany the river's flow. So in his privileged moment of revelation, the man who comes upon the buried life experiences a metaphysically determined change of climate:

"a lull" in the unabated heat of life's race and, best of all, "An air of coolness plays upon his face."

Nonetheless, any journey to those more temperate regions should be undertaken with the utmost caution. For in these closing lines Arnold essentially reiterates the pessimist's counsel: to find relief from the pain that life in the world inflicts, we must withdraw from "[t]his uncongenial place, this human life" (*Empedocles on Etna*, 2.366) to a life of mere subsistence indistinguishable from its negation. Making this particular counsel of renunciation especially disturbing is that, in "The Buried Life," Arnold seems insidiously to designate love a metaphysical good in order to enlist love itself in the service of realizing his profoundly loveless metaphysical end. Perhaps more charitably, we may choose to look upon "The Buried Life" not as intentionally manipulative but as deeply conflicted. What Arnold apparently does here is conflate his most contradictory desires: the wish to love and the anxious counterlonging to escape its feared consequences, even by flight into what looks suspiciously like emptiness. Still, here, as elsewhere, conflictedness concludes not in a standoff but in a perceptible drift toward negation, the dissolution of the individuated human existence that alone can love within the undifferentiated waters of the "sea where" one's life "goes."

In his study of Arnold's "betrayal of language," David Riede observes a kind of deconstructive practice at work in "The Buried Life," where Arnold can be shown to empty "the language of his predecessors of its power" and, in doing so, "ends by emptying his own, ends with a return to silence."[57] But I would suggest another, still more fundamental way in which "The Buried Life" also lends itself to deconstructive scrutiny; for in that poem Arnold avails himself of just those kinds of philosophic strategies that create for themselves the attendant metaphysical perplexities that Derrida's instruments of deconstructive analysis are designed to uncover. One of the forces clearly driving Arnold's argument is an undisguised hunger for presence, a motive central to metaphysical inquiry in Western philosophy since Plato. Even more strikingly, the way Arnold arrives at this deeply longed-for metaphysical end is by privileging speech over what in this poem, I would suggest, stands for writing, the language of the ordinary self as it plays out its life of inauthenticity, a language presumed to be ungrounded and emptied of signification, those identifying characteristics that convey us to the scene of writing. Finally completing Arnold's metaphysical scenario is that crucial moment when the presence so hungered after, here designated the buried life, actually manifests itself—a

claim validated for us by the authority of speech, since the effect of
that manifestation is, in the terminology of Derrida, that we experience "the undecomposable unity of the signified and the voice,"[58]
or, stating much the same thing in Arnold's own words, "And what
we mean, we say." Unsurprisingly, though, the argument of "The
Buried Life" does not present us with further revelations of how
language and life in the world might be spoken and lived in accordance with the newly uncovered truth of the buried life. Instead, we
find ourselves confronted with an aporia by which the metaphysical
argument deconstructively reverses itself, a process which, on Derridean principles, inevitably follows any such revelatory claims that
we are in the presence of the real, that some ultimate signified has
been disclosed to us.

From the very first, the poem's emerging ontology of the self has
been developed linguistically. Inauthenticity of speech, like the
"mocking words" that the lovers exchange at the poem's beginning,
is seen to indicate not only some failing in what is to be expected
of them as committed lovers but also, far more significantly, their
epistemological entrapment in the phenomenal, the implicitly apparent and unreal. Such a language may try to mimic what a language of truly meaningful speech might be; but it is ultimately
ungrounded, its signs essentially severed from what they signify,
thus performing the function assigned writing, as it has been repressed and debased, within the oppositional structures of logocen-
tric metaphysics.

The language sounded from the "many thousand lines" (57) along
which men enact their mistakenly chosen lives is heard in the world
as mere cacophony, "the din of strife" (46). Even intimate and
affectionate discourse, as the lovers' "war of mocking words" (1)
illustrates, is necessarily inauthentic, "play" unconnected to *jouis-
sance*, conveying no sense of Nietzschean joyousness or Derridean
freedom, that free play of signifiers by which writing is constituted.
The "play" of the lovers is instead to be castigated as merely "capri-
cious" (35) and "frivolous" (31), in part because the language of
"play" expresses only life's ontologically unmeaningful surface and
is wholly dissevered from those inaccessible depths where that
meaning that alone is truth resides. In a melancholy concession, Arnold acknowledges that, even when language and action are at their
seeming best, when "what we say and do / Is eloquent, is well" (65–
66), every such deployment of language and performance of action
is still subject to condemnation on the ontological ground that " 'tis
not true" (66).

Though Arnold, throughout "The Buried Life," would maintain

that the truth, which until now has been "nameless" and "unexpressed," has consequences for us, drives us on "our true, original course" (50), only when it becomes linguistically expressible does the buried life acquire the meaningfulness that he had sought from it at the poem's outset. But it is when the buried life shows and speaks itself that we are made truly aware that, for all of his professed modernity, Arnold, like many others who are professedly modern and are critics of traditional schemes of metaphysics, is himself writing another chapter in the history of a failed onto-theology, asserting the "undecomposable unity" of the spoken and some nonlinguistic ultimate signified that constitutes both meaning and truth.

As I indicated earlier, never once after the buried life manifests itself, that magic moment when "what we mean, we say" (87), are we shown how the language of the lovers who sit hand in hand differs in sincerity from the language uttered earlier, when the speaker's "world-deafened ear / Is by the tones of a loved voice caressed" (83–84). Paradoxically, those caressing tones that free "[o]ur heart" and unchain "our lips," releasing us from the ordinance of Fate that has sealed them, are uttered at what is implicitly an ontologically defective moment prior to the revelation uncovering the buried life and its consequent production of authenticity. The precipitating utterance, according to the logic of Arnold's metaphysics here, actually took place at a moment when our life still proceeded on an inauthentic line, since the buried life had not yet become a discernible object of knowledge. Yet those tones must even then have already been of sufficient noumenal efficacy to conjure up the essentially noumenal buried life. But if Arnold never manages to explain how the old and thus presumably still-defective language, even when it is the language of love, effects this magically transformative raising of the buried life into our field of metaphysically enlightened vision, neither does he really shown us how, after having become discernible, the buried life will translate its sheer ongoing movement into what would be for us a semantically meaningful utterance. The "murmur" (89) of "our life's flow" (88) is undoubtedly less discordant than the "din of strife" (46) we hear in "the world's most crowded streets" (45). However, we are left with no clue to understanding how that "murmur" is, in its obvious undifferentiatedness, convertible into a human utterance that depends for meaningfulness on phonic particularity and differentiation. Much as in "A Summer Night," in "The Buried Life," too, Arnold seems to make claims that life's outcome can accord with our desires, only to put them in question by the very strategies by which these claims are articulated.

In the end, "The Buried Life" does deconstruct itself as any such metaphysically ambitious project—one that, optimistically, would culminate in revelation and certitude—inevitably must. But what almost certainly must have led Arnold to embark on such a project— and claim success for what he must surely have known was a metaphysical undertaking destined for failure (or so the body of his poems tell us)—was once again, as I have suggested throughout this chapter, the presence of that woman who might well be Marguerite and the possibility raised by her presence of an implicitly libidinal fulfillment in love. Since the speaker's discourse on ontology begins at the very point that he asks Marguerite to give him her hand, we can only conclude that the revelation of the buried life, that stream of pure flow uncontaminated by lived experience, is at bottom a mere figment of anxiety, a characteristic substitution by Arnold of the safe and undifferentiated for the desired and desirable, but ever so threatening, scenario of love that may very well have been on the verge of enactment.

5

History

THOUGH METAPHYSICAL PESSIMISM REPRESENTS ITSELF AS A PHILOSOPHY for all seasons, its propositions and precepts universally valid, it should not surprise us that its moment of emergence was the mid-nineteenth century, the heyday of an optimistic historicism. Certainly many of those who most influenced mid-nineteenth-century attitudes—Carlyle, Comte, and, of course, Schopenhauer's great nemesis, Hegel—took it for granted that, in accordance with some linear or cyclical or dialectical principle, progress was either evident or imminent. But many disputed the possibility and even the desirability of progress, either mistrusting or disapproving of current social and political tendencies—especially democratization and the feared disappearance of a settled aristocratic order, a likely prospect for which the French Revolution was the unhappy harbinger—or else believing that the endemic misery inherent in the human condition far outweighed the benefits of any hypothetical improvement in material circumstances. For these doubters of progress, a metaphysical pessimism that axiomatically called into question the meaning and value of the life to be improved provided such a convenient rallying point that, by the second half of the nineteenth century, Schopenhauer had moved to center stage in European intellectual life to contend for dominance with no less a figure than Hegel.

Any reader familiar with Schopenhauer's contempt for "the senseless sham wisdom of Hegel" (*WWR*, 1:437) cannot be surprised by his confidence that Hegelianism would collapse in the face of his withering exposure of its empty pretensions and transparent philosophic errors. On Kantian principles, Schopenhauer would call into question the legitimacy of the Hegelian project, the reading of the metaphysical principle, things-in-themselves, into temporal history—an impermissible move on Kantian grounds, since, of course, time exists only within the phenomenal, as one of the a priori forms of perception, and is never present in the unknowable realm of things-in-themselves. Furthermore, Schopenhauer vigorously insisted that any optimistic historicism can be shown to be fatally flawed by the very historical data on which historicist claims rested. "The content of history," as Schopenhauer read it, discloses, not the grand design of the Absolute Idea working itself out in time, but a series of random and frequently brutal events amounting to no more than a "European cat fight."[1]

The success of the pessimistic challenge to Hegelianism and cosmic optimism is primarily a late-nineteenth- and early-twentieth-century phenomenon, as Nietzsche and Freud supplant Hegel and Comte, and Hardy and Conrad replace Tennyson and Browning at the center of European intellectual and British literary life. But with Arnold, the general movement of mind that leads from an optimistic historicism at midcentury to metaphysical pessimism in subsequent years is surprisingly and idiosyncratically reversed. As prose writer and Victorian sage in the last half of the nineteenth century, Arnold brought unmistakably historicist presuppositions to virtually all of his major concerns—politics, social relations, culture, and religion—contending that the present epoch of concentration stood ready to give way to a forthcoming epoch of expansion resting on a gathering "current of true and fresh ideas." The Hebraism in which the British spirit had imprisoned itself seemed ready at long last to relax its hold upon British life and to be displaced by a culturally invigorating Hellenism, albeit a modern-day Hellenism spiritually fortified by a long ascendant Christian morality. With reservations, Arnold also saw the age's increasing tendency toward political democracy and social equality as an intrinsically good thing, indispensable to bringing about "the humanisation of man in society." More broadly, in "Obermann Once More," he envisioned the most metaphysically tinged of all his historicist expectations, foreseeing an age in which religion rests on a "joy whose grounds are true" (238).[2]

According to both Culler and De Laura, evidences of that turn to history were present still earlier. Both critics find, even in the years when Arnold was dedicating himself almost exclusively to poetry, a narrative of "conversion very similar to Carlyle's."[3] Culler, in fact, locates with great exactness the very moment of Carlylean transformation, a "spiritual crisis in Arnold's life corresponding to the episode in the Rue St. Thomas de l'Enfer in *Sartor*," dated as falling between September 24 and 27 of 1849, when Arnold made his "soul-searching expedition up into the Bernese Alps," during which he "exorcised the spirit of Obermann."[4] Less precise in working out the analogy with *Sartor*, De Laura simply suggests that "Arnold's

early poems—to say, about, 1852—represent his own version of the
'Centre of Indifference,' " while "Arnold's 'Everlasting Yes' was to
be delayed twenty years, until the religious writings of the 1870s."[5]

These conversion narratives have never been much concerned
with the ideas that went into the poetry that came before the saving
turn to history, treating them as little more than a vague negation,
a querulous "Everlasting No." The argument of this study though
has been that through the articulation of his "No," Arnold presents
a pessimistic vision of things of greater depth, complexity, and
(above all) intellectual adventuresomeness than we find in the cautiously crafted and tenuously expressed beliefs of those late religious writings that we are asked to regard as Arnold's "Everlasting
Yes." I would only add, insofar as the poetry is concerned, that, if
there is anything in 1849 that we can meaningfully call a conversion, it is certainly less absolute, less right-angled, than the analogy
with Carlyle suggests. While evidences of an implicitly optimistic cyclical historicism may be discerned in "Dover Beach," "Stanzas
from the Grande Chartreuse," and "The Scholar-Gipsy," even in
these poems a significant residue of metaphysical pessimism and
psychological anxiety still remains active and potent, undermining
and undoing these emergent beliefs.[6]

Several leading critics of Arnold have precisely fixed the moment of
the turn to history, the event occasioning it a poetic journey into the
Alps in 1849, undertaken in apparent homage to Étienne Pivert de
Senancour, and in imaginary pursuit of Senancour's fictional hero,
the melancholy Romantic solitary Obermann. Yet once in Obermann
country, wandering the same valleys, ascending the same heights,
and indeed inhabiting the very same rarefied spiritual atmosphere
as the fictional Obermann, Arnold chooses to turn away, to renounce Obermann and his Alpine solitude in a gesture that Culler
calls "the most important spiritual act of his entire life, for it put
behind him all the turbulence and unrest, the Sturm and Drang, that
had troubled him in previous years."[7] For David Riede too, "Stanzas
in Memory of the Author of 'Obermann' " is similarly pivotal in Arnold's development; its truest analogues are "such palinodes as
Wordsworth's 'Elegiac Stanzas,' " in that it is to be properly read
as "more a farewell to his own earlier self than to Obermann."[8] Yet
as sharp as that turn away from Obermann and all he stands for
seems to be, an exclamatory "Away!" marking the poem's peripe-
teia and apparent point of no return with the utmost exactness, Arnold so complicates and qualifies his break, so carefully reinscribes
earlier beliefs and attitudes assumed to have been discarded even

after it is made, that, by poem's end, the distance between the speaker and Obermann does not finally seem so great after all.

In *"The Strayed Reveller" and Other Poems*, the writer-models Arnold would emulate were apparently chosen because they were inarguably geniuses like Shakespeare or Sophocles, who possess implicitly transhistorical qualities that surmount all barriers of space and time and, therefore, still speak directly to us from the now-vanished ages in which they lived. At first glance, Obermann may seem at least symbolically to possess the requisite identifying mark of Arnold's earlier sages—a mountaintop habitation with which many of the designated sages to this point have been identified—and therefore those special qualities of mind for which the speaker yearns. In this case, though, what draws the speaker of "Stanzas in Memory of the Author of 'Obermann' " to the heights are not those special mountaintop qualities with which the Arnoldian sage has until now been endowed. The speaker seeks to acquire from Obermann neither the transcendently intuitive powers "[o]ut-topping knowledge" ("Shakespeare," 3) possessed by Shakespeare nor even that special comprehensiveness of vision that enables the Sophocles of "To a Friend" spiritually to master all he surveys from the summit. The metaphoric heights on which Obermann dwells are relatively easily ascended by Arnold's poet-speaker, but once the summit is gained, what he finds there yields cold comfort. Turning the pages of Senancour's work, the speaker discovers neither Sophoclean calm nor Shakespearean triumph but the familiar symptoms of the common malady, a fundamental likeness to ourselves in the depth and unassuageability of his misery— the special appeal of the writings of Senancour being the exceptional clarity with which these symptoms manifest themselves and can therefore be diagnosed:

> A fever in these pages burns
> Beneath the calm they feign;
> A wounded human spirit turns
> Here, on its bed of pain.

(21–24)

As if to reiterate that likeness of his suffering to our own, the trait that most profoundly typifies Obermann is associated not with the summit and its figurative transcendence but with the base, that level (and doubtlessly darkling) plain to which humankind has been remanded for the unhappy days of its life. While reading Senancour, one may be put in touch with the restorative sights and sounds of the mountains and may even breathe "the virgin mountain-air" that "[f]resh through these pages blows" (25–26), but what most attracts the speaker to seek out Obermann are "sobs" that convey the depth of the general plight, the melancholy "ground-tone / Of human agony" (35–36). Of course, Arnold's reluctance to endow a comparatively minor writer such as Senancour with anything like the seemingly unique and virtually transcendent capabilities of a Sophocles or a Shakespeare should come as no surprise, for surely it is the indisputable stature of the latter two—their virtually transcendent fame over time—that, at some deepest level, makes Arnold's extraordinary and extraliterary claims for them seem not altogether unreasonable. But after the publication of *"The Strayed Reveller" and Other Poems*, Arnold seems to revise his criteria for selecting models and sages, with the suitability of historical circumstance a more relevant principle of selection than the earlier criterion of some form of seemingly transhistorical and therefore intuitively universal understanding. As model or sage, Arnold will, after 1849, give us Obermann, the historically bruised and embittered hero of a relatively minor poet;[9] or that fantastic amalgam of fact and legend, the scholar-gipsy, whose flight from society coincides with the onset of the modern world; or even the darkly ambiguous Empedocles, who though living in antiquity is endowed by Arnold with a premature modernity of temperament (which becomes the stated rationale for the omission of *Empedocles on Etna* from the 1853 edition of the poems).

The extent to which, from 1849 onward, historical considerations enter into Arnold's choice of a possible model becomes even more apparent in that curious process of elimination by which he explains the surprising selection of Obermann over seemingly far greater writers, Wordsworth and Goethe. Though Wordsworth is one of the three who "have attained," along with Obermann, "to see their way" (47–48), his adequacy as model "in this our troubled day" (46) is summarily challenged on the grounds that his is only a partial vision, having failed by the sage's measure to see life whole, since "Wordsworth's eyes avert their ken / From half of human fate" (53–54). Goethe, on the other hand, the one writer of the age whose literary reputation most nearly approaches that of a Shakespeare or a Sophocles, would seem surely in both his life and work to combine the seemingly inborn superiority as an artist with the complementary austerity of vision that we have come to associate with the model; Goethe would certainly therefore seem better suited than Senancour to serve as guide and sage to an age in search of an intellectual deliverance. Yet for reasons never deemed applicable

to Sophocles or Shakespeare, Goethe is effectively disqualified as
guide and sage for Arnold's age on the grounds that dissimilarity of
historical circumstances, a crucial generational difference, renders
Goethe's lonely way one that cannot be emulated by the speaker or
the other members of his own lost generation, the fact that

> though his manhood bore the blast
> Of a tremendous time,
> Yet in a tranquil world was passed
> His tenderer youthful prime.

(65–68)

Of the three "spirits who have reigned" over the first half of the
nineteenth century, it is Obermann, then, who is the most appropriate, or at least the historically most imitable model for a generation "brought forth and reared in hours / Of change, alarm,
surprise" (69–70), his despairing melancholy being the perfect
match for that generation's sense of historically enforced impotence. At this point in "Stanzas in Memory of the Author of 'Obermann,' " the notion that the source of our plight is a purely
metaphysical causation whose effects at all times and in all places
are everywhere the same has plainly given way to more localized
explanations based on observable historical differences and apparent historical determination. We can not "attain Wordsworth's
sweet calm or Goethe's wide / And luminous view" (79–80) because
changed historical conditions have placed such solutions out of
reach. But history, as Arnold thinks about it in these early lines
from "Stanzas in Memory of the Author of 'Obermann,' " is clearly
not yet historicism, an immanent telos that directs human events to
some intelligible and desirable end. In this case, history offers only
a seeming record of decline, with the "tranquil world" in which
Wordsworth and Goethe were nurtured forever lost to those of Arnold's generation who were "brought forth and reared in hours / Of
change, alarm, surprise" (69–70), and therefore can only despairingly ask, "What shelter to grow ripe is ours? / What leisure to grow
wise?" (71–72).

Indeed, Arnold's representation of the historical process in
"Stanzas in Memory of the Author of 'Obermann' " has really
changed little since his earlier figurative rendering of history in "To
the Duke of Wellington," where he spoke of Wellington keeping his
"track, across the fretful foam / Of vehement actions without term
or scope / Called history" (11–13). In the later poem, history is
again represented as the implicitly hostile workings of a sea "[o]f

vehement actions," the turbulence of this later sea spawning only a "change, alarm, surprise" that ceaselessly buffet those subject to its effects:

> Like children bathing on the shore,
> Buried a wave beneath,
> The second wave succeeds, before
> We have had time to breathe.
>
> (73–76)

By representing those who confront the sea of history, in "Stanzas in Memory of the Author of 'Obermann,' " as children overwhelmed by the strength of this antithetical force, Arnold has clearly chosen to read the historical process in the postrevolutionary age pessimistically, as another version of our human beleaguerment by otherness, an account that emphasizes the helplessness and victimization of those who must submit themselves to that process, a category that would seem to amount to nothing less than humanity at large in Arnold's own age.

At first, Arnold seems to look upon the imagined autobiography of Obermann as showing how at least one specially gifted inhabitant of the present age, a "seer" (106), avoided being overwhelmed by flux. His remedy: a flight to a solitary Alpine retreat where nature's restorative influence was sufficiently therapeutic for Obermann to find himself "grown young" (127) there, a flight, moreover, that the speaker himself intends ritually to reenact to attain that same end. Yet just when he seems on the verge of fully and finally identifying with Obermann (a bonding deemed indispensable to the speaker as poet), Arnold's speaker abandons the implicitly regressive strategies that had guided him until now, renouncing the seer with whom he would identify by something akin to an act of exorcism (this is the term used by Arnold's critics), decisively heralded by the single word "Away!" (128) and pointedly reiterated in the lines that follow: "Away the dreams that but deceive / And thou, sad guide, adieu!" (129–30).

David Riede is surely right in noting a likeness between these particular lines from "Stanzas in Memory of the Author of 'Obermann' " and "such palinodes as Wordsworth's 'Elegiac Stanzas,' "[10] another poem of recantation that bids farewell to nature and Romantic poetry as "dreams that but deceive." Moreover, giving this conversion narrative, as Culler conceives it, its seemingly Carlylean thrust is the speaker's announcement of a fundamental life choice: "I in the world must live" (137). By turning toward the world and away from Obermann and the life "grown young," Arnold, in effect, would seem to ask us to believe he has put regressive fantasies and childish things behind him, repudiating them for the sake of adult responsibility, perhaps the duty to do the work nearest at hand, the work of the world in a perilous hour. On the basis of this same Carlylean parallel, one might conclude as well that Arnold is also cautiously drawing up his own revised version of the historical process, putting forward the hinted-at beginnings of his own myth of progress. Behind his decision to live in the world might very well be the belief or, perhaps, just the hope that present decline is not the end of history but merely a cyclical stage on the way to a future that must be presumed immensely superior to the joyless present and quite possibly to a nostalgically recollected past as well. But such a future can come into being only through the freely willed labors of those willing to carry out the work that needs to be done in the world.

Yet despite the seeming decisiveness with which the speaker bids himself "Away!" the scenarios of exorcism and conversion that should be introduced by that word are not as clearly delineated as Riede and Culler imply by their Wordsworthian and Carlylean parallels. With characteristic tentativeness, Arnold carefully blunts the logic that would lead him to cast his lot with adulthood and the possibilities of history by positing two countervailing arguments that radically qualify the poem's seemingly pivotal assertion. Though for Culler that journey to and break with Obermann is nothing less than "the central spiritual crisis in Arnold's life, corresponding to the episode in the Rue St. Thomas de l'Enfer in *Sartor*,"[11] in one crucial respect the two ostensible conversion experiences could not be more unlike; for when Diogenes Teufelsdröckh in his "Baphometic Fire-Baptism" stands up in defiance of the mechanistic devil who would possess him, it is made unequivocally clear that the basis of that self-transforming defiance is the intuitive consciousness of his own free will: "I am not thine but Free, and forever hate thee."[12] But while Arnold's exclamatory "Away!" certainly bears the accent of freely willed choice, his speaker explains it deterministically, ascribes it to forces beyond his control—to "fate" (131):

> We, in some unknown Power's employ,
> Move on a rigorous line;
> Can neither, when we will, enjoy.
> Nor, when we will, resign.

(133–36)

Further blunting the decisiveness of that break with Obermann is the speaker's surprising avowal that, even after his descent from the mountains, he shall maintain a deep-seated spiritual identification with Obermann by reason of their continuing membership in a select brotherhood, the curiously named "Children of the Second Birth" (143), a group indifferently composed of "Christian and pagan, king and slave / Soldier and anchorite" (149–50), and "[w]hose one bond is, that all have been / Unspotted by the world" (155–56). Though, psychologically, coming down from the mountains and away from Obermann would seem to be, first and foremost, a rejection of disablingly regressive longings and an acceptance of adult responsibilities, by this assertion of ongoing affinities with Obermann, Arnold essentially reconstitutes these regressive longings at what he would have us believe is a more fundamentally spiritual level. To be a Child of the Second Birth is to remain inviolate amidst the corruptive pressures of a soiling world. (In a letter to Clough, Arnold equates the Children of the Second Birth with those who have heeded Christ's exhortation, "Except a man be born again, he cannot see the kingdom of God." In the secular atmosphere of the Obermann poem, however, such religiously freighted echoes do little more than add a sanctifying gloss to a phrase obviously imported to legitimize anxiously regressive desires that had apparently been discredited only a few stanzas earlier.) In electing himself to the Children of the Second Birth, Arnold's speaker again seems to be adopting a defensive strategy that would also be called upon at critical junctures in the roughly contemporaneous "Marguerite" poems, a supposedly spiritual flight from an adult world anxiously perceived to be filled with dangers. The world is no longer construed, in Carlylean terms, as the site of social and moral transformation or of necessary and perhaps saving labors. Instead, any reference to the world is now to be taken as a term of disparagement (as it is so often in Arnold, especially in poems of love where it is the world against which the lovers must be shielded). This term is clearly associated with that contaminating spotting and soiling that the Children of the Second Birth, retaining their childhood purity and innocence into adulthood, have somehow managed to resist.

Arnold has thus left us little reason to believe that the break with Obermann constitutes a conversion or exorcism in any intellectually meaningful sense, or that it marks any clearly demarcated passage from pessimism to a more or less optimistic historicism, the most crucial turn that his career over forty years actually takes. In fact, what the Children of the Second Birth—"Christian and pagan, king and slave, / Soldier and anchorite" (to say nothing of Obermann and Arnold)—have most in common, besides an obliviousness to social distinctions "we esteem so grave" (151), is a similar obliviousness to cultural and historical differences, connected as all the Children of the Second Birth are by a kinship of essential spiritual inviolateness that transcends every consideration of time and place. Indeed, by defining the Children of the Second Birth in such wholly negative terms, singling out as their most distinguishing attributes their being "unspotted" and "unsoiled" by the world, Arnold may once again be offering us another version of "the buried life" proceeding on its autonomous course, unaffected by the events of an antithetically conceived and spiritually debasing phenomenal world. Yet, in the end, Arnold is careful to eschew considerations of metaphysics, to keep the action and concerns of the poem firmly in the world, however harshly judged that world may be. While "Stanzas in Memory of the Author of 'Obermann' " is not really the exorcism or decisive turning-away from his past self that his critics would have it, in that poem Arnold can at least be said to make certain cautious, preliminary overtures to possibilities of a meaningful life in the world and even of general human progress—possibilities he philosophically raises for the first time in the poetry in relative independence of the offsetting negations of Arnoldian metaphysics.

But the emergence in the poetry of Arnold of such cautiously voiced historicist tenets and hopes in the fall of 1849 did not mean that historicism would quickly supersede that mix of philosophic pessimism and psychological anxiety that until then had shaped his poetry of suffering. Less than two years later in "Dover Beach," a more than residual metaphysical pessimism, an emerging historicism carefully calibrated to Arnold's seemingly constitutional melancholy, and the anxiety that in Arnold always attends upon occasions of love are allowed to stake their claims in a contest that neither intellectually nor emotionally is ever fully resolved. Despite the skill with which Arnold works the figurative oppositions of light and dark, land and sea, and sight and sound into a unified imagistic design and finally a miniallegory of the utmost intricacy (that intricacy and perceived unity doubtlessly the reason for the poem's high standing among Arnold's usual detractors, the New Critics), I would finally suggest that it is in the conflictedness found beneath its carefully wrought surface of apparent unity, in the pain of the speaking voice, and (above all) in its unmitigable desperation that the art (rather than the artfulness) of "Dover Beach" most truly resides.

Once again we have the characteristic Arnoldian setting, a cloud-

less night of total serenity in which the waters of the sea are illumi-
nated by moon and stars, a scene that in almost every appearance
in the poetry of Arnold directs the mind toward new beginnings,
toward hopes and possibilities that seem directly generated by the
seascape before him:

> The sea is calm to-night.
> The tide is full, the moon lies fair
> Upon the straits; on the French coast the light
> Gleams and is gone; the cliffs of England stand,
> Glimmering and vast, out in the tranquil bay.
> Come to the window, sweet is the night-air.
>
> (1–6)

The stars and moon, considered separately, in the splendor of their
isolation, provide a seemingly idealized representation of the autonomy and self-dependence that Arnold on innumerable poetic occasions professes to be the highest goal and good of the individuated
consciousness; and the sea, considered separately, is almost invariably looked upon as the fundamentally undifferentiated in contrast
to the individuated and, in most situations, as antithetical to the interests or values of the Arnoldian voyager or onlooker adrift or enisled within that sea. But in rare moments of almost suprasensuous
calm, the light of the stars and moon seems to merge with the visual
surface of the almost motionless sea, and these two immeasurably
distant and irretrievably separate realms are seemingly transformed into a single, glimmering level plain. It is not surprising that
at such a moment we would imagine the individuated life as almost
magically conjoined to the noumenal, the goods and values of our
earthbound human existence at one with the metaphysically real,
the world to which we have been awakened by this catalyst to possibilities becoming nothing less than "a land of dreams" (32).

Of course, such a figure necessarily carries the seeds of its own
unmaking, with this appearance of cosmic unity being inevitably
subject to dissolution by every accident of wind and light. But the
figure is flawed in a still more obvious way. Only in its idealizing
fantasies and dreams can humankind claim for itself any such identification with moon and stars, heavenly bodies whose operations
are carried on at a distance as immeasurable from us as they are
from the sea. From the outset, Arnold knows that the humanity to
which he belongs in "Dover Beach" is really consigned to the land,
whose relationship to the sea that continually impinges upon it
must be unceasingly and, no doubt, necessarily inimical. Even in

that introductory seascape, the framing coast (as almost all those who have written on the poem have noted) is carefully differentiated from the sea, so that the evening's light, while steadily fixed upon the sea, shines intermittently and brokenly on "the cliffs of England," which "stand / Glimmering and vast," and is even more impermanent to the viewer whose eye moves across the Channel to the "French coast," to a "light" that "[g]leams and is gone."

But the speaker is only truly apprised of how very much a being of the land he is after he calls his companion to the window to share in the special sweetness of that visually engendered moment. Just this once, he tells her, she shall be able to breathe unconstrictedly from an atmosphere ordinarily choked by "[d]ust and soil" ("A Summer Night," 82), that familiar earthly atmosphere presumably purified in "Dover Beach" by the cosmologically harmonizing powers that manifest themselves through the light that emanates from that night sky. But just as he bids her look out, the sounds of the earthly near-at-hand,

> the grating roar
> Of pebbles which the waves draw back, and fling,
> At their return, up the high strand,

(9–11)

must by their proximity, their unignorable "gratingness," claim our attention, supplant the visual and enticing as the intentional field of our observations, as the percepts that most demand to be conceptualized, to be fitted to our human concerns. As creatures of the earth, our truest affinities are plainly with that near-at-hand: with the pebbles of the shore, flung aimlessly and indifferently by the sea. This makes a fitting emblem for our harsh cosmological circumstances, circumstances to which that temporary appearance—indeed, that optical illusion—generated by the effect of moonlight on the sea is intuitively understood to be wholly irrelevant. In fact, the implicit irrelevance of the moonlit sea to our predicament is already indicated by the temporal distinction between the transitoriness of the visual, a calm holding true only for the present, for "to-night," and the contrastingly privileged "eternal note" conveyed by the "grating roar / of pebbles."

So by the end of the first stanza of "Dover Beach," we find ourselves situated, just as in "To Marguerite—Continued," at the point of convergence of sea and land, a setting doubtlessly better suited to represent what Arnold deems our general human predicament of cosmic hostility and beleaguerment. Though nothing in that particular scene *necessarily* gives rise to Arnold's basic metaphysical allegory of cosmic hostility and beleaguerment, his predisposition to draw the most pessimistic of inferences from the details of landscape is nowhere more strikingly illustrated than in the first stanza of "Dover Beach." Listening attentively to that movement of pebbles thrown back on the beach by the endlessly repeated action of the waves, he gleans not simply the fact of natural conflict and dissonance that the sounds of the sea striking the shore would seem to suggest. Instead, he claims to recognize in that "grating roar" a single, unvarying, blended undertone, "the eternal note of sadness," a message apparently intelligible only to its human listeners, those who dwell on the shore, to whom it speaks of an overwhelming of life and unceasing defeats, an inference natural enough for any listener already attuned by experience to the sufferings endemic to human existence.

But in one crucial particular, the metaphysically determined circumstances of the speaker in "Dover Beach" differ markedly from that of his counterpart in "To Marguerite—Continued." From its very opening line, "To Marguerite—Continued" declares itself a philosophical allegory in which enforced separation from others is the fated consequence of our necessary subjection to that blind, striving noumenal will that determines all phenomenal relationships. "Dover Beach," of course, does not begin as allegory. While the speaker of "Dover Beach," like the speaker of "To Marguerite—Continued," is similarly positioned at the point where sea and land converge, that point of convergence in "Dover Beach" is the poem's literal setting. He is actually there, in a room at Dover shared with another, and therefore the epistemological assumption of isolation with which "To Marguerite-Continued" opens, the natural concomitant of Arnold's allegorical representation of human life as an island, need not hold true. Indeed, the invitation by the speaker, "Come to the window," evokes possibilities of community and solidarity and, most of all, love, even in a setting that otherwise so readily lends itself to scenarios of cosmic denial and defeat.

But Arnold would still have his readers acquiesce in his apparently pessimistic claims that what is to be heard in that sound given off by the pebbles flung up on the beach is a note of world sorrow. To that end, he turns for instruction in the meaning of that dissonant grating to an acknowledged authority on suffering, to one who in Arnold's earlier poetry had already served as tutor and model: to Sophocles, who

> long ago
> Heard it on the Aegean, and it brought
> Into his mind the turbid ebb and flow
> Of human misery.
>
> (15–18)

For the great tragedian—and any reader of his plays needs no one specific citation to demonstrate this—misery is the permanent and essential condition of humankind, following its own "ebb and flow" to be sure and thus present at different times to a greater or lesser degree, but always indelibly even if but latently there, and there no doubt as a consequence of the harsh fatality under which we must live. The Sophocles of "Dover Beach" is apparently a pessimist *avant la lettre,* seemingly ready to render as a judgment valid for all times and in all places the proposition that life—at least human life—is necessarily suffering.

But between the summer of 1848, when Sophocles appeared in "To a Friend" as one of those "[w]ho prop . . . in these bad days, my mind" (1), and the summer of 1851, the generally accepted year of composition for "Dover Beach," the power and authority of the Arnoldian model diminished considerably. While the message Sophocles gleans from the sounds of the sea, that the law of life for humans is "misery," might seem a plausible and predictable Arnoldian conclusion, in "Dover Beach" that message carries none of the persuasive force usually associated with the findings of the model. It is a message that has its origins for Sophocles not in any flash of Shakespearean insight or as one of the gipsy child's innate a priori truths but in a casual associative connection, the seemingly random linkage of the sea's repetitive cadence to the apparently regular fluctuations of our fundamentally unhappy human lot—a regularity no doubt confirmed for Sophocles by Antigone and Oedipus and Philoctetes. But not only does the wisdom of the sage seem diminished; the relationship of the Arnoldian speaker as would-be disciple is also obviously and drastically revised in "Dover Beach." This second Sophocles does not really compel discipleship; the Arnoldian speaker never really relies upon him as a "prop." Acutely conscious of the insurmountable gulf of history and geography that separates him from Sophocles, the speaker of "Dover Beach" asserts his own time-bound and place-bound associative connections, finding in the sound of pebbles flung up on the beach at a far different time and place—"[h]earing it by this distant northern sea" (20)—a thought radically unlike that of Sophocles, a thought of "human misery" historically determined rather than valid for all times and places.

The relegation of this later Sophocles to the status of an important but not necessarily privileged voice is perhaps the most revealing index Arnold gives us to how far he has moved toward historicism by the time of "Dover Beach." While the Sophocles of "Dover Beach," like the gipsy child and Shakespeare, appears to offer a universally valid judgment, extracting from the sounds of the sea moving across the shore the general truth that to dwell in a misery that merely ebbs and flows is the unrelievable burden of human existence, the speaker quickly sets aside that presumably timeless Sophoclean wisdom to voice his own preoccupation with the consequences of the decline of the Christian faith in the nineteenth century. By proposing such very different origins for our suffering, he makes it clear that we are now—at least provisionally—to understand meaning to be historically conditioned, that each age appropriates from the semantically indifferent noises of the sea that message that best serves its own historically delineated needs and interests.

As an incipient mid-nineteenth-century historicist, Arnold almost certainly assumed that Sophocles would have been conditioned by the pessimistic predisposition of antiquity to believe that a harsh cosmic governance was ultimately responsible for the order of things and the outcome of events, for an ultimately irremediable human misery that held true universally. But to the historicist, any assumption of universality must be viewed skeptically and (in the case of Sophocles) charitably looked upon as the product of an unavoidable historical innocence; for the Christian faith which prevailed for centuries following antiquity held human misery to be not essential but accidental—at most an unfortunate and irksome prologue, if faith or conduct warranted, to an eternity of happiness. Consequently, the speaker may reasonably surmise that the source of his newly arisen sadness is not the unclouding of the metaphysical understanding but simply the spiritually diminished historical circumstances of those, disabused of faith, who live in the present, the unhappiness actually entailed for them by the loss of that promise-filled Christian paradigm. What Arnold speaks of here is not the human condition existentially conceived but the ache of modernity, its distinguishing characteristic, besides its disbelief, an achingly unhappy consciousness of faith withdrawing that infiltrates all present experience.

With this shift to northern sounds and thoughts, we are introduced to the first of the major cruxes in interpretations of "Dover Beach," what Ruth Pitman calls "the vexed question of Arnold's tides."[13] That is, there is an unexplained transition from the ebb and flow of waves to the ebb and flow of tides in "Dover Beach," a casual figurative shift that has left Arnold open to accusations of inconsistency or forgetfulness or confusion. Initially, the sounds to which the speaker calls our attention are made by the virtually constant motion of the waves flinging pebbles up on the beach at intervals only seconds or fractions of a second apart; and Sophocles, too, hearing a similar sound "long ago" (15) while "on the Aegean" (16), must similarly have assumed its source also to be the motion of the waves, since it calls to mind the analogous rhythms of "the turbid ebb and flow of human misery," a repetition so closely spaced that, in that constant commingling, there hardly seems time to distinguish ebb from flow, the greater from the lesser misery.

But when the speaker begins to analogize from these sounds, he now somewhat surprisingly attributes the sounds generated by that meeting of wave and beach to the larger and more broadly spaced movement of the tides, a movement to be measured not in seconds but in hours, thus enabling him to make that speculative leap by which he can equate the sound he hears to thoughts of a century-long withdrawal of faith from the modern world. In this case, though, it is surely the seemingly casual associative movement of the poem that is responsible for the reconceiving of what was originally perceived. It is an easy and apparently random progression of thoughts that carries the speaker from the sounds heard on the beach at Dover and the sadness they bring to his mind to remembrances of his great pessimistic forerunner and previously adopted model, Sophocles—who, as his plays tell us, was prompted to similar thoughts of the pervasiveness of human misery, when "on the Aegean" he had "long ago" listened to that very same sound of waves flinging pebbles up the beach. Then in a final shift we are brought back to the speaker, listening once more just as Sophocles once had, hence the associative connection. But now the speaker, once again associatively calling to mind thoughts of human misery, recognizes the historically conditioned, basic unlikeness between his own assumptions about the origins and nature of human suffering and those of Sophocles. Born twenty-two centuries later in mid-nineteenth-century Britain, the speaker must stand at this time and in this place, his consciousness necessarily and disturbingly touched by the knowledge of the intervening epoch of a waning Christian faith, when there had been comfort and even hope, a comfort and hope whose uncompensated loss he now holds responsible, in large measure, for his sorrow.

Thus, as Arnold's new paradigm of historical explanation is at last brought forward and foregrounded—a paradigm that attributes his suffering not to a buffeting forever inherent in the nature of things but to localized circumstances of mid-nineteenth-century life that deny him a happiness once available to others—he turns once again to the sounds of the sea that had initiated his rambling meditation. But with this concept now clearly shaping percept, what he believes himself to hear must finally be reconstituted, the noises of the sea sorted out so that only those elements that accommodate themselves to that governing paradigm are now attended to by the listening consciousness. Thus, the shift from the incessantly battering motion of waves to the slow ebb and flow of tides in "Dover Beach," though leaving Arnold undeniably liable to the accusation of inconsistency, is in fact a significant index to fundamental changes in ways of conceptualizing experience that occur in the poem. These changes lead us from the Sophoclean mode of analyzing significant human events in terms of a supposedly direct and immediate metaphysical determination to an emerging nineteenth-century predisposition to interpret them as the varied effects of an ongoing historical causality.

A second aspect of the "question of Arnold's tides" in "Dover Beach" has proven no less vexing. Because tides that ebb must eventually return, critics of the poem since George Saintsbury have understandably argued that, despite the manifestly melancholy lesson Arnold draws from the sounds of the withdrawing sea, the image of the tide, even in ebb, must necessarily contain the seed of future hopes. If these historical tides are organized by some principle analogous to the uniform laws of nature (for, if history is not to be read as movement and countermovement, the use of the figure seems pointless), then someday they surely will be "at the full" again, providing humanity with a historically sanctioned security and even a historically sanctioned joyfulness. To be sure, in a wonderfully resourceful essay, Pitman has argued that nineteenth-century geological science does not require such an inference, that Lyell's theory of erosion allows us to understand Arnold's tides as evidence for the unrelievedly melancholy conclusions that Arnold draws from the ebbing tide of history: "If the tide is essentially eroding, it will always be destructive; as it ebbs it reduces the land, and promise of its flow is simply promise of further encroachment."[14] Though Pitman's reading has the virtue of preserving the Arnoldian melancholy of "Dover Beach," one is still hesitant to regard Arnold as other than geologically commonsensical, perhaps even scientifically naïve, disposed to interpret the tides of history as a contrasting ebb and flow endlessly repeated, with the epoch to come predictably similar to the epoch just past and certainly superior in its tidal fullness to our sadly diminished present.

For in other poems where Arnold conceives of history cyclically, he clearly assumes that the future that shall come into being, after the "spark from heaven" shall "fall" ("The Scholar-Gipsy," 120) or after the world now "powerless to be born" ("Stanzas from the Grande Chartreuse," 86) emerges, will be immensely superior to the present. Even more strikingly, in the relatively late "Obermann Once More," where the ebbing of the tide also represents the passing of the Christian era under an unsparing Enlightenment scrutiny—"that tide of common thought, / Which bathed our life, retired" (189–90)—Arnold obviously employs his tidal metaphor traditionally, in terms of ebb and flow, telling us that present loss shall be offset by the tide's return and the cycle's renewal, *"One common wave of thought and joy / Lifting mankind again"* (323–24).

Far more credible than the counterintuitive claim of Pitman, however impressive its scientific credentials, is the simpler assessment of R. H. Super, who concludes that, while "the spiritual state of England is indeed distressing," such distress may be only transitory, since the tidal metaphor "might be taken in fact to imply that the remedy lies with time."[15] Yet if the historical section of "Dover Beach" conveys a hope missing from the earlier sections, where "sadness" is deemed eternal and "human misery," according to Sophocles, continually present, either in "ebb" or in "flow," that hope seems to carry with it the Kafkaesque qualification that there may be hope—but not for us. Turning at long last to the woman who presumably stands beside him, Arnold apparently feels himself free to ask why, if our present unhappiness is not metaphysically entailed, could we not seize the moment, take refuge from the world and thus the historically determining conditions that now beset us within the sanctuary of purely personal relations, and find through love the happiness that otherwise will come only in some future moment of cyclical renewal.

With this turn to his companion, their relationship now made perfectly clear by the term of endearment—"love"—we have arrived at the point most in dispute in discussions of "Dover Beach." Somewhat surprisingly, a good many commentators, perhaps a majority, apparently deciding that the speaker's gesture toward love and commitment—his plea that they "be true to another"—must outweigh all other factors, take the poem finally to affirm more than it denies. Thus, William Cadbury begins his influential essay by insisting, "The surprising thing about 'Dover Beach' is that, like Matthew

Arnold himself, it is so cheerful despite the gloom of what it says."[16] And in his well-known psychoanalytic reading of "Dover Beach," Norman Holland finds the poem "peaceful" and "satisfying," effects that are unexpectedly produced in "a poem at least partly about disillusionment, loss of faith, despair" by the "heavy, massive set of defenses" Arnold brings to bear against these distressing elements.[17] Dorothy Mermin also emphasizes the "extraordinary charm of 'Dover Beach,'" a charm engendered by "the retreat into private, domestic life and personal affections that is the usual alternative in Victorian fiction to the evils of the social world."[18]

The man and the woman who stand together at the window are plainly not islands permanently dissevered by principles apparently intrinsic to the ordering of things. Their present intimacy, together with the speaker's avowal of love, surely indicates that there is love now, and therefore no necessary or even probable reason why the speaker and his companion should not remain "true to one another." Yet the lines that follow that declaration and appeal present the darkest in the poem's series of dark visions:

> Ah, love, let us be true
> To one another! for the world which seems
> To lie before us like a land of dreams,
> So various, so beautiful, so new,
> Hath really neither joy, nor love, nor light,
> Nor certitude, nor peace, nor help for pain;
> And we are here as on a darkling plain
> Swept with confused alarms of struggle and flight,
> Where ignorant armies clash by night.
>
> (29–37)

Those who read "Dover Beach" as "cheerful" or as "peaceful" and "satisfying" remain untroubled by the disconfirming logic implied by this sequence of negations, arguing that Arnold's affirmation of love more than offsets the seeming nihilism that succeeds it. Indeed, the distinguished psychoanalytic critic Norman Holland painlessly solves this problem by maintaining that in "Dover Beach" "the poem defends before it presents its disturbance."[19] But I would contend that Arnold's declaration of love and appeal for love's continuance is not a precautionary defense against the disturbance to follow but is itself that which must be defended against.

To understand why and how love, seemingly such an unalloyed good in this heartfelt evocation of it, actually functions as a disturbing element in the closing stanza of "Dover Beach," we need to turn once more to that scenario of signal anxiety repeatedly enacted in the "Marguerite" poems, where a seemingly imminent kiss or embrace actually called forth the defensive strategies designed to thwart the speaker's desires before the psychological dangers invariably attendant upon love could work their irreparable harm. So, too, in "Dover Beach" the sexually promising situation of being alone with the woman one loves is suffused with an anxiety that serves as a signal of imminent danger, a warning to the speaker of the need for guardedness lest an earlier episode of unpleasure be painfully repeated.

At two crucial points in this final stanza, the anxiety thereby created and the mechanism of defense it calls forth manifest themselves with particular clarity. Of the saving attributes absent from a world that has "neither joy, nor love, nor light, / Nor certitude, nor peace, nor help for pain," the most conspicuous is obviously "love," and we can only wonder how the speaker's appeal for love and fidelity can ever be made good if the absence of love is a given of human existence. Critics of Arnold usually slide over the contradiction implicit in this second reference to "love" (though as every teacher of "Dover Beach" knows, students do not), or else they treat this second love as abstract, philosophical, Platonized, a "universal love," as J. Hillis Miller calls it, which, if it existed, would "guarantee particular acts of love."[20] But Miller goes on to argue that the absence of this second love does not mean that the "particular act of love" attested to by the speaker is not really love but only "a modern 'existentialist' kind of love which says, 'Since there is no love, in the sense of a power transcending man, let us create love out of nothing in spite of the insecurity and even absurdity of such love.' "[21] But if the claim that the other attributes enumerated in that list are absent from the world is to be considered in any way meaningful, then they must be absent not just in some cosmically general way but in their particular instances. Surely Arnold would not find the absence of certitude so devastating if we were allowed a truly existential certitude, nor would he find a purely existential "help for pain" less comforting because it lacked transcendent validation.

Indeed, attempting to salvage Arnold's earlier affirmation of love by such arguments runs the risk of trivializing the bleakness of "Dover Beach"'s unsparing, final revelation. That revelation, by unobtrusively including love as one item in a list of goods absent from the world, surely asserts that love is an illusion to be discarded and denied. And the underlying logic justifying that denial, I would suggest, is the logic of signal anxiety, the declaration of love inducing in the speaker here, as in so many of Arnold's other poems, an anxiety that rapidly mobilizes his psychic defenses against the threat that love is instinctively felt to represent. To ward off the danger posed by love, Arnold here adopts a strategy of *undoing*, a defense that allows one to " 'blow away' not merely the *consequences* of some event (or experience or impression) but the event itself."[22] By asserting as an apparently universal maxim the proposition that there is no love, Arnold in effect cancels his original avowal of love, unsays and undoes it by declaring that there could be no such love as that he has professed because no such love could ever exist in the world.

The most compelling evidence for regarding this second reference to love as a self-canceling act of undoing is Arnold's reinscribing of this fundamental gesture of psychological denial in the famous simile of the fantasized night battle with which "Dover Beach" closes. In Arnold's source, the account by Thucydides of the Battle of Epipolae, we are told how, fighting in darkness, the Athenians were unable to distinguish friend from foe, so that, "thrown into confusion," they finally came "into collision with their own comrades in many different parts of the army" and "not only became panic-stricken but came to blows with one another."[23] What most likely would have associatively triggered Arnold's remembrance of this bit of schoolboy history is the obvious pertinence of the action that took place on that "darkling plain" to his own private situation, as he has parenthetically disclosed it during his general meditation. For what that narrative of confusion and consequent suffering—of comrade striking comrade—offers us in its prescribed function as a paradigm for our relationships in the world at large is a cautionary tale of the potential untrustworthiness and propensity to betrayal of those to whom we are bound by ties of community and love. And the bearing of this narrative of humanity at cross-purposes on the speaker's own imaginings of the projected outcome of his initial plea for constancy in love is only too obvious. Confined as we are to the "darkling plain," we shall inevitably find that those we would love will return us hurt for our love, however well-meaning their seeming intentions.

Readers who would take cheer from the apparently high valuation Arnold places on love in "Dover Beach" have generally argued that the lovers are spectators, beings apart, who have managed to maintain a saving distance from the confusion that rages around them. But what surely calls to mind the passage from Thucydides is the resemblance the speaker instinctively seizes upon between his companion and himself, "here" in a room at Dover, and the soldiers at Epipolae, locked in desperate struggle, the outcome unsure and their comrades-in-arms only too likely to become their adversaries. On the darkling plain there is no separate space for the detached and observing; if the lovers' "here" is akin to that Thucydidean setting, it is because, in some profoundly disturbing sense, the lovers know that they too are combatants and subject in their relation to one another to the accidental betrayals of darkness.

One further note on that relationship seems in order. In his essay on "Dover Beach," Holland—a critic no reader would charge with prudishness—insists on treating the lovers as "asexual,"[24] so that the key line, "And we are here," has the effect (according to Holland) of keeping the lovers "quite distinctly separate from what conflicts with that solid, constant trust—the ignorant armies with their sexual undertones."[25] But that view of the lovers' relationship seems strikingly at variance with their circumstances as Arnold describes them—the speaker and the woman he professes to love alone at night in a room at a resort, circumstances that manifestly call for an accounting in sexual terms—and with the probable biographical context of that occasion at Dover—the honeymoon stopover in Dover by Arnold and his bride in June of 1851.[26]

Against Holland's contention that this closing stanza describes an asexual love—one invoked as a precaution against subsequent primal-scene fantasies aroused by sounds that conjure up fearful childhood memories of things that go bump in the night—I see no reason to place the defense before rather than, more logically, after the anxiety that had called it forth. Finding himself in a situation that apparently requires him to behave sexually as a lover, the speaker of "Dover Beach" reacts with an inhibiting anxiety that calls into play defenses that might release him from his obligations as lover, seeking first by a return to the safe ground of metaphysics to undo his original pledge, and then constructing a fantasized scenario of unavoidable conflict that calls into question the very possibility of the fidelity set forth as a presumably necessary condition of genuine love. Undoubtedly precipitating this moment of sexually disabling anxiety—as the allusion to the night battle so plainly indicates—is a psychologically familiar cause (one whose sexually disabling consequences we have already observed in the Marguerite poems): fear of loss of the loved object's love. This concern in turn leads us back to fragmentary remembrances of that original loved object for whom every subsequent love must be, in some sense, a never fully adequate substitute. If Arnold resorts in "Dover Beach" to asexual defenses as Holland suggests, they are defenses mustered, not in behalf of his love for and with the woman who presumably is to spend the night with him at Dover, but against the dangers

that necessarily adhere to success in that love—a love uncon-
sciously recognized as a reenactment of our first infantile attachment and, like that earlier love, instinctually apprehended as both
impossible and debasing.

In "Dover Beach," all three of Arnold's major principles of explanation—the metaphysical, the historical, and the psychosexual—
are granted significant and seemingly equal hearings. Yet by
placing the psychosexual last in the poem's sequence of ideas, Arnold gives it a certain primacy; he intimates that even if the other
causes for our sorrow could be somehow negated or modified—if
the metaphysical explanation could be found in error or even in-
complete, or if the historical cycle could reverse itself and some historically acceptable new ground of faith were to flow back and
establish itself—our unhappiness would not necessarily be therefore lifted or, perhaps, even lightened. The most fundamental and
probably irremediable cause of our sorrowful predicament, this
highly encoded closing allusion suggests, lies in ourselves, in the
unpredictability and untrustworthiness of our desires and compulsions, in the inherently tragic nature (and here Arnold seems at one
with Freud) of the erotic life.

Arnold concluded the volume published as *Empedocles on Etna,
and Other Poems* with "The Future," and, given that poem's title
and subject matter, it might at first glance seem the poem of these
years best suited to illustrate how far Arnold had traveled down the
road to historicism by 1852. Indeed, convinced of Arnold's essentially historicist orientation, Culler treats "The Future" as a distill-
ation of Arnold's basic vision, its sequence of riverside settings
clearly analogous to what Culler had designated as the major regions of Arnold's myth, "the Forest Glade, the Burning or Darkling
Plain, and the Wide-Glimmering Sea." And the three distinctive regions that line the banks "of the river of Time" (3) are for Culler
similarly assimilable to what he regards as the organizing conceptual hypothesis of Arnold's poetry: "a threefold pattern of history
which arose from the alternation of vital or organic periods, which
are periods of faith and imagination, with mechanical or critical periods, which are periods of skepticism," with these alternating cy-
cles further broken down into the familiar "threefold cycle of thesis,
antithesis, and synthesis, repeating itself over and over again" (a
linking of Arnold to Hegel that can hardly be overlooked).[27]

Yet even in this presumably future-looking poem, Arnold's basically pessimistic predisposition seems to reassert itself at almost
every point along the way. Indeed, in the poem's first line, "A wan-

derer is man from his birth," Arnold preemptively asserts limits to historicism, making plain his sense of our homelessness in the history through which we wander and his doubts as to whether historical process really possesses the telic directedness usually associated with it in the nineteenth century. In the 1853 and 1854 editions of his poetry, Arnold reinforces that introductory disclaimer with a prefatory motto that even more explicitly and strikingly makes this same point, dropping the figure of the voyage for a metaphor that still more directly expresses the feelings of homelessness associated with life in the world: "For Nature hath long kept this inn, the Earth / And many a guest hath she therein received."[28]

Having inserted this apparent disclaimer, Arnold is free to take up the real business of "The Future," a highly condensed account of our basic human history from its imagined beginnings. What is undoubtedly most surprising about the phenomenal consciousness in "The Future" is just how environmentally conditioned the epistemological transaction that makes man a historical being is: "As is the world on the banks / So is the mind of man" (17–18), he tells us, pointedly restating a still-earlier assertion, "As what he sees is, so have his thoughts been" (7). This is not simply a case of the empiricist setting limits on human knowledge, insisting that all we can know must derive from objects and events perceived. Arnold's theory of knowledge is more skeptically restrictive than any simply "distinctly Lockean"[29] account of mind requires. The individuals of each separate historical epoch can know only the present, being effectively debarred from any substantial or significant memories of past events or any informed inferences about future possibilities: "But what was before we know not, / And we know not what shall succeed" (69–70).

Denied any meaningful access to the past (and still less to the future), Arnold's historically conditioned voyager can only

> Fable and dream
> Of the lands which the river of Time
> Had left ere he woke on its breast,
> Or shall reach when his eyes have been closed,

(20–23)

but he must do so "[v]ainly" (19), since

> Only the tracts where he sails
> He wots of; only the thoughts,
> Raised by the objects he passes, are his.

(24–26)

Thus, those special qualities we "fable and dream" the past did and the future might possess—their freshness, calm, and vigor—being unknowable are essentially irreplicable and, therefore, unavailable to the present generation, a loss that must increase our pain, intensify our sense of alienation and homelessness, make us grasp even more starkly our own insufficiencies.

Since Arnold has already told us in "The Future" that what the individual knows in journeying down "the river of Time" depends wholly on what he perceives on the shore directly opposite, any attempt to predict what our human future will be can only be wildly conjectural. Our natural tendency is simply to extrapolate from the present, to see the din and confusion of the cities of the plain that now make up the shoreline across from us becoming ever more oppressive as we journey down "the river of Time," believing

> That cities will crowd to its edge
> In a blacker, incessanter line;
> That the din will be more on its banks,
> Denser the trade on its stream,
> Flatter the plain where it flows,
> Fiercer the sun overhead.
>
> (60–65)

Yet the empirically skeptical limitations on knowledge that Arnold has posited, reiterated, and then underscored make it plain that his wasteland extrapolation from our present experience is neither a necessary nor even probable outcome of the continuation of the journey but a mere surmise, neither logically nor empirically more valid than any other. No less experientially plausible (especially to a resident of London) is what might be termed "the surmise of the estuary," the seemingly more hopeful supposition, introduced by a cautious "Haply" (71), that at the next stage in its movement "the river of Time" will leave the noise and confusion of its bordering cities behind it, becoming, as it approaches that point at which the river's currents and the sea's tides converge, "a wider, statelier stream" (74) and acquiring in its progress,

> if not the calm
> Of its early mountainous shore,
> Yet a solemn peace of its own.
>
> (75–77)

According to the surmise of the estuary, in the future that may await "man" the "wanderer," the waters that carry him may begin to supersede "the banks" that "fade dimmer away" as the principal object of his attention and source of his knowledge, relieving him of his recent distress and confusion, striking "[p]eace to the soul of the man on its breast" (82). Such a shift in the poem's basic figure indicates a corresponding shift in emphasis in the terms of the poem's implied philosophic dualism, that hypothesized future of man marking a turn that shall carry him away from the phenomenal, which until now has wholly claimed his attention, and toward that noumenal dwelling place where he most truly belongs. Of course, by that surmise Arnold effectively abandons that concern to which the historicist writer who ponders the future of humanity in the nineteenth century is usually drawn: concern about social conditions and how to improve them. Though he finds in the increasingly urbanized society of the present a life of din and confusion, his desired aim here is not to rectify but to escape it. But that to which he would escape, abandoning earthly life, is not the highly individuated stars of the heavens with their supposed affinities to the individual human consciousness but the undifferentiated waters of "the infinite sea" (87). This is, of course, journey's end for a "river of Time" that, unknown to the unattending consciousness, has secretly impelled humanity through the entire course of its journey through history.

In "The Future," then, the figure of the estuary enables Arnold to show how time-bound humanity, while still living out the last phase of its historical life, can nonetheless experience genuine metaphysical enlightenment, be made cognizant of the noumenal while still within the phenomenal. At this figurative last stage of the journey in time, not simply the future but a culmination and end, humanity will have arrived at that place where both orders converge, the place where "the river of Time" by being now "spotted with foam" (80) actually provides the observer and voyager with the first discernibly manifest signs of the "infinite sea" toward which that river has always flowed. Amidst "the hush" (78) of the river, which "may strike / Peace to the soul of the man on its breast" (82–83), only one sound is detected, "[m]urmurs . . . of the infinite sea" (87) that "the night-wind / Brings up the stream" (85–86). Neither the phonically particularized and differentiated sound of human language nor the sheer dissonance of the "din" (62) that emanates from the cities of the plain, "murmur" is a term frequently associated by Arnold with life's flow or its figurative movement of waters, charged for him with noumenal resonance, and thus most often heard in moments of enlightenment or even as a harbinger to remergence in the noumenally undifferentiated. Some examples: in "Resignation," the poet

who watches the "general life" (191) "unroll" before him, "[a]
placid and continuous whole" (189–90), at the same time can hear
in that unfolding whole "[t]he murmur of a thousand years" (188);
in "The Buried Life," at the time "[a] man becomes aware of his
life's flow" (88), he also "hears its winding murmur" (89); in "The
Youth of Man," the vital principle in Nature the poet calls on to re-
lieve the sorrow of the aged couple before him is addressed by a
sequence of increasingly exalted and implicitly noumenal references, the first of which points again to that wordless signifier that
stands as the conventional phonic sign of the Arnoldian noumenal:

> Murmur of living,
> Stir of existence,
> Soul of the world!
>
> (51–53)

To the "wanderer" who listens to the "[m]urmurs . . . of the infinite sea" he now approaches, the scene before him has not been
altogether divested of phenomenal hopes. Because "the banks fade
dimmer away," on which until now he "[r]ivets his gaze," he is able
to shift attention, to note that "the stars come out" (85), carrying
with them expectations of the imminent sighting of a glimmering
sea, for Arnold that imagined point of juncture in which the noumenal ground and the individuated life appear to demonstrate an essential commonality and, thus, an image that functions for Arnold
as a perennial catalyst to dreams of possibilities that might yet be
fulfilled within the parameters of phenomenal existence. But the
possibilities raised by that figure are invariably quickly dispelled,
seen through as illusion. And in "The Future," Arnold, in the pre-
figurative synopsis of human history of the second stanza, has already announced the destiny that awaits the individuated life when
it leaves river and bank behind it and enters finally on the waters
of what he ominously terms the "swallowing sea" (17). Immersion
in the deep, the incorporative "swallowing" of the life of consciousness within the antithetical element—this would seem to be the destiny that awaits not only the individual but humanity as a whole. If
the flow of "the river of Time" is determined by any immanent tele-
ology or eschatological goals, these are most certainly antithetically
conceived, the effects of metaphysical purposes sharply at variance
with human reason or desire and, by extension, at variance with the
wishes, interests, and needs of human society as a whole. Despite
the portent of promise that might be anticipated from its title, "The
Future," contrary to most critical speculation, does not "sound a

note of hope,"[30] provides no prospect of general social improvement that might rescue us from the sweltering cities of the plain. Confronting history, it chooses to retreat into the implicit hopelessness of a pessimistic metaphysics, providing us with simply another instance of Arnold's fundamental quarrel against life.

Only with "Stanzas from the Grande Chartreuse" and "The Scholar-Gipsy" is metaphysical pessimism finally supplanted as a primary explanatory concept and history at last truly foregrounded by Arnold. Occasionally figures and motifs from the poetry of pessimism resurface in these primarily historicist poems, but such figures and motifs seem largely vestigial and are quickly displaced by the governing arguments of these poems. In "Stanzas from the Grande Chartreuse," for example, the speaker at one point assumes one of the most familiar of Arnoldian roles, that of voyager upon a "sea of time" (122), which "round us raves" (125). At first glance, that raving sea may seem just another version of those earlier allegorized seas in the poetry in which human life has been carried on since time's beginning, that metaphysically real conceived by Arnold as cosmic nemesis, an antithetical element that at any moment may overwhelm the individual voyager.

But the figure is soon dropped, its usual metaphysical implications unpursued. In developing his essentially historicist argument, in "Stanzas from the Grande Chartreuse," Arnold does advert to this habitually recurrent figure but divests it of its earlier metaphysical significance, employing it instead as a convenient vehicle for representing the European wanderings in exile of his immediate Romantic predecessors: Byron, Shelley, and Obermann. Then, after serving this thematically limited purpose, the figure of the "sea of time" is set aside altogether for a newly constituted landlocked setting. This setting provides the poem's most enduring and defining image: not some "darkling plain" juxtaposed fearfully against an enticing but illusory "moonlit sea," but a sunlit landscape composed of a forest glade, a hunting lodge, and a road that carries men of action "[t]o life, to cities, and to war!" (180)—a landscape whose conceptual mapping-out seems perfectly suited to addressing the question of whether or not to plunge into historical time and embark upon a life that seems rich in possibilities

The core situation of "Stanzas from the Grande Chartreuse," like that in so many of Arnold's other poems, might loosely be thought of as a relationship of speaker to model. Again we have a low-pulsed meditative speaker whose identity is as yet unformed, and who, therefore, in his psychological dependency looks to others for guidance. Again, too, as the object of his meditation, we have a potentially exemplary figure or, in this case, figures, whose ways of life the speaker might wish to follow, though such longings, the Arnoldian speaker knows even as he articulates them, must be unavailing for reasons rooted deeply in their differing natures. In the earlier poems, the insurmountable barrier between speaker and model was epistemological, disparities in fundamental endowments of mind that render the intuitively gifted model and the individual of ordinary talents seemingly different in kind. But here the principal obstacle between the speaker and his prospective models is basically historical, a fundamental and determining difference in eras and epochs that renders it impossible for the individual of one age ever to assume the identity of the individual of another, however great their affinity of temperament. Sharing his own age's disbelief, Arnold's speaker can only second the world's judgment, albeit mournfully and reluctantly, that the faith on which the Carthusians' life choice is based is a mere anachronism, "a dead time's exploded dream" (98).

Moreover, within the major epochs themselves, we find similarly determining and dividing subcategories of historical periods that keep individuals of the present age irrevocably separated even from those who, broadly speaking, belong to the same epoch of doubt. Even the great Romantics—Byron, Shelley, and Obermann—though all doubters, are ruled out as possible objects of imitation for their Victorian successors, not because they are beings placed somehow transcendentally beyond our reach, like Shakespeare and Sophocles and the gipsy child, but because those of the Arnoldian present can never recover those historically originary moments of doubt and disorder and sorrow whose novelty and immediacy precipitated Romanticism's remarkable testimonials of outrage and denial and lamentation. Inured by the passage of time to the irremediableness of their post-Christian and post-Revolutionary situation, Arnold's "kings of modern thought" (116), intellectual counterparts in his own age to Byron, Shelley, and Obermann, have been reduced by their own historical moment to a fretful but mute acquiescence in the workings of history, seeking neither to arouse nor console their own contemporaries or the generations that might come after them against the depredations of the historically inevitable.

In having replaced a philosophy of metaphysical pessimism by a philosophy of history that places his own age at the nadir of a cycle of historical change, Arnold in "Stanzas from the Grande Chartreuse" appears to have done little by such an exchange to better his own unhappy circumstances or those of the humanity among whom he must live. Once again we are presented with an irresistible external causality to whose determining agency Arnold and his contemporaries, born too belatedly not only for any assumption of faith but even for any outcry against its loss, can only passively submit. In fact, in the most famous lines of "Stanzas from the Grande Chartreuse," just such a familiar sense of personal impotence and victimization by forces beyond his control is explicitly stipulated to be the inescapable consequence of the cyclical movement of the historical process as it works its way through Arnold's own age:

> Wandering between two worlds, one dead,
> The other powerless to be born,
> With nowhere yet to rest my head,
> Like these, on earth I wait forlorn.

> (85–88)

History is not something made by humanity, the sum of our human actions, but a clearly hypostatized entity, proceeding by its own intrinsic laws so that all broad historical change, and especially the coming into being of a new world to replace the lost world of departed faith, is understood as a self-engendering activity of the hypostatized historical process itself. For the humanity forced to live in this interval between worlds, before the new is gestated, there is only estrangement, insecurity, helplessness, the anxiety of separation from a regressively sought-after object of infantile trust.

But this austere and implicitly inhumane account of a fundamentally deterministic historical process is not the only conception of history posited by Arnold in "Stanzas from the Grande Chartreuse." Later in the poem, imagining the coming into being of the desired future, Arnold somewhat tentatively prophesies:

> Years hence, perhaps, may dawn an age,
> More fortunate, alas, than we,
> Which without hardness will be sage,
> And gay without frivolity.

> (157–60)

Such change for the better, such progress, the emergence of a world roughly comparable in wisdom and joy to the world we have lost, is unquestionably conceived of as a product of human agency, its coming to be possibly hastened by the actions of humanity as it is now or, at least, of those men whom Arnold labels "Sons of the World" and implores to "speed those years" (161). Yet the speaker is careful to set himself apart from those "Sons of the World," treating their efforts and accomplishments with the fastidious irony of one obviously their superior in sensitivity. Turning to those he had earlier charged with hardness—with having callously derided not only the faith of the Carthusians but his own poet's tears—Arnold, while sardonically avowing his admiration for the "Sons of the World," makes it clear that the world apparently waiting to be born, that presumably secularized equivalent of a vanished age of faith, is one that he almost certainly would not wish to enter, at least if the coarseness of those to whom the task of bringing that future into being has been delegated is any harbinger of things:

> We admire with awe
> The exulting thunder of your race;
> You give the universe your law,
> You triumph over time and space!
> Your pride of life, your tireless powers,
> We laud them, but they are not ours.
>
> (163–68)

Why the pride and power of those who now rule over and will eventually transform the world should be finally undesired is presumably to be explained by the troubling coda with which "Stanzas from the Grande Chartreuse" concludes, a relatively detailed mini-allegory whose transformations of time, place, and character produce more problematizing complications than clarifications or answers. With that allegory we are conveyed from the intellectual and cultural disturbances of the mid-nineteenth century to a medieval world in which neither the monks of the Grande Chartreuse nor the spiritually reclusive poet who visits them are to be judged either anomalous or anachronistic because they abjure the world. To that end, the monastery on the heights itself is transformed into an "old-world abbey" (170) recessively cloistered in the "greenwood," one of those locales designated by Culler as a shaded grove and shown to be especially congenial to Arnold in his self-conception as poet,[31] while Arnold and those he claims to speak for are converted into children who dwell nearby.

Moreover, monk and poet are not the only ones rendered less beleaguered and fretful by this softening medievalizing process; their principal antagonists and critics are correspondingly rendered less strident and less trifling, too. Where Arnold in his sour ruminations on the modern pursuit of pleasure had found only frivolity, the empty enjoyments of "[t]he eternal trifler" (155), he now grants an indisputable attractiveness to the spectacle presented by their

medieval counterparts, hunters and "[g]ay dames" (185), their
presence disclosed by "[l]aughter and cries" (186) and a "bugle-
music" (189) that arrestingly woos Arnold's shyly reclusive audi-
tors "with a charmed surprise" (190). Those who carry out the business of the world, the pursuers of worldly power who have been
castigated by the speaker for vanity and insensitivity and hardness
during almost the whole length of the poem, are similarly rendered
far more appealing by Arnold's allegorical turn. Their lives of narrow, bourgeois ambitiousness are transformed by the sensitive poet
into a second enticing spectacle of glittering pageantry and chival-
ric endeavor:

> Of passing troops in the sun's beam—
> Pennon, and plume, and passing lance!
> Forth to the world these soldiers fare,
> To life, to cities, and to war!
>
> (177–80)

Of all these changes, the most surprising and inexplicable in this
supposedly elaborating coda is the transformation of the speaker
himself and that "we" he puts forward as his spiritual kindred (an
elite coterie of similarly sensitive souls that must tacitly include the
reader); for in the course of the poem, they are regressively transformed from intellectually fully formed adults—men of sound judgment who have been successfully persuaded by the reasonings of
"rigorous teachers" (67) of the errors of an "exploded" faith—into
beings who are "like children" (167) "reared" not in the secular city
by "rigorous teachers" for the intellectual combat of the nineteenth
century but

> in shade
> Beneath some old-world abbey wall,
> Forgotten in a forest-glade,
> And secret from the eyes of all.
>
> (169–72)

Moreover, as they now are, so shall they apparently always remain,
children dwelling in proximity to and maintaining an innate sympathy with the poem's monastic fellowship, but living out their lives as
something considerably less than sworn and intellectually committed members of any religious order.

Even in the first of his major historicizing poems, "Stanzas in
Memory of the Author of 'Obermann,'" Arnold had already be-
trayed ambivalence toward any wholehearted yielding to the zeit-

geist, qualifying his decision to live in the world by declaring that at
some spiritually privileged level both he and Obermann were "Children of the Second Birth," inviolate and innocent and thus pro-
tected against the dangers of worldly contamination. But in
"Stanzas from the Grande Chartreuse," where Arnold knows he
must forsake his sympathetic attachment to the Carthusians,
"[l]ast of the people who believe" (112), if he is to help "speed" the
dawning of "an age, / More fortunate," he backs away altogether
from his obligations to society and history, retreating instead to
childhood through the most immobilizingly regressive of strategies.
Though powerfully wooed by "banners flashing," which "[m]ake
their blood dance and chain their eyes" (187–88), and by "bugle-
music on their breeze," which "[a]rrests them with a charmed surprise" (189–90), Arnold's cloistered children respond to these undeniably inviting summonses to join the world with a refusal based on
an apparently constitutional belatedness:

>   too late ye come!
> Too late for us your call ye blow,
> Whose bent was taken long ago.

(196–98)

That at the time of his visit to the Grande Chartreuse Arnold
should imagine himself resisting these glamorized allurements of
"[a]ction and pleasure" is not at all surprising. If we think of them
translated into their conventional nineteenth-century equivalents,
love and work (for Freud the principal means by which humanity
attains whatever modicum of happiness is available to it), these ostensible goods are exactly what Arnold realized was the life that
awaited him after his night's stay at the Grande Chartreuse. As
Honan tells us, Arnold had timed a long-wished-for visit to the monastery at the Grande Chartreuse to coincide with his honeymoon
tour of Europe. But the rules of the monastery stipulated a rigid
segregation of the sexes during any overnight stay, so that the recent bridegroom had to spend a honeymoon night away from his
bride in order to satisfy his curiosity by observing the rituals of the
Carthusians at first hand. While she was left alone in "a small
house" just outside the monastery, Matthew was given "a cell to
sleep in" and allowed to hear "midnight mass."[32] Neither the presence of his bride during his ascent to the monastery nor her absence during his actual visit there is really alluded to by Arnold; yet
the very omission of the woman he has just married from a poem
that closes with a retreat by the speaker into a fantasy of eternal

childhood suggests that his night alone at the Grande Chartreuse
provided Arnold with a sort of psychological moratorium, breathing
room before renewal tomorrow of the demands of marriage, with
its obligatory pleasures, and the commencement little more than a
month later of the long hours and inevitable drudgery of the post
of inspector of schools, which influential friends had obtained for
him.[33]

That Arnold should first romanticize what he would renounce,
"action" and "pleasure," is an obvious and striking clue to his profound ambivalence toward that life he had chosen. For all the attractiveness of the "[a]ction and pleasure" that woo him, he does
reject them in fantasy, finally and fully, declaring himself unsuited
by nature to embark upon either, too compulsively fixated upon the
cloistered security of childhood to live otherwise. But the strength
with which Arnold resists that call from the world and regressively
clings to an imagined childhood suggests that the source of his anxiety may not only be adult uncertainties about marriage and career
but also dimly glimpsed childhood conflicts of the utmost distress-
fulness. One can certainly envision Thomas Arnold, certainly as we
have seen him through his son's eyes in "Resignation," urging his
children to go forth like "soldiers" "[t]o life, to cities, and to war";
but against that paternally imposed obligation to choose, like his
father before him, a socially sanctioned love in marriage and an ethically strenuous work, there was surely posed a competing desire
to remain safely lodged within the protective confines of a maternal
security and trust. That the speaker as child feels his "blood dance"
at the sight of the world's banners is perhaps our most reliable
index to the depths of ambivalence he feels toward that call from a
father whose own life in the world was so highly prized and with
whom the son must surely have often identified. But it is a call that,
however enticing, must be refused, a refusal, he adds, not of his own
making but predetermined and long ordained.

We do know that after staying overnight at the Grande Chartreuse Arnold really did return to life in the world, to marriage and
to work. We may reasonably infer though that the fantasy of childhood recaptured that concludes the poem provides a doubtlessly
wishful scenario in which Arnold can forsake those obligations,
compelled by the intractable dictates of his nature to remain within
the abbey and its religious life. Yet the role he assigns himself as
perennial child can only mean that he is to be always among but
never of that imagined abbey's order, a perpetual acolyte, perhaps,
but never the priest or monk who has made his professions and
taken his vows. Indeed, his presence within the boundaries of the

religious life has been regressively determined by a "bent" that "was taken long ago," and though he shall watch "yellow tapers" (200) that are "[e]mblems of hope over the grave" (201) and listen to organ tones with their "accents of another sphere" (201), he is effectively debarred by his self-assigned status as child from ever rationally assenting to the hopes and dogmas that these sights and sounds signify.

Of course, long before his visit "[t]o the Carthusian's world-famed home" (30), the speaker tells us that "rigorous teachers" had "seized my youth, / And purged its faith, and trimmed its fire" (67–68), bidding him aspire to the "high white star of Truth." To be sure, that regressively determined turn to a reconstituted childhood in the abbey in the "forest-glade" would appear an attempt to undo the spiritually and psychologically withering effects of those rigorous teachings by restoring the speaker to a childhood ease he knew before the purgation of his faith and the trimming of his fire. Still, by remaining a child, he never actually reneges upon the consent he gave to the truths taught him by his "masters of the mind" (73), never really becomes a Newmanite, even in imagination. Undoubtedly, one reason for withholding assent from the creed of the Carthusians is that looming behind his nameless "masters" is once again almost certainly the figure of the poet's famous father, Thomas Arnold, a severe critic of Catholic tendencies in the English church, someone who would hardly have reacted to the defection of Newman and his followers to Rome with anything less than consternation and condemnation. So for his son to journey to a monastery and seemingly cast his lot with Newman—if only in fantasy—would imply a greater break with his father's remembered authority than Arnold is willing to risk.

But probably the most psychologically persuasive explanation of that strangely inconclusive gesture of religious commitment with which "Stanzas from the Grande Chartreuse" concludes is to be found not in these foregrounded nineteenth-century religious disputes but within the conflicted structure of recollected family relationships. In fantasizing himself a child living within the sanctuary of a romantically medievalized religious life, Arnold seems less interested in overturning the teachings of those "masters of mind" who had "purged" his youthful "faith" than in satisfying a nostalgic longing to return to a time before paternal authority had inculcated itself, when religious belief was part of that cluster of values associated with the maternal presence. At this remarkable moment—a honeymoon night not spent with his bride but in the monastery of the Grande Chartreuse—Arnold's wish is not to challenge the paternal authority to which he had in youth acceded but rather to leap across time and thus annul that intellectually decisive moment when, by the purging of his faith, he in essence identified with the father. He would regressively restore himself to a time before any responsibilities or demands were imposed upon him, when to be cared for and loved he needed to be neither a liberal in religion nor a worker nor a husband, the roles assigned him by those overseeing masters formed in his father's image.

So at this moment of crisis, which registers itself by a sense of infantile helplessness, it is not surprising that the adult Arnold, finding "nowhere yet to rest my head," should seek refuge against present ills by retreating to a time of imagined innocence and simplicity within the sheltering protectiveness of a mother's undemanding and unquestioning love, an innocence somehow associated with the monastic life, "Forgotten in a forest-glade, / And secret from the life of all" (171–72). What had precipitated this sense of crisis was a visit to a monastery that had indeed raised the spirit of the dead and perhaps temporarily forgotten father as a supervising and disapproving presence, ready to warn the young poet against any backsliding from those austerely rationalistic lessons that had "purged" his "faith." Further, it is almost inevitable, psychologically, that such a fantasized denial of a father's authority should call up his love for his mother (herself the daughter of a clergyman and more conventionally religious during marriage than her notoriously doubting husband) and that Arnold should imagine himself remaining true to her and her faith by living out his life within an abbey's walls, possessed of an innocent and unthinking childhood piety, a faith unpurged that a mother's affection had inculcated. Such a fantasized regressive turn, moreover, provides another psychologically compensatory gain in that the sexual obligations that marriage now imposed and that threateningly impinged upon the idealized image of the mother might be similarly wished away by that imagined reversion to an innocent childhood purity apparently to be sustained permanently by a something akin to a subsequent life of monastic celibacy.

Like "Stanzas in Memory of the Author of 'Obermann,' " "Stanzas from the Grande Chartreuse" may be thought of as the record of an event crucial in Arnold's turning from an unsparingly bleak metaphysical pessimism to a modestly optimistic historicism, a coming to terms with the spirit of the age. But in this latter case we have not even the qualified and faltering step forward of the poem addressed to Obermann but an apparent step backward, a refusal to play the assigned part in the making of the future for implicitly psychological reasons that may be much the same as those that led him to adopt metaphysical pessimism as the intellectual premise of his poetry in the first place. Thrust into life and the world by the interrelated social necessities of marriage and work, Arnold, at least in imagination, poetically recoiled from what was required and sought release in a more benign version of those regressive fantasies that had earlier urged him to seek release from life's demands by drawing "homewards to the general life" ("Resignation," 252). Such depth of refusal, as we know from his subsequent writings over a long and productive lifetime, was only temporary, and yet its presence in "Stanzas from the Grande Chartreuse" indicates how profoundly Arnold resisted the call of life, even after he had ostensibly demonstrated a willingness to play the part assigned him by his station and his heritage, committing himself intellectually to the possibility of historical progress, as his father had before him, and choosing like his father to marry and to work, in short, to live in the world.[34]

Like "Stanzas from the Grande Chartreuse," "The Scholar-Gipsy" is a poem whose fundamental conceptual premise is also a cyclically conceived historicism. Its speaker, too, finds himself in the bottoming-out of a historical cycle and thus in the spiritually melancholy circumstances of being "between two worlds," each implicitly superior to the present but sadly unattainable, "one dead, / The other powerless to be born" (85–86). As we know from Arnold's subsequent prose, the mid-seventeenth century is the appropriate starting point for our historical epoch of cyclical decline and, therefore, an especially fortuitous moment for just such a flight from the prevailing culture as (we are told by Joseph Glanvill in the poem's source, *The Vanity of Dogmatizing*) the scholar-gipsy has chosen. It was then that Renaissance Hellenism, with its free play of intellect and spontaneity of consciousness, its clarity of wit and gaiety of life, received a seemingly fatal check in England from the Hebraizing spirit of Puritanism; and an essentially Protestant Philistinism, with its twin impulses (as we have learned from Max Weber and R. H. Tawney) toward strictness of conscience and the making of money, began to dominate English life, so that one who was born when "life ran gaily as the sparkling Thames" (202), and who had become "tired of knocking at preferment's door" (35), might well have chosen to leave behind him a society that was both Protestant and acquisitive.

Moreover, and perhaps even more germane to Arnold's point in "The Scholar-Gipsy," at the same historical moment a scientifically grounded skepticism had begun to put in question the supernatural tenets of a Christianity that even in the early phases of the Renaissance served as the basis for much of the seeming cohesiveness of European culture. Apparently foreseeing that these culturally dispiriting changes would produce, on the one hand, a socially stultifying Protestant Philistinism and, on the other, the scientifically generated "languid doubt" (164) that would typify the intellectual life of modernity, the young Oxford scholar (at least as Arnold imagined him) had chosen to opt out of this unhappy, between-worlds span of history and hold himself in readiness for the advent of a happier age waiting to be born.

Arnold tells us very little about what that better world waiting to be born will be like, but, as with any cyclically conceived historicism, it will apparently come about not through any merely contingent human endeavor but by the workings of some immanent necessity, inexorable historical laws that no individual or individuals can hasten, impede, or alter. The triggering signal for this upward turn of the historical cycle shall be the "fall" of a "spark from heaven" (171), a heralding event performing the same kind of annunciatory function in "The Scholar-Gipsy" as the birth of a god does in two-thousand-year reversals of the Yeatsian gyre. Yet human agency does apparently collaborate in this Arnoldian schema of change, with the scholar-gipsy himself assigned a leading role in the working-out of this historically transformative process. When the "heaven-sent moments" (50) do come, he "will to the world impart" (49) arts he has learned from the gipsies, presumably indispensable to humanity's long-awaited betterment but which until now had remained a closely guarded secret, supposedly possessed by the gipsies alone, who are apparently under no like obligation to disseminate it to humanity at large.

From Arnold's earliest considerations of the scholar-gipsy as a subject for poetry, the special and secret art he had acquired from the gipsies—hypnotism or mesmerism as the Victorians termed it—had been a principal reason for the poet's interest in the little-known tale from Glanvill. Indeed, as a notebook entry of 1848 tells us, the title originally contemplated by Arnold for a poem on the scholar-gipsy was the "The first mesmerist."[35] Taken literally, the scholar-gipsy's explanation of what he will do with "the secret of" the gipsy's "art" (48)—that is, mesmerism—at that critical juncture when the new world stands on the verge of being born, is that he will "impart" it "to the world" (49), transmit the secret of the gipsies to everyone, thus making all humans mesmerists. But since the end of mesmerism for those possessed of such powers is "to rule as they

desired / The workings of men's brains" (45–46) so that "they can
bind them to what thoughts they will" (47), it is more likely that it
is submission to rather than the acquisition of such powers by the
generality of mankind that is to be culturally transforming. To have
all humans mesmerized rather than all humans mesmerists—
figuratively speaking—seems the goal implicit in this admittedly im-
precise formulation of that better future called into being by the fall
of "the spark from heaven" (171).

Since Glanvill himself attributes the hypnotic wonders performed
by the gipsies to "the power of imagination,"[36] it seems reasonable,
following Culler, to read the story of the scholar-gipsy, as Arnold
retells it, as "a myth of the Romantic imagination."[37] We may further infer that the cultural function Arnold speculatively contemplated for the mesmerizing imagination at that momentous point at
which the historical cycle begins its upward turn is probably much
like that high destiny he will later assign to poetry itself in "The
Study of Poetry": that is, at a date not far in the future, "most of
what now passes with us for religion and philosophy will be replaced by poetry itself," which will be then employed "to interpret
life for us, to console us, to sustain us" (*CPW*, 9:161) as religion and
philosophy had once done. Certain that the metaphysical explanations of Christianity had been exploded once and for all by the
scientific rationalism and philosophic skepticism of the Enlightenment, and yet hopeful (as many nineteenth-century historicists
were) that the unity of culture that Christianity had once fostered
could be reconstituted under secular auspices, Arnold saw in a
poetry more generally disseminated to a better educated public a
vehicle for restoring a cultural and spiritual cohesiveness now lost.
In "The Scholar-Gipsy," too, these later conclusions are already intimated: when "the spark from heaven" (171) falls, signaling the
emergence of a new epoch, the human community shall find its
"thoughts" again bound into cohesiveness, this time by succumbing
to the mesmerizing powers acquired by the scholar-gipsy, which
themselves symbolically represent those powers widely ascribed in
the nineteenth century to the poetic imagination, especially given
its axiomatically assumed mythopoeic capabilities.

Commentators have often noted the strong resemblance of "The
Scholar-Gipsy" to the great odes of Keats, especially "Ode to a
Nightingale,"[38] through Arnold's imitation of both the meter and
stanzaic form of the odes along with an atypical lushness of natural
description, a trait usually associated with Keats. But the most interesting of Arnold's borrowings is his appropriation of the highly
distinctive dramatic design of the odes, where the desiring self

imaginatively reaches out toward empathic communion with some implicitly sacralized symbolic object, a nightingale or a Grecian urn, only to be ultimately thwarted because the imagination has ascribed to these objects attributes and powers that cannot be empirically justified or because it has wildly overestimated its own powers.[39] Thus at poem's end the desiring speaker is essentially returned to the "sole self," wiser perhaps but immeasurably more "forlorn," though the interrogatory possibilities raised in the closing lines of "Ode to a Nightingale" and the ventriloquistic conclusion to "Ode on a Grecian Urn" leave the reader with the slenderest of hopes that things may be otherwise. For the first half of "The Scholar-Gipsy," Arnold's argument follows a roughly Keatsian trajectory. Having invested the scholar-gipsy with special mesmerizing powers of inestimable future usefulness, the speaker, anxious to claim these benefits for himself and his age, embarks on an imagined pursuit that culminates with surprising ease in his astonishingly improbable claim that "once, in winter" (121) he had actually seen the scholar-gipsy on a "wooden bridge" (123) near Oxford, an encounter plainly analogous to the empathic union that is the comparable goal of the desiring self in the odes of Keats. But here, too, the empathic trajectory concludes in the imagination's defeat, vanquished by the brute fact of man's mortality, a limited life span which renders any sighting of the scholar-gipsy utterly impossible because "[t]wo hundred years are flown / Since first thy story rang through Oxford halls" (131–32).

Yet in the end Arnold drastically reverses this seemingly common-sense conclusion and, going far beyond the problematic but tentatively hopeful closings of the great odes, simply flies in the face of the seeming fact of human finitude, declaring that the scholar-gipsy has "not felt the lapse of hours" (141) like the rest of us but rather possesses "an immortal lot" (157). Because he has never died but presumably shall live forever, he could have been seen not many winters past and perhaps will be seen again by the speaker and that modernity he represents. Still it is a strange and ultimately inconsequential immortality that emerges from "The Scholar-Gipsy," and no critic and perhaps no reader has probably ever taken its argument for immortality very seriously.[40] Surely none of us reads "The Scholar-Gipsy" as we read *In Memoriam* or "Cleon," where the claim that the soul of Hallam now lives or the intimation that the spirits of Cleon and Protos might continue to exist even after their deaths through the saving grace of Christ is implicitly understood as crucial evidence for a larger claim that the human soul survives beyond the grave. Nor does Arnold even go as

far as Keats, who, by leaving open the possibility that the nightingale might be an "Immortal Bird" or the Grecian urn (and possibly
the individuals depicted there) might endure forever, plainly teases
us toward speculation on the analogous possibility of a life for us
after death.[41]

But in "The Scholar-Gipsy," the prospect of immortality is clearly
confined to the scholar-gipsy himself. His "immortal lot" is not by
inference our immortal lot but an apparently unique exemption
from general laws that dictate our mortality. "The generations of
thy peers" (135), men also "born in days when wits were fresh and
clear / And life ran gaily as the sparkling Thames" (201–2), have
been granted no such exemption and are, as Arnold delicately puts
it, "fled" (136), gone to the grave and that death which presumably
is extinction. Then alluding to his own generation, Arnold ominously notes that their fate shall be our fate: "[We] ourselves shall
go" (156).

The significance of this extravagantly asserted claim of immortality derives, I would suggest, not from its applicability to the religious problem of the life hereafter but from its usefulness as a
vehicle for carrying forward Arnold's argument about history. In insisting that the scholar-gipsy has remained alive though "[t]wo hundred years are flown" (131), Arnold grants him not eternal life but
a longevity sufficient to bridge the positive phases in the cyclical
movement of the historical process. To achieve that narrower and
implicitly fictive end of establishing the scholar-gipsy's exceptional
longevity, Arnold does not feel that he needs anything like the complexly elaborated evolutionary arguments of Tennyson in "In Memoriam" nor even the scriptural authority that Browning calls upon
in "Cleon." Instead he offers a literary precedent of incontestable
greatness, Keats's odes, which recollected by Arnold's reader might
at least promote a suspension of disbelief and an act of poetic faith
that would allow him to accept at something like face value Arnold's
virtually unargued analogous claim that the scholar-gipsy, like the
nightingale of Keats, was "not born for death" ("Ode to a Nightingale," 61) but, possessing an "immortal lot" (157), remains "exempt
from age / And living as thou liv'st on Glanvill's page" (158–59).

But there is a more pertinent reason for Arnold's connecting the
matter of "The Scholar-Gipsy" with the figure and poetry of Keats.
As Culler has shown, the scholar-gipsy displays symbolic affinities
with other representatives of a recurrent Arnoldian type, especially
figures like Callicles and the strayed reveller (Culler's general term
for this type).[42] While Arnold's strayed revellers can usually be identified by their symbolic locale (the shaded grove) and by a disposi-

tion toward solitude, two of them, Callicles and the strayed reveller himself, are poets who sing songs or recite poems of a very special character. Unlike Sophocles and Shakespeare, poets who are sages, the strayed reveller as poet is essentially a celebrator of natural magic and concomitantly a purveyor of myth, a teller of quasi-religious tales designed to render human existence with all of its enigma and pain somehow intelligible, if possible bearable, and, at rare moments perhaps, even pleasurable, as it would seem to have become in the orgiastic bacchic celebrations with which "The Strayed Reveller" concludes.

Of the poets who meant most to Arnold, Keats was the one most closely associated with natural magic and the mythmaking imagination, thus with the poet as strayed reveller. (Even before Culler proposed his dramatis personae of basic Arnoldian types, Leon Gottfried in *Matthew Arnold and the Romantics* had entitled his chapter on Keats and Arnold "The Strayed Reveller: Keats.")[43] Admittedly, in his 1853 preface Arnold does single out Keats's *Isabella, or the Pot of Basil* as a bad example, an instance of the harmful influence of Shakespeare, which had led modern poetry to misguidedly emphasize felicity of expression and no less misguidedly disregard "*Archetectonicè* in the highest sense, that power of execution, which creates, forms, constitutes" (*CPW*, 1:9). But as the homage that is imitation in "The Scholar-Gipsy" clearly shows, by 1853 Arnold almost certainly had already recognized that quality in Keats on which he would base his 1880 encomium: "that in one of the two great modes by which poetry interprets, in the faculty of naturalistic interpretation, in what we call natural magic, he ranks with Shakespeare" (*CPW*, 9:214).[44]

Magic, indeed natural magic, its possession by those most profoundly in contact with the natural order, the gipsies, whose mesmerism can control "[t]he workings of men's brains" and ultimately "bind them to what thoughts they will"; its acquisition by the Oxford scholar who would apparently keep it wholly to himself until he could direct it to socially useful ends; and finally its projected deployment by him at a propitious and seemingly sanctified moment to achieve a new cultural cohesiveness: these in a sense constitute the principal conceptual action in "The Scholar-Gipsy." Furthermore, just as the scholar-gipsy possesses certain discernible affinities with Keats, so too, as I have already suggested, does the magic the scholar-gipsy has acquired bear a certain obvious likeness to the poetic imagination at its most magical, as it manifests itself in poems like those in which Keats himself most brilliantly employed it. Carrying this analogy a step further, I would maintain too that just as the magic of mesmerism will be imparted by the scholar-gipsy "to the world" (49) at a moment designated by heaven for its deployment, so too, at a similarly fated moment, will the signified counterpart to his gipsy magic, the poet's power of imagination, be similarly deployed to bind men to the poet's imaginative will and bring humankind into the new cultural and spiritual cohesiveness of that coming epoch whose unifying agency shall be not religion but poetry.

It is to keep imagination inviolate, to preserve intact those powers handed down from the past for their designated employment in that culturally transformative "project" that in his closely guarded solitude he "nurses in unclouded joy" (199), that the scholar-gipsy has chosen to lead a life apart and flee those who would seek to persuade him to exercise his powers prematurely, before the arrival of the "heaven-sent moments" when the secrets of his art are to be imparted. From the very first, the scholar-gipsy would seem to have adopted the artist's self-alienating strategy of "silence, exile, and cunning" as his way of guarding his special and ultimately indispensable powers. With the least sophisticated, those closest in their relationship with nature to the gipsies, he may maintain a certain contact: with the housewife who quietly darns "[a]t some lone homestead in the Cumner hills" (101) or the "[c]hildren, who early range these slopes / And late for cresses from the rills" (105–6), and hand flowers to "[m]aidens, who from distant hamlets come / To dance around the Fyfield elm in May" (82–83). But even then, the scholar-gipsy keeps essentially to himself, remaining "pensive and tongue-tied" (54). When those he encounters might upset that equanimity, draw him away from his chosen pensiveness and silence, whether they are noisy shepherds at some lonely country alehouse or "Oxford riders blithe" (72), his strategy is already one that shall become even more pronounced in the poem's second half, flight into a still deeper solitude.

In fact, in the poem's second half, the scholar-gipsy is never again seen with another person but is either depicted in solitary flight or encouraged to continue so; hence David Riede suggests that we look upon the second part of "The Scholar-Gipsy" as a "misreading"[45] of the first part, by which the scholar-gipsy is arbitrarily transformed from "happy wanderer" to "zealous quester." What is most remarkable, though, about the second half of "The Scholar-Gipsy" is that after the poem's great reversal—the denial and then reassertion of the scholar-gipsy's immortality—it is the speaker himself, whose earlier ruminations were only intended to pass the time until nightfall when he could "again begin the quest," who most strenuously

exhorts the scholar-gipsy to a flight that must leave the goals of the
speaker's quest unattained if its object were to heed his counsel.
For success in overtaking the scholar-gipsy would mean not the im-
parting of a special wisdom by that exemplary figure to his would-
be disciple but the destruction of that wisdom before its possessor
could fulfill the special purpose of his mission to the future. For the
scholar-gipsy personally, success in the quest would mean exposure to the fatal contagion of modernity—its feverishness and,
above all, "the infection of our mental strife" (222)—endangering
one who up to this time had remained free of that contagion by living (at least for the duration of the modern period) within a natural
order that seemingly stands outside the historical process altogether. While the speaker may be compelled by his own historical
predicament to persist in his quest after the scholar-gipsy, he
knows that the least he can do if he is truly concerned with the
scholar-gipsy's well-being is to warn him away, implore him to "fly
our paths, our feverish contact fly!" (221). Furthermore, if it should
happen that the scholar-gipsy were unlucky enough to come within
sight of his ardent pursuers, he is, nonetheless, still urged to remain
"[a]verse" (208), to "[w]ave us away, and keep thy solitude!" (210)
because contact would mean transmission of that endemic and inevitably fatal ailment, "this strange disease of modern life," with the
result that "then thy glad perennial youth would fade, / Fade, and
grow old at last, and die like ours" (229–30).

   At this point, we might usefully reconsider our governing analogy
that connects "The Scholar-Gipsy," its titular figure, and his mesmerizing magic with Keats and poetry and the poetic imagination.
In carrying that analogy to its logical conclusion, we would undoubtedly wish to argue that just as success by the speaker in his
quest, the overtaking of the scholar-gipsy and appropriation of his
powers, would fatally impair the efficacy of those magical powers
whose proper application is to make the world now waiting to be
born as healthy and whole as that better world that existed prior to
modernity, so too would the allegorically comparable pursuit of
poetry by the modern poet (and most especially by Arnold himself)
similarly impair the analogously magical powers of the poetic imagination and prevent it from realizing the high destiny that awaits it
in that better future which it will help to bring about. In fact, a danger very much like this would seem to have been on Arnold's mind
in the preface to the *Poems* of 1853, an essay probably written in
the same year as "The Scholar-Gipsy." For in the closing paragraphs of that essay, he explains that his purpose in commending
the ancients as the best model for the modern poet is not so that the

modern poet may equal them in excellence but that he may do as little harm as possible to the art with which he has, for so brief a time, been entrusted before he must turn it over to those generations that will succeed his.

Not the advancement of poetry but its transmission undamaged and intact is thus the most satisfactory outcome Arnold can foresee for the poets of his own age (doubtlessly including himself), those who because of their historical situation, "these damned times" (*Letters*, 1:156), can never become more than dilettanti. Appealing to Goethe as the final authority on modernism, Arnold writes:

> Two kinds of dilettanti, says Goethe, there are in poetry; he who neglects the indispensable mechanical part, and thinks he has done enough if he shows spirituality and feeling; and he who seeks to arrive at poetry merely by mechanism, in which he can acquire an artisan's readiness, and is without soul and matter. And he adds, the first does the most harm to art, and the last to himself. (*CPW*, 1:15)

For Arnold, that the poets of his time, living as they do in "an age wanting in moral grandeur" (*CPW*, 1:14) and amid "bewildering confusion" (*CPW*, 1:14), cannot be anything other than dilettanti seems indisputable; and therefore their only real choice—that is, which kind of dilettanti they are to become—should be decided not by their own private desires or interests but by what Arnold takes to be their larger obligations to their art and to that posterity who shall be its future practitioners and beneficiaries:

> If we must be dilettanti: if it is impossible for us, under the circumstances amidst which we live, to think clearly, to feel nobly, and to delineate firmly; if we cannot attain to the mastery of the great artists—let us, at least, have so much respect for our art as to prefer it to ourselves. Let us not bewilder our successors; let us transmit to them the practice of poetry, with its boundaries and wholesome regulative laws, under which excellent works may again, perhaps, at some future time, be produced, not yet fallen into oblivion through our neglect, not yet condemned and cancelled by the influence of their eternal enemy, caprice. (*CPW*, 1:15)

Reading these cautionary instructions to modern poets back into the figurative argument of "The Scholar-Gipsy" requires surprisingly little modification. The speaker himself provides a self-rebuking admission of what must be judged his own dilettantism, of his having been condemned by "the circumstances amidst which we live" to that waywardness and "caprice" inherent in a modernity in which "each strives, nor knows for what he strives, / And each half-lives a hundred different lives" (168–69). Though doubtlessly inclined to aspire to the "spirituality and feeling" the scholar-gipsy apparently enjoys, the speaker understands that his own obligation to the future mandates restraint, compels him to sound the warning signal, urge the object of his pursuit to speedier flight, more cunning evasions. Here too we sense a fear that the good that the scholar-gipsy is to disseminate when the time is ripe will be fatally impaired if he should unluckily come into contact with any of those unhappily condemned by the circumstances of history to an age to which moral grandeur has been denied. To take the final leap, we may say that "The Scholar-Gipsy" itself may be read as a set of self-constraining instructions to poets lest they spoil the future, the upward phase of the historical cycle, and, more poignantly, it may be read as a set of self-constraining instructions that Arnold, engaged "in the dialogue of the mind with itself" (*CPW*, 1:1), addresses to himself as well, instructions that seem to have taken hold in that petering-out of Arnold as modern poet in the years after the writing of "The Scholar-Gipsy." Indeed, what Arnold as poet and the poets of his own poetically ill-starred age have been entrusted to do, according to the preface of 1853, is ensure that no harm befalls poetry in their own unpoetical age, that what has been handed on to them from a more inspiriting and morally superior past will be passed on intact—uncontaminated by the modern poet's own hunger for "spirituality and feeling"—to that more inspiriting and morally superior future that poetry shall help bring into being. Yet it is clear from "The Scholar-Gipsy" that, if these modern poets (and especially Arnold himself) do persist in pursuing their vocation, the probable outcome will be not just failure in their obligation to the future but the very ruin of its hopes.

But to account for a disease so contagious and virulent that contact with those who carry it must undo the course of historical necessity and prevent the poetry and society of the future from coming into being, the reader conditioned by the personal and private melancholy of Arnold's earlier poetry is probably best advised to seek the ultimate source of that disease not in history per se but in deeper and more primal longings, in the latent psychological conflicts and anxieties that determine so much of the manifest content of Arnold's poetry prior to 1853. If we do so seek what we shall doubtlessly find is that in "The Scholar-Gipsy," just as in earlier poems, that latently determining psychological matter would seem to lie closest to the surface of consciousness in just such troublingly

unassimilable materials as the two notoriously perplexing similes
with which "The Scholar-Gipsy" closes.

In the first of these, the scholar-gipsy is implored to turn away
from his pursuers as absolutely as Virgil's Dido in Hades had
turned away from Aeneas, the man who having wronged her and
driven her to suicide would, nonetheless, in the nether world, still
call her back:

> Still fly, plunge deeper in the bowering wood!
> Averse, as Dido did with gesture stern
> From her false friend's approach in Hades turn,
> Wave us away, and keep thy solitude!
>
> (207–10)

Most commentators on "The Scholar-Gipsy," following the lead of
G. Wilson Knight, have quite rightly seen in this a reassertion of the
most basic thematic oppositions in Arnold's poem and a reaffirma-
tion of its most fundamental values in its siding with Dido, "a figure
of feminine appeal and oriental glamour," who, in a final, heroic
show of integrity, rebuffs the young Aeneas, even then on his way
to "fulfilling his destiny as the founder, through Rome, of Western
efficiency and organization."[46] But Arnold's sympathy for Dido carries implications that resonate far beyond the poem's manifest cultural oppositions and choices.

With that Rome, whose values Dido repudiates, Arnold would almost certainly have associated his father as scholar and teacher
and advocate, an association that may help us to understand why
at so crucial a moment in his own poem Arnold would recall the
Aeneid. "The Scholar-Gipsy" had, of course, been written at a
highly stressful time, when Arnold's decision to marry and work
would have stood most obviously in opposition to his diminishing
hopes for himself as a poet, so that this particular episode from the
Aeneid, which he had doubtlessly studied as a schoolboy, must have
seemed a psychologically compelling way of expressing such conflict. On one side was the figure of Aeneas, the embodiment of the
masculine spirit and its associated values of duty to and involvement in the world, a notion forever identified for Arnold with his
father and his father's teachings; on the other was Dido, clearly associated with a countervailing and deeply seductive image of poetry
that presented itself to Arnold not merely as unmanly but as dangerously feminized. Yet Arnold's own inclinations seem abundantly
clear, with the paternally identified Aeneas characterized as "false
friend" (209) and the injured and abandoned Dido granted an aus-

tere and defiant integrity that leaves little doubt where our sympathies are to lie. But a psychologically still more disturbing resonance attaches itself to this encounter, through its framing context: the larger love story of Dido and Aeneas themselves, a narrative that in all of its compulsions, resistances, interweavings, and overdetermination provides one of the most complexly rich instances in all of literature of the scarcely displaced oedipal masterplot.

The love story of Dido and Aeneas is above all else a tale of primal sexual transgression and contamination. Initially the widowed Dido herself insists that self-pollution and desecration must follow if her dead husband were to be supplanted in a marriage bed in which love would now be trespass. Though Aeneas may be the "only one" since her husband's death "who has stirred my senses and sapped / My will" (4.22–23),[47] the divine ordinance that commands sexual abstinence in widowhood must be obeyed:

> I feel once more the scars of the old flame.
> But no, I would rather the earth should open and swallow me
> Or the Father of heaven strike me with lightning
>   down to the shades—
> The pale shades and deep night of the Underworld—before
> I violate or deny pure widowhood's claim upon me.
>
>   (4.23–27)

Faithful to that ordinance, Dido reiterates the inviolability of the claim of her first and thus only husband: "He who first wedded me took with him, when he died, / My right to love: let him keep it there in the tomb for ever" (4.28–29).

Taboos against the desecration of widowhood are themselves, Freud tells us, readily assimilable to fantasized oedipal prohibitions against supplanting the mother's husband in his privileged position as sexual partner. Even more germane to the oedipal scenario are the night terrors Aeneas himself recounts after attaining his sexual ends and becoming Dido's lover, the appearance to him of "the troubled ghost of my father, Anchises" (4.352), who "[c]omes to me in my dreams, warns me and frightens me" (4.352). Only here does Virgil, in fact, mention those political and patriotic responsibilities to the founding of Rome that we are accustomed to regard as the real grounds for the abandonment of Dido by Aeneas. But even this act of duty to the state is rooted in more narrowly patrilinear obligations passed on to him from his father that Aeneas, in his turn, owes to his son, Ascanius. "Disturbed no less by the wrong I am doing

Ascanius" (4.354), Aeneas fears he is "[d]efrauding him of his destined realm in Hesperia" (4.355) by dallying for the sake of a pleasure desired (and indeed enjoyed) but impermissible.

This, then, is the overarching context for the encounter in Hades between Aeneas and the ghost of Dido alluded to in "The Scholar-Gipsy," and it must have been a context deeply etched into the cultural memory of Arnold's educated readers, since study of the *Aeneid* was so prominent a staple of their early education and especially of the education of Arnold himself, the son of the schoolmaster. Moreover, that scene of encounter in Hades picks up many of the compulsions, inhibitions, and pained ambivalences seen earlier in book 4 of the *Aeneid*, undoubtedly complicating and, to some degree, undermining the manly and patriotic resolution that apparently had been negotiated earlier with the flight of Aeneas. Pained at seeing the ghost of Dido, Aeneas tearfully insists in "tender, loving tones" (4.455) that the decision to leave her "was not of my own will" (4.460) but was rather an involuntary yielding to some implacable external agency: "Heaven's commands" (4.461) that "drove me / Imperiously from your side" (6.462–63). (In the Marguerite poems too, the speaker seeks to exonerate himself by attributing his forsaking of his lover to the seemingly arbitrary ordinances of a god.) But when Aeneas tearfully pleads with Dido to "let me see you a little longer" (6.465), Dido, contemptuous of his excuses, coldly rejects him and returns to the husband she had earlier forsworn:

> She would not turn to him; she kept her gaze on
>   the ground,
> And her countenance remained as stubborn to his appeal
> As if it were carved from recalcitrant flint or a
>   crag of marble.
> At last she flung away, hating him still, and vanished
> Into the shadowy wood where her first husband, Sychaeus,
> Understands her unhappiness and gives her an equal love.
>
>   (6.470–74)

Thus, Arnold introduces into his narrative of his poet-speaker's feared betrayal of the scholar-gipsy a disquieting and undermining subtext in which the poet-speaker's figurative counterpart, Aeneas, clearly bears personal responsibility for a seemingly analogous betrayal, whose apparent source is the inevitable transgressiveness that resides in the deepest recesses of the sexual life. It is not just the historically accidental but contagiously fatal disease of modernity that the speaker—himself infected—would have the scholar-gipsy flee. Recasting that imperative to flee as the sexually charged tale of Dido and Aeneas suggests nothing so much as that anxiety-driven pattern of reaching toward and drawing away in aversion from the woman with whom he is romantically involved, found so frequently in Arnold's poems exploring sexuality and the psychology of love. Moreover, that broader thematic concern of the Arnoldian speaker that he might dishonor or impair the poetic responsibilities with which he has been entrusted, through its framing by the allusion to Dido and Aeneas, may similarly be seen as a variant of more fundamental and psychologically primary warnings against oedipal violation and the feelings of guilt such violation invariably produces. In the speaker's cry to the scholar-gipsy—and the spirit of imagination he embodies—to "flee," we may see remembered residues of fears of polluting a marriage bed from which Arnold, like Aeneas, was forbidden by the law of prior possession, fears of transgression of a father's prohibitions and his stern exhortations to duty, exhortations clearly incompatible with a career of poetry as Arnold had pursued it.

The simile of the Tyrian trader similarly provides a mirroring image of the poem's primary narrative which, more closely observed, also discloses undermining traces of the psychologically transformative. Plainly, its ostensible intent is to have us regard the flight by the Tyrian trader from the advancing civilization of the Greeks and his heroic voyage to the edge of the world and the margins of culture in quest of some traditional wisdom as an essentially parallel enactment of the primary narrative, the scholar-gipsy's abandonment of seventeenth-century Oxford to live with and like the imaginatively empowered gipsies, acquiring and husbanding their arts until he can use them for socially beneficial ends when the cycle of history reverses itself. By insinuating a figurative likeness between the Tyrian trader, voyaging "[o]'er the blue Midlands water with the gale" (244) and, beyond that, "[t]o where the Atlantic raves" (246), and the scholar-gipsy as he wanders in the tame woods of the Oxford countryside, Arnold might seem merely to be endowing a very timid referent with something of the heroic character of the seafarer's courage. Moreover, in identifying the story of the Tyrian trader with that of the scholar-gipsy, Arnold also lends credibility to the primary narrative's claim that history does repeat itself and, by extension, to the hope that the distressful present of modernity shall give way to a better future when the spark from heaven falls, just as the irreverent science and demoralizing skepticism of antiquity finally gave way to the epoch of Christian faith, an epoch that Arnold perhaps implies came into being through something like preservation and transmission of the shy Iberians' traditional faith.

From the preliminary assertion of likeness stipulated by the "As" of the simile, we might logically expect that each major figure in the primary narrative has a clearly resembling counterpart within the simile: the scholar-gipsy, for example, can be matched with the Tyrian trader (as they grammatically are by the connecting subordinating conjunction); the inhabitants of a now ascendant modernity from whom the scholar-gipsy flees similarly can be matched with those "young lighthearted masters of the waves" (241), the encroaching Greeks; and the aloofly reclusive gipsies, with the still more mysterious inhabitants of little-known regions beyond the western straits, "shy traffickers, the dark Iberians" (249).

Yet while the Iberians and gipsies, who lead traditional lives close to nature, seem enough alike to make sense of the simile, neither of the other two parallels really holds. Even Culler, while strongly committed to the simile's logic of likeness, admits that the scholar-gipsy, "as we originally knew him, more closely resembles the Grecian coaster than the Tyrian trader."[48] Indeed, the "grave Tyrian trader" seems most to resemble not the scholar-gipsy in his "glad perennial youth" (229) to whom he is expressly likened but the speaker himself, similarly grave in his forbearance, his "[s]ad patience, too near neighbor to despair." Nor, finally, do "[t]he young light-hearted masters of the wave" (241) seem at all like their tacitly designated counterparts from the original narrative, those neurasthenic moderns who in their wretchedness and misery exemplify Arnold's own phase of the historical cycle—which, by the logic of the simile, would most closely parallel the epoch of Greek ascendancy.

What these intimations of difference amidst claims of a signifying likeness suggest is that what Arnold has given us is not a mirroring narrative but a covert counterplot; not merely divergent, but oppositional. In "Stanzas from the Grande Chartreuse," too, he had also used his simile to undermine—indeed, even to undo—implicitly historicist premises that that simile was ostensibly to elaborate. There his strategy had been to take his speaker and the between-worlds generation, forlornly awaiting that cyclical reversal through which "may dawn an age, / More fortunate, alas! than we," a generation for whom he purports to speak, and reconstitute them literally as children, desiring and perhaps destined to live out their lives in regressive changelessness "[b]eneath some old-world abbey wall" (170). Standing in opposition to the reconceptualized speaker and that "we" is a surprisingly attractive set of very different figures:

men of action, apparently able to live successfully in the world, who, with banners flying, vigorously step forward in quick time "[t]o life, to cities, and to war" (180). They are plainly men of the present, living cheerfully in the here and now, seemingly unconstrained by the between-world limitations that Arnold and his like must passively endure, unless they choose the implicitly neurotic course of an immobilizingly regressive flight back to childhood.[49]

The coda to "The Scholar-Gipsy" also has suggestions of regressive flight, but one more complex, more highly displaced, and less fully effectuated than the immediate and absolute transformation of speaker into child in "Stanzas from the Grande Chartreuse." The regressive implications of the voyage of the Tyrian trader are to be found not in the reversion to childhood of the voyager but in the object of his voyage, in his projected transaction with the reclusive and presumably childlike Iberians from whom the Tyrian trader apparently hopes to acquire (in return for his own unspecified offerings) some good that bespeaks their own innocently uncorrupted nature, some antidote to spiritual devastation by a dangerously encroaching civilization. Of course, whether the trader's heroic voyaging is to be successful remains highly problematic. Whereas in the poem's initial quest the scholar-gipsy had made contact with those he sought and gleaned what their crucial secret was, the Tyrian trader does no more than set out the commodities he would barter, uncertain whether or not the contents of his "corded bales" (250) will prove acceptable items of trade to these "shy traffickers" (249) and, more important, whether those greatly desired goods (though never identified nor seen) he has come so far and through such dangers to obtain will be offered in exchange.

One other striking point of likeness between the codas to "Stanzas from the Grande Chartreuse" and "The Scholar-Gipsy" is the prominence in both of a set of lighthearted, adventuresome, and seemingly masterful men, the "passing troops" whose entreaties the children of "Stanzas from the Grande Chartreuse" refuse, and, correspondingly, the Grecian sailors from whose intrusion the Tyrian trader actually takes flight. Yet they seem figures without parallels within the primary narratives to which the similes refer. Where the poet-speaker in each poem had initially cast himself as spokesman for his generation, those listlessly unhappy men and women accidentally cast adrift in the between-worlds circumstances that are the inescapable lot of those born into the joylessly transitional epoch of modernity, the similes seem to alter drastically that historically deterministic argument. The passing troops and the Grecian sailors are clearly members of the child-speaker's and the Tyrian trader's own generation, and yet they still manage to exhibit energy in abundance, an energy enabling them to create history rather than remain its passively suffering victims. In fact, the real contrast in the concluding similes of the two poems is not between hypothesized representatives of opposed phases of the historical cycle, but it is between two sharply differentiated segments of contemporary humanity: the strivers and doers (whether soldiers or seafarers) and those held in check from any commitment to action by an innate diffidence, remaining wary and anxious, desirous only of evading or escaping the claims upon them of life and the world.

In effect, in the similes Arnold seems to put the assumptions of historicism behind him, to rule out the cyclical movements of the zeitgeist as the ultimate determinant of human behavior. Instead, he seems to indicate that that behavior ultimately depends upon what is intrinsic, the characteristics an individual brings to the historical circumstances under which he lives. Thus, in these two final similes, the Arnoldian speaker, who had previously represented himself as spokesman for the unhappy collective humanity of the transitional epoch, reverts to type, and—whether child or trader—he again becomes the melancholy, solitary "I" so often observed in the earlier poetry. Essentially isolated from others not for reasons of history but from causes that we can assume lie within, he also seems beset by the usual Arnoldian amalgam of desire and anxiety, the prospect of contact with another calling forth the stock defenses of regression or flight. Moreover, with the appearance of "the merry Grecian coaster" manned by "[t]he young light-hearted masters of the waves," there are intimations that the earlier theory of history, with its despairing sense of the present and its relegation of hope to an unattainable future, was badly misconceived. From the confidence and evident mastery of these heroic voyagers, we would guess that the future is now, that the turn that advances civilization has, in fact, already been taken by these men of action (whose similarly confident and similarly masterful Victorian counterparts Arnold was only too well aware of), and that it is from the men of his own time who most resemble them, those who are most likely to be agents of progress and potential benefactors of their society, that the speaker of "The Scholar-Gipsy" is actually and perhaps culpably most profoundly estranged.[50]

Thus, the simile with which "The Scholar-Gipsy" closes in effect revises its apparently historicist and forward-looking referent in ways that actually bring "The Scholar-Gipsy" into intellectual and psychological alignment with what is bleakest and most personally painful in the earlier and avowedly pessimistic poetry. With the Tyrian trader having displaced the speaker as the poem's point of subjective reference, human life is again imagined as a solitary voyage, as it was in "Human Life" and "A Summer Night." Moreover, from the fact that, unlike the scholar-gipsy, the Tyrian trader never actually completes his crucial transaction with those he has sought out, we can only conclude that by the poem's end Arnold has drawn back from his cautiously intimated faith that the shattered culture of historical man shall, through the imaginative magic of poetic myth, be restored again to something approaching its lost unity, or, still worse, that the poet will ever really affect a world that is ruled over by men of energy and power, "[t]he young lighthearted masters of the waves." Given the poem's latent counterargument surreptitiously compounded of the most troubling elements of the primary narrative and the materials of the two equally troubling closing similes, "The Scholar-Gipsy" can be seen, finally, for what it proves to be: a kind of valedictory to the major part of Arnold's poetic career, a turning away from a poetry that until now had primarily been made out of the profoundly conflicted but courageously authentic products of "the mind's dialogue with itself" and a turning instead toward a poetry and prose more responsible, more dedicated to ameliorating the social needs of the larger community, more in keeping with paternal wishes and commands.

In the very same year, in the preface to the *Poems* of 1853, Arnold finally does appear at last to break decisively with his own past attitudes, his inner doubts and discouragements and anxieties.[51] Thus it is not surprising that, just as he renounces his most ambitious poem, the grimly conceived *Empedocles on Etna*, tacitly eliminating it from circulation in apparent penance for past intellectual errors and poetic misdeeds, so too would he seek to devalue the best of its kind among those poems that express his own uniquely developed and despairingly construed historicism, "The Scholar-Gipsy," fearful that its very charm might assist in the propagation of views of which Arnold himself only months after its completion clearly no longer approved. Taking up Clough's kindly intended words of praise for "The Scholar-Gipsy," in a letter dated November 30, 1853 (just a month before publishing his preface), Arnold responds with a statement that echoes the positions taken in the preface and seems still more remarkable, not just for its ungracious response to Clough's praise, but for the startling self-characterization of what Arnold would have Clough take to be not only his poetics but his nature:

I am glad you like the Gipsy Scholar—but what does it *do* for you? Homer *animates*—Shakespeare *animates*—in its poor way I think Sohrab and Rustum *animates*—the Gipsy Scholar at best raises a pleasing melancholy. But this is not what we want.

> The complaining millions of men
> Darken in labor and pain—

what they want is something to *animate* and *enoble* them—not merely to add zest to their melancholy or grace to their dreams —I believe a feeling of this kind is the basis of my nature—and of my poetics. (*Letters*, 1:282)

Allowing for certain minor changes of phrase—in the letter to Clough the goal of poetry is to "*animate* and *ennoble*" men rather than to "inspirit and rejoice the reader" (*CPW* 1:2) as the preface puts it—the programs of these two statements of Arnold's poetics in the fall of 1853 sound much alike. He would repudiate a poetry of "doubt" and "discouragement" and eschew "melancholy" in favor of a poetry self-consciously designed to raise the flagging human spirit in a dark time. Indeed, in the letter to Clough censuring "The Scholar-Gipsy," the poet's obligation to assist in ameliorating the misery of an age in which "complaining millions of men / Darken in labour and pain" is asserted more emphatically than in the 1853 preface.

In the preface, Arnold assures us that his insistence that the poet "inspirit and rejoice the reader" does not mean that he must limit himself to purely cheerful or uplifting subjects because, as our literary experience teaches us, "In the presence of the most tragic circumstances, represented in a work of art, the feeling of enjoyment, as is well known, may still subsist" (*CPW*, 1:2). Extending that argument a stage further, Arnold offers an even more paradoxical principle to explain the strangely counterintuitive derivation and development of literary pleasure from representations of the palpably unpleasurable, indeed from what one ordinarily would take to be the unhappiest of human experiences: "[T]he more tragic the situation, the deeper becomes the enjoyment; and the situation becomes more tragic in proportion as it becomes more terrible" (*CPW*, 1:2). But from the catalogue that follows of terrible situations that should yield a proportionately high degree of tragic enjoyment, Arnold—in a notorious act of self-censuring that sounds very much like recantation—expressly excludes one familiar type, the unrelievedly terrible that is wholly subjective. This category, of course, includes virtually all of his own best poetry to this time. "What then are the situations, from the representation of which, though accurate, no poetical enjoyment can be derived?" Arnold asks, and then, in reply, singles out "those in which suffering finds no vent in action; in which a continuous state of mental distress is prolonged, unrelieved by incident, hope or resistance; in which everything is to be endured, nothing to be done." Differentiating such situations from those deemed to be intrinsically tragic by invoking that distinction between the merely painful and the genuinely tragic (which critics of an Arnoldian cast of mind ever since have used to deny tragic status to the writings of an Ibsen or a Beckett or any truly modern writer), Arnold then adds: "When they occur in actual life, they are painful, not tragic; the representation of them in poetry is painful also" (CPW, 1:2–3).

What is most remarkable about the principles annunciated in this preface and in that letter to Clough that reaffirms them is how little they have to do with the poetry written by Arnold before it—aside from the one special case of *Sohrab and Rustum*—and how closely Arnold adheres to them in those poetically anticlimactic years that follow it. While he does return to the seemingly unpleasurable viewed as the intrinsically tragic on two later occasions, it is to an unpleasurable assumed insulated against any threat from an aesthetically corrosive subjectivity by his care in selecting an action whose appeal to past ages should provide assurances of its probable permanent interest and, therefore, its likely appeal to readers of Arnold's own age. With his precedent *Sohrab and Rustum*, which in "its poor way" supposedly "*animates*" after the fashion of Shakespeare and Homer, Arnold turns again to old stories impersonally narrated: to a myth about the age preceding the birth of human history for the matter of *Balder Dead* and to a legend set in antiquity as the basis for his one completed attempt at reproducing classical tragedy with *Merope*. The notorious failures of these two works, Arnold's most ambitious poetic enterprises after 1853, perhaps testify not so much to the inherent defectiveness of the principles set down in the preface (though general poetic practice since then might speak to their irrelevance) as to their essential incompatibility—despite his protestations to the contrary in the letter to Clough—with what we might deduce from that sizable body of poems written between 1843 and 1853 to be, in the deepest sense, the basis of Arnold's own "nature" and his "poetics." Both of these long narratives recount familiar Arnoldian themes: in *Balder Dead* Arnold returns to the subject of "Mycerinus," the untimely death of the young and gifted, a fate here too found to be irreversible, even though its victim is a god; and in *Merope* we are brought back to what many of us believe to be one of the most fundamental of Arnoldian concerns, the death of a father and a son's obligations to assume his duties and carry on in his place. But the premise of authorial distancing seemingly entailed by the epic manner of *Balder Dead* and the classically dramatic form of *Merope* leaves Arnold's treatment of these themes atypically unanguished and thus disappointingly listless, the inevitable consequence of a theory designed to protect the poetry against what is deepest though darkest in Arnold's poetic nature. Moreover, since these poems carry forward Arnold's after-the-turn historicist attitudes, the tragic effect is surprisingly blunted: in *Balder Dead* by Balder's concluding optimistically "millenial vision"[52] of "[a]nother Heaven" still to come; and in *Merope* by the play's unqualifiedly happy ending in which mistaken identities are at last cleared up, mother and son reunited, the usurping pretender deposed and punished, and the wronged heir allowed finally to avenge his father and assume a throne rightfully his by inheritance.

Of the poems written by Arnold in his own voice, only one, "A Southern Night," retains anything like the mood or atmosphere of the earlier poetry. This is more a matter of its somberly elegiac tone and a return to the familiar imagery of sea and stars—imagery Arnold would naturally draw upon when writing about the death of his brother during the return voyage from India to England, rather than the result of any real philosophic continuity with an earlier poetry of pessimism or any persisting psychological likeness between the self-effacing mourner of "A Southern Night" and those anxious or embittered or self-deprecating lyric speakers found almost everywhere in the poetry written before the 1853 preface.

The two best-known and probably most important of the later poems, "Rugby Chapel" and "Thyrsis," display an optimism and propose counsels of hope and good cheer that seem little short of astonishing coming from the poet of "To Marguerite-Continued," "Dover Beach," and, indeed, even "The Scholar-Gipsy." In "Rugby Chapel," Arnold presents a portrait of the long-dead Thomas Arnold that is essentially divested of all ambivalence and virtually every trace of oedipal complicatedness, a portrait of the father as unalloyed Carlylean hero, remembrance of him alone sufficing to serve as the source of a son's belief "[i]n the noble and great who are gone" (146). That father whose spirit had hovered so ominously over "Resignation"—the obvious psychological prototype for that life of striving and mastery from which Matthew, the son, draws back in distaste and aversion and from which he would rescue his only too susceptible sister—in this later poem is raised up as one of those "[b]eacons of hope" (192) whose irrepressible will to strive and to master, qualities once regarded as expressions of self-re-gardingly aggressive impulses, is in this public gesture of filial piety to be looked upon as a clearly unqualified and inspirational good. Indeed, in 1857 Thomas Arnold is not merely praised and honored as a father but placed in the historical vanguard of humanity, with those who encourage and exhort the "host of mankind" (171), shor-ing up its "feeble, wavering line" (171–72) as it continues on its un-steady but, nonetheless, historically determined progress, "On, to the bound of the waste, / On, to the city of God" (207–8).

Purportedly a sequel to "The Scholar-Gipsy," "Thyrsis" is, if any-thing, more highly contrived and forced in its reassuringness than even "Rugby Chapel." As proof of the crucial claim that the scholar-gipsy yet lives, Arnold no longer finds it necessary to fall back upon the convolutedly unlikely but still poignantly self-critical explana-tion that human mortality is an unhappy consequence of our human susceptibility to change, a susceptibility from which the scholar-gipsy, by his single-minded dedication to his obligation to the future, has been somehow happily exempted. Instead, now in "Thyrsis," Arnold even more improbably bases his claim for the survival of the scholar-gipsy into the present on the assertion of a transparently arbitrary and wildly incongruous surrogacy by which a tree, the fa-mous and predictably long-lived signal-elm, may stand for a man. Furthermore, by the strange logic of that surrogacy, the signal-elm's continuing existence is to serve as conclusive proof that the scholar-gipsy still nurses his project and survives. But, of course, it is the radical unlikeness of the signal-elm not just to the scholar-gipsy but to the human species generally that insulates the later poem against the doubts and questionings of its highly problema-tized original. It is the fact that the signal-elm is never really threat-ened by the perilousness of human relationships that enables Arnold to end "Thyrsis," not with anything like his frantic instruc-tions in the earlier poem urging the scholar-gipsy to "[f]ly hence, our contact fear!" (206) (or the closing simile reinscribing that ad-vice), but with the confidently voiced non sequitur: "Our tree yet crowns the hill, / Our Scholar travels yet the loved hill-side" (239–40). Probably nowhere in the later poetry is the profound difficulty Arnold had (despite what he asserted to be his "nature" and his "poetics") in writing a poetry that would serve his avowed purpose of *animating* and *ennobling* his readers more strikingly mani-fested than in his use of that transparently arbitrary and clumsy contrivance of the signal-elm to draw hope from what, in the complex formulations of fifteen years earlier, had ambiguously but ultimately presented itself as grounds for at least personal despair.

By 1866, the year in which "Thyrsis" was probably completed, it was obvious that Arnold already plainly understood that if he was to serve the needs of "[t]he complaining millions of men" who "[d]arken in labour and pain," it would not be through his poems, even those written in the manner of *Sohrab and Rustum*. His duty, as he now perceived it, was to prepare the way for a poetry that would truly "*animate* and *ennoble*" by an enabling act of criticism that would create the cultural conditions needed to make such a poetry possible. To that end, he had already published his first collection of *Essays in Criticism* a year earlier and would begin *Culture and Anarchy* a year later. It was through this great and growing body of prose that Arnold now knew he would finally fulfill what he understood to be his responsibility to society and what he undoubtedly also understood to be his long postponed obligation to the memory of his father.

But if the writing of prose was to be an almost exclusive preoccupation henceforth and, finally, the source of a gratifyingly increasing fame, Arnold could certainly recognize that his career as a poet was essentially over, and thus he seemed able retrospectively to evaluate it with a surprising mixture of confidence and objectivity. In that letter of 1869 to his mother from which I quoted at the beginning of this study, Arnold offers an assessment of his poetry and his probable place among the poets of the age. His assessment seems nothing less than a recantation of the principles of the 1853 preface and that contemporaneous letter to Clough in which Arnold proposed *Sohrab and Rustum* as the most appropriate illustration of what he wished others to regard as his "poetics" and his "nature." It will not be because of his fidelity to the example of the ancients or his choice of subjects of a permanent interest—and therefore, most probably, subjects from an earlier age—that he shall be remembered, he tells his mother, indeed more than remembered, but numbered with Tennyson and Browning as one of the first poets of the age. With very few poems remaining to be written— "Westminster Abbey," an elegy even more wooden than "Thyrsis" that he would write in tribute to the memory of his friend Arthur Stanley, and a series of elegies to his pets the most prominent— Arnold in 1869 can raise her hopes for the most gifted of her children by explaining that the "turn" he believes himself "likely to have," as Tennyson and Browning "have had theirs," will come about because his own "poems represent the main movement of mind of the last quarter of a century, and thus they will probably

have their day as people become conscious to themselves of what
that movement of mind is, and interested in the literary productions
that reflect it" (*Letters*, 3:347). And surely that preceding "quarter
of a century," whose "movement of mind" his poems represent and
reflect, must have been in 1869 still understood just as it was in
1853, as an age of "confusion," "bewildering" in its "multitude of
voices counselling different things" (*CPW*, 1:8). Nor would Arnold's
claim in 1869 seem to be that he had merely followed the practice of
the ancients, transmitted our poetic heritage intact to the future,
undamaged by any quintessentially modern defectiveness of "spirituality and feeling" (*CPW*, 1:15).

From that letter to his mother, it seems probable that by 1869
Arnold saw himself as the posterity that would share his own self-
valuation would see him, at least those of us who regard him as a
poet to be ranked with Tennyson and Browning—indeed, a poet
who in our own usually unspoken assessments finally surpasses
them. He seems to know in that letter that readers would go to him
not for his inspiritingness but for his anxiety, for his conveying of
that "modern nervousness"[53] that so much resembles their own. We
may very well also suspect that in 1869 Arnold recognized that the
poems to which they would therefore turn would not be *Sohrab and
Rustum* or *Balder Dead* or *Merope* but "To Marguerite-Continued," "The Scholar-Gipsy," the recently published "Dover Beach,"
and the recently republished *Empedocles on Etna*.

Even in the face of the threat of Victorian censoriousness and the
still more inhibiting constraints of his own personal fastidiousness,
in his very best poems Arnold shows a willingness to look inward
that commends him to us, to examine the psyche's dark corners,
even to offer otherwise forbidden glimpses of those secret depths
from which the impulses of sexual desire and the forces that would
repress them emanate. From one perspective we may regard him
as the first of our confessional poets, a genuine modern by the candor with which he is willing to admit personal failings, psychological
inadequacies, the tentativeness with which desire arouses itself,
and the frequency with which it is thwarted. But Arnold's superiority to those we may consider his modern successors in the line of
confessional poets—indeed the basis for his claim to be honored as
one of our major poets—resides in those very characteristics that
most strikingly identify Arnold as a poet of the nineteenth century.
Like those Romantic predecessors whose heir, even in his most
doubting poems, he knew and acknowledged himself to be, Arnold
wished not only to describe that world he so darkly observed but to
understand and explain it, to trace his own most personal thoughts

and feelings, desires and doubts, back to their origins, not merely in the privacy of his own human psyche but in the nature of things. So he too gave in to the metaphysical impulse, to the Romantic bent for world-making, and out of his own decidedly unromantic doubt and despair produced a dark cosmology and then an equally dark philosophy of history, each philosophy rich, complex, dynamic.

Certainly what made the Arnoldian vision possible was undoubtedly a rare convergence of the man and the moment, the emergence of intellectual conditions that not only would generate a philosophy like Schopenhauer's but, beyond that, would allow such dismaying tenets to have broad dissemination and a surprisingly wide acceptance. If the period of Arnold's poetic achievement was brief and only a handful of great poems were produced within that span—and these are larger in number than he is usually credited with—surely that is because so austere and forbidding a philosophy would seem virtually unsustainable over a long and full poetic lifetime. Yet of the major Victorian poets, Arnold alone chose, from the possibilities made available to him, that metaphysically pessimistic option that, as Nietzsche recognized, most truly represented the main movement of mind in his own age (though few of Arnold's contemporaries understood that), insofar as it pointed most accurately to that future still to come. It is not only an act of prescience for which he reaps the reward that we moderns shall always return to him but, beyond that, an act of intellectual courage in which he clearly surpasses his rivals and for which he shall forever deserve our admiration and our praise.

Notes

CHAPTER 1. INTRODUCTION

1. Of the three, Arnold's place among the major poets has probably been the most frequently challenged. Even twenty-five years ago, in his authoritative survey of criticism of Arnold's poetry, David J. DeLaura conceded that "Arnold's claims as an artist in verse and as spokesman in his poetry for an essential aspect of the modern experience are even now not secure beyond debate" ("Matthew Arnold," in *Victorian Prose: A Guide to Research* [New York: Modern Language Association, 1973], 261).

2. Norman Holland, *The Dynamics of Literary Response* (New York: W. W. Norton & Co., 1975), 116. Only four articles on "Dover Beach" are listed in the *MLA Bibliography* for the 1990s. The only substantially innovative reading of the poem in very recent years is an essay by Joseph Bristow, " 'Love let us be true to one another': Matthew Arnold, Arthur Hugh Clough, and 'Our Aqueous Ages,' " *Literature and History*, 3d ser., 4 (1995): 27–49. In keeping with current tendencies, Bristow proposes a reading in which "[t]he 'Love' invited to 'Come to the window' (6) and 'Listen,' to the 'grating roar / Of pebbles' could not so implausibly be Clough," though Bristow is quick to disclaim any desire to "concoct a previously unknown homoeroticism between Arnold and Clough" (31).

3. Gerald Graff, *Beyond the Culture Wars: How Teaching the Conflicts Can Revitalize American Education* (New York and London: W. W. Norton & Co., 1992), 37–41.

4. David Riede, *Matthew Arnold and the Betrayal of Language* (Charlottesville: University Press of Virginia, 1988).

5. Nicholas Murray, *A Life of Matthew Arnold* (London: Hodder and Stoughton, 1996); Ian Hamilton, *A Gift Imprisoned: The Poetic Life of Matthew Arnold* (London: Bloomsbury, 1998); *The Letters of Matthew Arnold: 1829-70*, ed. Cecil Y. Lang, vols. 1–3 (Charlottesville: University Press of Virginia, 1996–99); Donald D. Stone, *Communications with the Future; Matthew Arnold in Dialogue* (Ann Arbor: University of Michigan Press, 1997).

6. Clinton Machann, *The Essential Matthew Arnold: An Annotated Bibliography of Major Modern Studies* (New York: G. K. Hall & Co., 1993), 60.

7. For gender-based readings, see especially Mary Ellis Gibson, "Dialogue on the Darkling Plain: Genre, Gender, and Audience in Matthew Arnold's Lyrics," in *Gender and Discourse in Victorian Literature and Art*, ed. Anthony H. Harrison and Beverly Taylor (De Kalb: Northern Illinois University Press, 1992): 30–48; Martin Danahay, *A Community of One: Masculine Autobiography and Autonomy in Victorian Britain* (Albany: State University of New York Press, 1993); and Bristow, " 'Love let us be true to one another.' "

8. Carl Dawson, *Victorian Noon: English Literature in 1850* (Baltimore: Johns Hopkins University Press, 1979), 73.

9. Quoted from Murray, *Life of Matthew Arnold*, 98–99.

10. Ibid., 74.

11. Stefan Collini, *Arnold* (Oxford: Oxford University Press, 1988), 27.

12. Paul Turner, *Victorian Poetry, Drama, and Miscellaneous Prose* (Oxford: Oxford University Press, 1989), 76.

13. A. Dwight Culler, *Imaginative Reason: The Poetry of Matthew Arnold* (New Haven: Yale University Press, 1966), 41.

14. For each of these positions, see G. Robert Stange, *Matthew Arnold: The Poet as Humanist* (Princeton: Princeton University Press, 1967); William Madden, *Matthew Arnold: A Study of the Aesthetic Temperament in Victorian England* (Bloomington: Indiana University Press, 1967); William Buckler, *On the Poetry of Matthew Arnold: Essays in Critical Reconstruction* (New York: New York University Press, 1982). Among the major critics of Arnold's poetry—though his is not a full-length study of Arnold's poetry—only J. Hillis Miller, in *The Disappearance of God: Five Nineteenth-Century Writers* (Cambridge: Harvard University Press, 1963), 212–69, can truly be said to regard the poetry as essentially negative in its outlook.

15. Riede, *Betrayal of Language*, 29.

16. Ibid., 28.

17. Culler, *Imaginative Reason*, 4. Over two decades after Culler put forward this account of the Arnoldian poetic landscape, Collini would still describe it as "the standard modern commentary" (*Arnold*, 27).

18. Culler, *Imaginative Reason*, 4.

19. A. Dwight Culler, *The Victorian Mirror of History* (New Haven: Yale University Press, 1985), 124.

20. But in his very interesting *Communications with the Future*, Donald Stone has recently argued that "there are strong affinities between" Arnold and Nietzsche (81), though these are mainly treated in connection with the prose.

21. Friedrich Nietzsche, *The Will to Power*, ed. Walter Kauffman, trans. Walter Kauffman and R. J. Hollingdale (New York: Random House, 1967), 15.

22. Ibid., 15.

23. Ibid., 16.

24. Arthur Schopenhauer himself provides us with a pessimist's honor roll of those writers from Theognis to Byron who have written best on the "wretchedness of human existence" (*The World as Will and Representation*, trans. E. I. F. Payne, 2 vols. [New York: Dover Publications, 1958], 2:585–88).

25. Sophocles, *Oedipus at Colonus*, trans. Robert Fagles (New York: Viking Press, 1982), 341.

26. The Bible: Authorized (King James) Version, ed. Robert Carroll and Stephen Prickett (Oxford: Oxford University Press, 1997), 609.

27. Thomas Hardy, *Jude the Obscure*, ed. Norman Page (New York: W. W. Norton & Co., 1978), 320.

28. William Shakespeare, *Hamlet*, in *The Complete Works of Shakespeare*, 4th ed., ed. David Bevington (New York: HarperCollins, 1992), 1.2.134. All quotations from Shakespeare are from this edition and are cited by act, scene, and line number.

29. Shakespeare, *King Lear*, 4.6.183.

30. Ibid., 5.3.312.

31. Thomas Carlyle, *Sartor Resartus: The Life and Opinions of Herr Teufelsdröckh*, ed. Charles Frederick Harrold (New York: Odyssey Press, 1937), 164.

32. Carlyle, *Sartor Resartus*, 167.

33. Ibid., 168.

34. Alfred Tennyson, "The Two Voices," in *The Poems of Tennyson*, ed. Christopher Ricks (London: Longmans, 1969), 522–41. All quotations from Tennyson are from this edition and are quoted by line number in the text.

35. The one critic who does mention Arnold's possible relationship to Schopenhauer is Stone, who writes that Arnold found "unsatisfying Schopenhauer's view that life is no blessing" (*Communications*, 83). While the Arnold of the later prose may have thought life a blessing, this does not seem true of the Arnold of "Resignation."

36. For a highly informed discussion of the influence of Johann Fichte's *Die Bestimmung des Menschen* (The vocation of man) on *Sartor Resartus*, see Elizabeth M. Vida, *Romantic Affinities: German Authors and Carlyle, A Study in the History of Ideas* (Toronto: University of Toronto Press, 1993), 77–88. Vida persuasively argues that "[i]t is, however, in the central chapters of Book II, 'The Everlasting No,' 'Centre of Indifference,' and 'The Everlasting Yea,' containing Teufelsdröckh's spiritual autobiography, that the closest affinity of *Sartor* with *Die Bestimmung* is reached" (77–78).

37. John Oxenford, "Iconoclasm in German Philosophy," *Westminster and Foreign Quarterly Review* (spring 1853): 401.

38. Ibid., 405.

39. Isobel Armstrong, *Victorian Poetry: Poetry, Poetics, and Politics* (London: Routledge, 1903), 255.

40. Dawson probably comes closest to offering a Schopenhauerian explanation for the situation Arnold describes in "To Marguerite—Continued" by saying, "Arnold, like Hardy after him, seems to imply both an arbitrary fate and a fate directed by a less than generous will" (*Victorian Noon*, 71).

41. Gian Piero Baricelli, *Giacomo Leopardi* (Boston: Twayne, 1986), 195.

42. *A Leopardi Reader*, ed. and trans. Ottavio M. Casale (Urbana: University of Illinois Press, 1981). All quotations from Leopardi are from this edition and are cited by page number in the text.

43. The passages from both Jenyns and Johnson are found in Basil Willey, *Eighteenth-Century Background: Studies in the Idea of Nature in the Thought of the Period* (London: Chatto and Windus, 1940), 52–53.

44. Coleridge offers what would seem his most exalted commendation of Wordsworth, that "he is capable of producing" "the FIRST GENUINELY PHILOSOPHIC POEM," in the concluding chapter of *Biographia Literaria: or Biographical Sketches of My Literary Life and Opinions*, in *The Collected Works of Samuel Taylor Coleridge*, vol. 7, ed. James Engell and W. Jackson Bate (Princeton: Princeton University Press, 1983), 156.

45. For a helpful discussion of suicide in the nineteenth century, see Linda Ray Pratt, "Empedocles, Suicide, and the Order of Things," *Victorian Poetry* 26 (1988): 75–90. But in her account of those who assess suicide as a "moral solution" (77), Pratt does not include Schopenhauer's important essay.

46. Arthur Schopenhauer, *Parerga and Paripolemena*, ed. E. J. F. Payne, 2 vols. (Oxford: Oxford University Press, 1974), 2:622.

47. Sigmund Freud, *Beyond the Pleasure Principle*, in *The Standard Edition of the Complete Psychological Works of Sigmund Freud*, trans. James Strachey (London: Hogarth, 1955), 18:50.

48. Peter Gay, *Freud: A Life for Our Time* (New York: W. W. Norton & Co., 1989), 365. As Gay reports, Freud's reply on "that occasion was that he owed his originality to his 'meager reading' " (365). On the question of the extent of Scho-

penhauer's influence on Freud, Brian Magee provides a reasonably balanced judgment: "To do Freud justice, he never, in his maturity, equivocated over the fact that Schopenhauer had preceded him with his most fundamental ideas, but only over the directness or indirectness of his debt. And as his greatest biographer, Ernest Jones, tells us, he openly regarded Schopenhauer as one of the half-dozen or so greatest men who ever lived" (*The Philosophy of Schopenhauer* [Oxford: Oxford University Press, 1983], 285.

49. In keeping with his general disposition to read Arnold's poetry positively, Culler, in his very brief comment on "Human Life," asserts that "[t]he winds of destiny which, in *Human Life*, reft from his side the 'unsuiting consort,' were actually guiding him by his own 'inly-written chart' " (*Imaginative Reason*, 132–33). Since that "chart" was given us by our "heavenly Friend," we may wonder how the "unknown Powers" into which the "heavenly Friend" is finally transformed have befriended us in forcing us to give up the "joys," the "friends," the "homes" that have been denied us in a life's voyage that seemingly serves only their own inscrutable purposes.

50. Somewhat surprisingly—since its city setting occupies only ten lines until Arnold carries us through memory to his more characteristic locale of "the moonlit deep"—"A Summer Night" is sometimes treated as a poem dealing primarily with urban circumstances. Stange, for example, in "The Victorian City and the Frightened Poets" (in *The Victorian City*, ed. H. J. Dyos and Michael Wolff [London: Routledge and Kegan Paul, 1973], 2:475–94), praises "A Summer Night" as "the only English poem of the time which invests the city with the symbolic depth and richness of Baudelaire's Paris" (485). Beginning with Kenneth Allott (*The Poems of Matthew Arnold* [London: Longman, 1979], 282), commentators on "A Summer Night"—including Arnold's major biographers, Park Honan (*Matthew Arnold: A Life* [New York: McGraw-Hill, 1981], 225–26); Murray (*Life of Matthew Arnold*, 130); and Hamilton (*Gift Imprisoned*, 133)—have tantalizingly localized the urban setting even further by identifying the "unopening windows" that the speaker of "A Summer Night" longingly looks up at with the Eaton Place house of Judge Wightman from which Arnold had been excluded during much of his courtship of Lucy Wightman. If this is so, then "A Summer Night" may be regarded as another, typically Arnoldian love poem, where the figure of the "moonlit deep" sets in motion a scenario in which, knowing that desire is preordained to be frustrated, the speaker, at the moment of reaching toward, draws back and turns instead to some highly attenuated and uneroticized alternative to love, in this case that idealized life of self-contained autonomy exemplified by the heavens, which (as the figure instructs us) can only succeed by being solitary and unshared.

51. It is, of course, an image that has drawn its share of commentary. In *Imaginative Reason*, Culler—commenting on its appearances at the close of *Empedocles on Etna*, in "The Forsaken Merman," and in "To Marguerite—Continued"—finds in it suggestions of a "renewed pastoralism" (176) an image similar to "the third phase of Arnold's world" (176–77), that is, similar to "the phase of reconciliation" (16) toward which Arnold's symbolic landscape finally points. However, it is difficult to square so positive a reading of the image with the unhappy outcomes of the poems Culler cites in which the image appears. In " 'The Moon Lies Fair': The Poetry of Matthew Arnold," *Studies in English Literature* 4 (1964): 569–81, Herbert R. Coursen, in analyzing this and other moonlight images, reaches conclusions that more closely parallel mine: "In Arnold's poetry, as in 'Philomela,' the moon is the great illusionist, begetting 'Eternal passion!' which must be followed by 'Eternal pain!' " (581).

52. R. D. Laing, *The Divided Self* (London: Pantheon Books, 1965), 46.
53. Ibid., 44.

CHAPTER 2. TOWARD PESSIMISM

1. Though determining the order of composition of the earliest-written poems in *The Strayed Reveller* must be conjectural, Murray has a helpful discussion of the dating of "To a Gipsy Child by the Sea-Shore" and concludes that it was "written probably in August 1843" (*Life of Matthew Arnold*, 49), which presumably would make it the earliest poem composed by Arnold to go into that collection.

2. The connection is noted by Kenneth Allott in Arnold, *Poems*, 23. In "Matthew Arnold's Gipsies: Intertextuality and the New Historicism," *Victorian Poetry* 29 (1991): 365–83, Anthony Harrison reaches a conclusion not so different from mine when he describes "To a Gipsy Child by the Sea-Shore" as "a pessimistic, if not morose, elegy that visibly reinscribes and transvalues Wordsworth's Intimations Ode" (369).

3. Quoted by Kenneth Allott in Arnold, *Poems*, 22.

4. In *A World of Possibilities: Romantic Irony in Victorian Literature* (Columbus: Ohio State University Press, 1990), Clyde de L. Ryals proposes a similar interpretation of "the models Arnold holds up": "These figures," Ryals explains, "have one trait in common: they do not break their silence to offer any counsel," failing to do so because "human language belongs to the phenomenal world and it can never encompass the noumenal world to speak God's word" (69).

5. There is an understandable tendency to see "To a Gipsy-Child by the Sea-Shore" as principally an expression of Arnold's concern for the poor, as Riede does, arguing that because the child "only knows hunger and poverty," that "far from being in communion with nature and the rural life," in fact "he is an alien and outcast" (*Betrayal of Language*, 56). But two facts call into question such an interpetive emphasis. One is that being an "alien and outcast" is for Arnold, at least in this case, a mark of the child's spiritual superiority to both the speaker and the "well-fed soul" of the poem. The other is the prospect that, despite his impoverished beginnings, Arnold seems to think that the child may very well succeed in the struggle of life, gleaning "what strenuous gleaners may, / In the thronged fields where winning comes by strife."

6. Culler, *Imaginative Reason*, 63–65.

7. Ibid., 65.

8. Ibid.

9. David J. DeLaura, "A Background for Arnold's 'Shakespeare,' " in *Nineteenth-Century Literary Perspectives: Essays in Honor of Lionel Stevenson*, ed. Clyde de L. Ryals (Durham, N.C.: Duke University Press, 1974), 146.

10. Riede sums up this paradox well: "Very strangely in a poem celebrating a poet, Shakespeare's most notable trait is an inscrutable silence" (*Betrayal of Language*, 43).

11. In *The Voices of Matthew Arnold: An Essay in Criticism* (New Haven: Yale University Press, 1961), Wendell Stacy Johnson long ago spoke of the claim of immortality that Arnold makes for Shakespeare as "a matter of some controversy among critics of Arnold" (65). Moreover, not long afterwards, Robert A. Greenberg, in "Patterns of Imagery: Arnold's 'Shakespeare,' " *Studies in English Literature* 5 (1965): 723–33, maintained that "[t]he 'immortal spirit' contrasts with the earlier 'mortality' and must signify Shakespeare as distinct from Arnold and others"

(729). But he then offered an explanation of immortality that has no metaphysical resonance, describing it only as "the consequence of inner wholeness" (730).

12. In "Patterns of Imagery," Greenberg had earlier noted the similarity between the two poems in this regard (730).

13. Quoted by Kenneth Allott in Arnold, *Poems*, 27.

14. Critics have long found a biographical underpinning for Arnold's choice of the story of Mycerinus from Herodotus as the subject of this poem of 1844 in the recent "death of Dr. Arnold and Tom's revelation that his brother received a doctor's warning that he too was 'doomed' " (Murray, *Life of Matthew Arnold*, 56).

15. Madden, in *Matthew Arnold: A Study of the Aesthetic Temperament*, seems almost alone among the critics in taking the pursuit of pleasure as the true choice of Mycerinus: "Rebelling out of cynical disillusion, Mycerinus turns to an abandoned life of the senses, to which the Powers are equally indifferent" (87).

16. Northrop Frye, "New Directions from Old," in *Fables of Identity: Studies in Poetic Mythology* (New York: Harcourt, Brace and World, 1963), 65.

17. Culler, *Imaginative Reason*, 59.

18. Ibid.

19. Ibid.

20. Ibid., 59–60.

21. Ibid., 60.

22. Alan Roper, *Arnold's Poetic Landscapes* (Baltimore: Johns Hopkins University Press, 1969), 92.

23. A highly suggestive piece of evidence for interpreting "Mycerinus" as advocating hedonism is a poem written shortly afterward, "The New Sirens," which was subtitled at the time of its first publication "A Palinode," presumably, in the words of Kenneth Allott, "a recantation of what Arnold had once believed in common with the new sirens" (Arnold, *Poems*, 33). But the only poem that both chronologically and conceptually can plausibly be said to express the belief that "The New Sirens" would recant, the moral superiority of the life of the senses, is "Mycerinus," at least when that poem is interpreted, as I have suggested, as fundamentally advocating hedonism.

CHAPTER 3. THE POETRY OF PESSIMISM

1. Northrop Frye, foreword to *Romanticism Reconsidered*, ed. Northrop Frye (New York: Columbia University Press, 1963), viii.

2. Upon surveying the criticism of "Resignation" in 1973, DeLaura, in his essay on Arnold in *Victorian Prose*, reaches just this conclusion: "Considering its inherent merits and importance in Arnold's development, 'Resignation' has received very little close analysis" (276). Since 1973, commentary on "Resignation" has been sparse; apart from my own 1988 essay on "Resignation" in *Victorian Poetry* (upon which I draw here), no other sustained analysis has appeared that would lead us to modify DeLaura's judgment.

3. As U. C. Knoepflemacher, probably the most influential critic of the poem, puts it, "Arnold's 'Resignation' is his version, or more properly his inversion of 'Tintern Abbey' " ("Dover Revisited: The Wordsworthian Matrix in the Poetry of Matthew Arnold," *Victorian Poetry* 1 [1963]: 17). Other critics who read "Resignation" as essentially a counterstatement to "Tintern Abbey" are M. G. Sundell in " 'Tintern Abbey' and 'Resignation,' " *Victorian Poetry* 5 (1967): 255–64; William, A. Madden, who describes "Resignation" as "consciously anti-Wordsworthian" in

"Arnold the Poet," in *Matthew Arnold: Writers and Their Background*, ed. Kenneth Allot (Athens: Ohio University Press, 1976), 53; Robert Langbaum, who reads "Resignation" as a record of "Arnold's break with Wordsworth's ideas about nature and the organic connection between nature and human identity," in *The Mysteries of Identity: A Theme in Modern Literature* (Chicago: University of Chicago Press, 1983), 68; and Thaïs E. Morgan, who (apparently unmindful that *The Prelude* was first published a year later than "Resignation") cites *The Prelude* and "Tintern Abbey" as the two poems by Wordsworth whose "proleptic rhetoric of experience" it is that "in 'Resignation' Arnold undoes," in "Rereading Nature: Wordsworth between Arnold and Swinburne," *Victorian Poetry* 24 (1986): 435.

4. *The Letters of John Keats, 1814-1821*, ed. Hyder Edward Rollins (Cambridge: Harvard University Press, 1958), 1:387. The rejection of Keats implied by the account of the poet in "Resignation" is noted by Stange in *Matthew Arnold: The Poet as Humanist*, 62; and by Madden in *Matthew Arnold: A Study of the Aesthetic Temperament*, 167. Both Stange and Madden believe that the source of Arnold's detached poet is to be found in Goethe, while James A. Berlin maintains that Arnold's poet "conforms closely to Schiller's naive model," in "Arnold's Two Poets: The Critical Contrast," *Studies in English Literature* 23 (1983): 622. Yet neither of these explanations really explains why the poet should so deeply "crave" the "general life."

5. The likeness of "the All" of the cosmos in which Empedocles seeks absorption through suicide and the general life of "Resignation" has been pointed out by Warren Anderson in *Matthew Arnold and the Classical Tradition* (Ann Arbor: University of Michigan Press, 1965), 44. Otherwise Arnold's concept of the general life is rarely analyzed in these terms: Stange, for example, explains it as the "the primal beauty at the heart of things" (*Poet as Humanist*, 64); Langbaum puzzlingly says that "Arnold seems to be saying that the poet should know . . . he cannot share nature's life" (*Mysteries*, 68–69); Knoepflmacher offers the most philosophically helpful definition when he describes the general life as "an impersonal power which demands the submission of all men" ("Dover Revisited," 19). But there has been no detailed philosophic explanation of the metaphysics implied by this concept.

6. Interpretations of the last line of "Resignation" vary radically. Honan, for example, regards it as nothing more than the suffering induced by the spirit of the age: "a tension in the individual who is at the mercy of the analytic *Zeitgeist*" (*Matthew Arnold: A Life*, 179); Roper, who reads the poem as mixing the pleasures of landscape with social protest, takes the last line to be an extension of that protest, a generalizing indictment against the "harshness of the general lot" as that lot is defined by the human characters in the poem (*Arnold's Poetic Landscape*, 137); and Langbaum cautiously gives Arnold's cryptic line an essentially psychological emphasis, admitting uncertainty as to whether Arnold's "something" refers to the "necessity that thwarts desire" or "desire" itself (*Mysteries*, 70). But none of these critics who see the closing lines in essentially human terms seems willing to include within that "world" (278) that has undergone this seemingly general infection the nature that—we are told only a few lines earlier—seems "to bear" (270) and, hence, that must surely suffer from the general malady along with earth's human inhabitants. Knoepflmacher, while certainly broader in his description, is not very helpful in his analysis, describing "the something that infects the world" as "the aggregate of all that is visible, an impersonal and tyrannical power which offers 'not joy but peace' to him who apprehends its operations" ("Dover Revisited," 20). The only critics who deal with Arnold's conclusions in gen-

uinely pessimistic terms are Stange, who believes the closing line points to "an evil immanent in things" (*Poet as Humanist*, 68); and Fraser Neiman, who declares Arnold's "something that infects the world" to be "a metaphysical evil" that is the "source of a malaise that is not attributable to death or chance," in *Matthew Arnold* (Boston: Twayne, 1968), 44.

7. John Locke, *An Essay concerning Human Understanding*, ed. Andrew Seth Pringle-Pattison (Oxford: Oxford University Press, 1956), 39.

8. In her 1988 essay, "Empedocles, Suicide, and the Order of Things," Linda Ray Pratt tells us that "[s]ince Walter Houghton's essay in 1958, critics have generally agreed that Empedocles charts a crisis produced by the 'social dislocation' of 'modern' times" (76)—an observation that serves as the starting point for her own stimulating attempt to place Empedocles' suicide within a framework of nineteenth-century attitudes toward suicide. Pratt's 1988 observation still seems to hold true.

9. In fairness, it must be noted that Arnold himself seems to side with Empedocles in judging the period and its philosophers, characterizing it in the preface of 1853 as "a time when the habits of Greek thought and feeling had begun to change, character to dwindle, and the influence of the Sophists to prevail" (*CPW*, 1:1).

10. Among the critics who essentially take Callicles' side, I would include Fraser Neiman, who maintains that Callicles expresses his conceptions through myths that are viable" (*Matthew Arnold*, 73); and Linda Lee Ray, who, in "Callicles on Etna: the Other Mask," *Victorian Poetry* 7 (1969): 309–20, finds in the songs of Callicles "a series of subtle mythological contrasts and comparisons warning Empedocles that the cosmic order will not sanction defiance" (310). Paul Zietlow, in his valuable essay, "Heard but Unheeded: The Songs of Callicles in Matthew Arnold's *Empedocles on Etna*," *Victorian Poetry* 21 (1983): 241–56, finds in Callicles' songs a "tone" that conveys the "[d]isinterested objectivity" (243) that will become the mainstay of Arnold's later critical theory but that, nonetheless, in the drama itself only serves to "exacerbate rather than soothe Empedocles' inner conflict" (251).

11. In his concluding speech, Empedocles tells us that he has "lived in wrath and gloom, / Fierce, disputatious, ever at war with man" (2.394–95).

12. This is the way Frank Kermode, in *Romantic Image* (London: Routledge and Kegan Paul, 1957), differentiates between the two central characters: "Empedocles is the Romantic poet who knows enough; Callicles the Romantic poet who does not know enough" (15). Culler, for whom the basic scenario of Arnold's poetry is an ascent from strayed reveller to sage, is even harder on Callicles, arguing that for Empedocles to linger in the shaded glen would "involve a descent to a lower form of existence, to man's life only in so far as it is a part of nature" (*Imaginative Reason*, 160).

13. Anderson, *Arnold and the Classical Tradition*, 45–46. The "discerning critic" Anderson cites is W. P. Ker, *The Art of Poetry: Seven Lectures* (Oxford: Oxford University Press, 1922), 157.

14. Both Jerome J. McGann ("Matthew Arnold and the Critical Spirit: The Three Texts of *Empedocles on Etna*," in *Victorian Connections*, ed. Jerome J. McGann [Charlottesville: University Press of Virginia, 1989], 146–71), and Riede (*Betrayal of Language*, 78–94) propose essentially deconstructionist readings of the work. Jennifer Wallace, in "Translations in Arnold's *Empedocles*," *Essays in Criticism* 45 (1995): 301–23, employs a Derridean theory of translation as her primary principle of explanation. Sara Suleri, in "Entropy on Etna," in *Matthew Arnold*, ed. Harold Bloom (New York, New Haven, and Philadelphia: Camden House, 1987), 139–49,

reads the drama in terms of the "hidden strategy of readership" (149) embedded there.

15. I take it that just such intelligence and concern is what Empedocles believes has been lost when, from his newly acquired scientific perspective, he laments that the stars shine "Above a race you know not—/ Uncaring and undelighted" (2.295–96).

16. Arnold, *Poems*, 149.

17. Brad Inwood, intro. to *The Poem of Empedocles: A Text and Translation with an Introduction by Brad Inwood* (Toronto, Buffalo, London: University of Toronto Press, 1992), 37. In a curious passage, Empedocles says that prior to coming together in a single individual, "heads and hands and all the other parts were gathered together in the earth, being alive and able to perceive" (114). Whether Empedocles thought this true of elemental being in general is never established in the fragments we possess.

18. See Culler, *Imaginative Reason*, 171; and Walter E. Houghton, "Arnold's 'Empedocles on Etna,' " *Victorian Studies* 1 (1958): 329. Strangely enough, McGann maintains that the goal of Empedocles is the "salvation of mind" ("Matthew Arnold," 164), when he seems to so clearly seek its annihilation.

19. Houghton, "Arnold's 'Empedocles,' " 331.

20. Anderson, *Arnold and the Classical Tradition*, 43–44.

21. Quoted by Culler, *Imaginative Reason*, 153. The most detailed attempt to establish parallels between the philosophy of Empedocles and the philosophy expressed in Arnold's poem about Empedocles is Gay Sibley's interesting essay, "A Matter of Ellipsis: Love, Strife, and the Pressure for Specialty in Matthew Arnold's 'Empedocles on Etna,' " *Nineteenth-Century Prose* 16 (winter 1988–89): 53–78.

22. Houghton, "Arnold's 'Empedocles,' " 312.

23. Inwood, *Poem of Empedocles*, 54.

24. Ibid., 47, 209, 213, 217, 217, 221.

25. Ibid., 52. For an excellent discussion of the relationship of reincarnation to immortality in Empedocles, see Inwood's introduction, 52–54.

26. Ibid., 52.

27. Ibid., 54.

CHAPTER 4. ARNOLD IN LOVE

1. Schopenhauer, "On Women," in *Parerga*, 2:618, 618, 617, 621, 622.

2. Magee, *Philosophy of Schopenhauer*, 10.

3. Peter Gay, *The Tender Passion*, vol. 2 of *The Bourgeois Experience: Victoria to Freud* (Oxford: Oxford University Press, 1986), 81.

4. Christopher Janaway, *Schopenhauer* (Oxford: Oxford University Press, 1996), 3.

5. Magee, *Philosophy of Schopenhauer*, 18.

6. Quoted from Kathleen Tillotson, "Dr. Arnold's Death and a Broken Engagement," *Notes and Queries* 197 (1952): 410.

7. Norman Wymer, reply to "Dr. Arnold's Death and a Broken Engagement," by Kathleen Tillotson, *Notes and Queries* 197 (1952): 504.

8. Tillotson, "Dr. Arnold's Death," 504.

9. Norman Wymer, *Dr. Arnold of Rugby* (London: Robert Hale, 1953), 192.

10. Honan, *Matthew Arnold: A Life*, 101.

11. Hamilton, *Gift Imprisoned*, 52–54.

12. Arnold, *Letters*, 1:lvii.

13. Tillotson, "Dr. Arnold's Death," 411.

14. Hamilton treats the poem very briefly but does suggest, noting these recent events, that in "Resignation" Arnold "urges on Jane a wise, stoical acceptance of her fate" (*Gift Imprisoned*, 88). The only other reference to these events that I am aware of in the criticism of "Resignation" appears in Gibson. However, she does not really use this information to interpret the poem but rather takes Arnold to task in his representation of the woman in the poem, because he "tells us very little about Jane Arnold's own experiences, which we can conjecture at this time to have been painful enough"—that is, as Gibson, drawing on Kenneth Allott, explains in a footnote, the poet does not tell us that his sister "had broken her engagement" ("Dialogue on the Darkling Plain," 48).

15. Honan, *Matthew Arnold: A Life*, 211.

16. Hamilton, *Gift Imprisoned*, 76.

17. Ibid., 103.

18. Peter Gay, *Education of the Senses*, vol. 1 of *The Bourgeois Experience: Victoria to Freud* (Oxford: Oxford University Press, 1984), 309.

19. Arnold, *Letters*, 1:xxxvi.

20. Gay, *The Tender Passion*, 3–43.

21. Writing about the Marguerite poems in *Imaginative Reason*, Culler argues that in them Arnold "discovers that he is not the passionate Byronic lover which his relation with Marguerite implies." Yet the real question would seem to be not whether someone "more preoccupied with ideas and things than with people"— who in these poems about love shows himself to be (in Culler's words) "asexual, passionless, cold"—is a Byronic lover, but whether he is in any meaningful sense a lover at all (131).

22. Because, in the prose paraphrase of the poem, Arnold tells us that his new sirens assert that their love is "romantic, and claims to be a satisfying of the spirit," earlier critics writing on "The New Sirens" have set aside the uncomfortable questions raised by the poem's obvious eroticism and sought higher and safer intellectual ground from which to discuss this strange, difficult, and troubling poem. Warren Anderson, for example, assumes that Arnold uses the term "romantic" to refer expressly to Romanticism, that major literary, philosophic, and cultural movement of the nineteenth century and, therefore, concludes that in Arnold's opinion "Romanticism" in this specialized sense "does not satisfy the spirit" (20). Yet having made Romanticism, thus conceived, a key issue in "The New Sirens," Anderson finds himself predictably forced to ask why the almost obligatory counterclaim of Classicism that should almost reflexively appear in tandem with any Arnoldian condemnation of Romanticism is in this case nowhere in evidence. In his extended commentary on "The New Sirens," Stange in *Matthew Arnold: The Poet as Humanist* also makes this linkage of the romantic and the spiritual in the prose paraphrase a primary interpretive key to the poem, which, he tells us, "is no more about 'romantic love' than it is about the contract between youth and age," claiming instead, "Its real subject is the attitude we must take toward experience, toward art, and toward the world" (52). Yet for all the importance assigned by the critics to these ostensible terms of paraphrase, the phrase in question seems a surprisingly poor fit with the lines from the poem it purports to explain. It should be noted that Riede, the critic who has written most recently on "The New Sirens," focuses (as I do) on the sexual elements in the poem.

23. Sigmund Freud, "The Most Prevalent Form of Degradation in Erotic Life," in *Sexuality and the Psychology of Love*, ed. Philip Rieff (New York: Collier Books, 1963), 58–70.

24. Controversy over who Marguerite was and whether there even was a lover in Switzerland who was the original for the Marguerite in the poems has been a long-debated and still divisive question in Arnold criticism. Arnold himself had complicated the issue by telling his daughters in his later years that "the lover of his passionate youth did not exist." However, as Murray points out, there are understandable reasons to regard the denial as "no more than a piece of judiciously fictive propriety" (*Life of Matthew Arnold*, 79), the most compelling that 1848 letter to Clough with its reference to "the blue eyes" of one of the "inmates" of the Hotel Bellevue in Thun, which Arnold visited on the following day and to which he returned the next year. In his 1981 biography of Arnold, Honan provides us with a further complication by nominating an Ambleside neighbor of the Arnolds, Mary Claude, for the role of Marguerite because of an admittedly tantalizing reference to her in a letter in November 1848 from Mary Arnold to her brother Tom in New Zealand; Mary Arnold mentions "Matt's romantic passion for the Cruel Invisible, Mary Claude" (quoted from Honan, *Matthew Arnold: A Life*, 151). But because there is no evidence that Mary Claude was in Thun during either of Arnold's visits in 1848 and 1849, Honan, to preserve the connection between the girl spoken of in Mary Arnold's letter and the Marguerite of the poems, is forced to construct a highly tenuous and almost wholly unsubstantiated itinerary for Mary Claude during Arnold's Marguerite period and an even more highly strained account of how Arnold's relationship with Marguerite expresses itself in the sequence known as *Switzerland*. According to Honan, the Mary Claude who is the original of Marguerite never did turn up in Thun, and in her absence Arnold wrote a series of love poems placing himself and the Marguerite he purported to love in situations that were basically imaginary, invented variations on the writings of the European " 'sentimental school' of Senancour, Richter, Chauteaubriand, and Foscolo" (152). Despite Honan's great and deserved prestige as Arnold's preeminent biographer, his identification of Mary Claude as Marguerite has not taken hold. It was vigorously challenged by Miriam Allott ("Arnold and Marguerite—Continued," *Victorian Poetry* 23 [1985]: 125–43), who concludes persuasively (at least to my mind) that on the basis of the available evidence there really was "a girl in Switzerland." Among those who have written most recently on the subject, both Lang (Arnold, *Letters*, 1:126n) and Murray (*Life of Matthew Arnold*, 81–82) explicitly reject Honan's contention, while Hamilton simply disregards it. Only Clinton Machann in his recent literary life of Arnold gives Honan any kind of hearing. Who Marguerite was or even whether she actually existed is not finally crucial to the account of the Marguerite poems that follows, since what concerns me most are Arnold's attitudes toward women, sexuality, and love and the underlying psychological origins of these attitudes, attitudes that are really independent of whether the events described in the poem are imagined or real. I would only add that in my opinion the explanation that probably best fits the available facts is that in the space of eighteen months, beginning in September 1848, Arnold would appear to have fallen in love with three different women: Mary Claude, a girl he met in Switzerland, and his future wife, Frances Lucy Wightman—a penchant for falling in love that does not seem out of keeping with the sexual turbulence and anxiety we find expressed in the love poetry written by him around that time.

25. Stange too is struck by the incongruity in a love poem of having the speaker "contemplate almost with pleasure the inevitable transformation of the experience of love into memory." But Stange manages to resolve this seeming contradiction by a dramatic distancing of the author from the speaker through turning the speaker into a "somewhat frivolous lover" (*Poet as Humanist*, 225).

26. Paull F. Baum, *Ten Studies in the Poetry of Matthew Arnold* (Durham, N.C.: Duke University Press, 1958), 62. Other critics, while not making the direct association with Dr. Arnold suggested by Baum, have still identified the voice with some internalized facet of the speaker: in Wendell Stacy Johnson's words, the voice is a "ventriloquist's, giving external authority to an 'inner-directed' but unexamined motive" (*Voices*, 53) or, as Riede characterizes it, "a projection of the speaker's own latent reservation" (*Betrayal of Language*, 108). In explaining why Arnold would "hear this voice" and "choose to obey it," Murray proposes an answer that is very much like Freud's signal anxiety: "In part it is a fear of the emotional disorientation that must come to one who believed of the opposite sex that 'we have known beforehand all that they can teach us' and yet are 'obliged' to learn it from them" (*Life of Matthew Arnold*, 84).

27. Sigmund Freud, *New Introductory Lectures in Psychoanalysis*, vol. 22 of *Complete Psychological Works of Sigmund Freud*, ed. James Strachey (London: Hogarth, 1964), 82.

28. Sigmund Freud, *Inhibitions, Symptoms, and Anxiety*, vol. 20 of *Complete Psychological Works of Sigmund Freud*, ed. James Strachey (London: Hogarth, 1959), 109.

29. Nathan G. Hale, Jr., *The Rise and Crisis of Psychoanalysis in the United States: Freud and the Americans, 1917-1985* (New York: Oxford University Press, 1995), 48. For a detailed account of Freud's changing views of anxiety and the uses to which these have been put by psychoanalysts since Freud, see the three long essays on anxiety by Allan Compton: "A Study of the Psychoanalytic Theory of Anxiety: I. The Development of Freud's Theory of Anxiety," *Journal of the American Psychoanalytic Association* 20 (1972): 3–44; "A Study of the Psychoanalytic Theory of Anxiety: II. Developments in the Theory of Anxiety since 1926," *Journal of the American Psychoanalytic Association* 20 (1972): 341–94; "A Study of the Psychoanalytic Theory of Anxiety: III. A Preliminary Formulation of the Anxiety Response," *Journal of the American Psychoanalytic Association* 28 (1980): 739–73. The one major exception to the list of major psychoanalysts after Freud who made Freud's later theory of anxiety central to their own theorizing was, of course, Jacques Lacan, with his strong preference for the early over the later Freud, and his virtually in toto rejection of the adaptive doctrines of the Anglo-American ego psychology that derived from the later Freud.

30. James Strachey, introduction to Freud, *Inhibitions*, 81.

31. Freud, *Inhibitions*, 136.

32. In discussing these lines, both Stange (*Poet as Humanist*, 237) and Johnson (*Voices*, 53) call Arnold "priggish." Riede stops just short of the Freudian analysis I shall propose, but he does hear in Arnold's words of renunciation "the stern patriarchal tones of a puritanically repressive ideology" (*Betrayal of Language*, 174).

33. Sigmund Freud, "The Most Prevalent Form of Degradation in Erotic Life," in *Sexuality and the Psychology of Love*, ed. Philip Rieff (New York: Collier Books, 1963), 62.

34. Ibid., 68.

35. See Matthew Arnold, *The Yale Notebooks*, ed. S. O. A. Ullmann (Ann Arbor: University of Michigan Press, 1989), 112. In this entry, Arnold not only lends credence to the view that he was romantically involved with a Frenchwoman named Marguerite by having the woman of the diary speak in French, but he also provides us with a "not very detailed" (113) drawing of the head of a woman that we are tempted to regard as the memory-picture of the Marguerite whom Arnold had left

behind. From the coarseness of the speaker's response to the wretchedness of the diarist—"poor child, let's go out and eat"—one is certainly inclined to view the young woman in the picture, who presumably is Marguerite, as the socially inappropriate Marguerite of tradition rather than the high-minded Mary Claude whom Honan takes to be the original of Marguerite.

36. Culler would also have us read the episode in terms of his basic symbolism: "To see Marguerite not as virginal and pure but as soiled, is to make her share in the transformation of nature from forest glade to burning plain" (*Imaginative Reason*, 125).

37. Freud, "Most Prevalent Form," 62–63.

38. Freud, *Inhibitions*, 120.

39. Riede has described with considerable force the dilemma that threatens to overwhelm Arnold's concluding claims: "The speaker's assertion that they are lonely but do not know it seems almost absurd since one can hardly be said to *be* lonely but not *feel* lonely" (*Betrayal of Language*, 173).

40. Arnold, *Poems*, 130.

41. In *Inhibitions, Symptoms, and Anxiety*, Freud says of regression: "If it succeeds in making an instinct regress, it will actually have done it more injury than it could have by repressing it" (105).

42. Otto Fenichel, *The Psychoanalytic Theory of Neurosis* (New York: W. W. Norton & Co., 1945), 160.

43. Fenichel, *Psychoanalytic*, 305.

44. In setting forth that symbolic landscape through which Arnold would seem to have organized his poetry, Culler chooses the remembered "continent" of "To Marguerite—Continued" as one of his illustrations of the "early stages" of "the glade," suggesting in terms very much like those I shall propose that in "their use of geological images and a subtle incest theme, they still suggest a Freudian unconscious or a time prior to individuation" (*Imaginative Reason*, 7).

45. Arnold, *Poems*, 131.

46. Ibid., 201.

47. The parallels between "Written in Butler's Sermons" and "To Marguerite—Continued" have been noted by Culler (*Imaginative Reason*, 7–8).

48. For Langbaum, Arnold's God is nothing more than a "rhetorical flourish," because "Arnold is really talking about the locked-up ego that prevents men and women from loving" (*Mysteries*, 71). Riede criticizes Arnold even more harshly for introducing "a mysterious God as an explanation for human suffering," a decision that Riede condemns as "a cheap and easy evasion" (*Betrayal of Language*, 170). Despite the harshness of these complaints, most readers of "To Marguerite—Continued" still regard it as one of Arnold's most successful poems, and for many readers it is one of the very best poems of the period. Dawson seems to me to come closest to the truth of our experience of the poem when writing of Arnold's earlier use of the word "bounds"; he tells us that " 'bounds' suggests something like Blake's manacles, with the difference that, for Blake, the manacles are 'mind-forged.' Arnold like Hardy after him, seems to imply both an arbitrary fate and a fate directed by a less than generous will" (*Victorian Noon*, 71). What Dawson concludes holds true not only in this instance but in those many other places in the poetry where Arnold insists that our failure to love or even, more generally, our failure to communicate with others is not the result of a decision freely made but of what is apprehended as some externally imposed constraint, a constraint imposed not just on each of us individually but on all of us, "we mortal millions" (4). Much of the interest of "To Marguerite—Continued" derives from the skill with

which, from the depths of his longings, Arnold brings to the poem's surface the psychological origins of what he would characterize as the nature of things, all the while sustaining his governing figure. But neither the psychology he proposes with its implicit narrative of maternal loss experienced as abandonment nor the metaphysics inferred from that psychology of a power greater than ourselves constraining our subsequent efforts to know others would in any way indicate that we ever have had free choice.

49. Citing those lines in which Arnold expresses the desire that he might eventually be able to refer to Marguerite as his sister, Culler remarks: "A biographer could hardly resist the interpretation that Arnold found his relationship with his mother and sister more satisfactory than that with Marguerite" (*Imaginative Reason*, 134). Leon Gottfried suggests that in this passage we find traces of a literary precursor, Shelley, but then acknowledges that in Shelley "this relationship is charged with philosophic and symbolic significance, whereas in Arnold it is hard to see much beyond the psychological" (*Matthew Arnold and the Romantics* [London: Routledge & Kegan Paul, 1963], 151).

50. C. B. Tinker and H. F. Lowry, *The Poetry of Matthew Arnold: A Commentary* (London: Oxford University Press, 1940), 195.

51. Critics of "The Buried Life," from Baum in 1958 to Riede in 1988, have contended that Arnold's core concept in this poem is so beset by intellectual confusions that the poem finally sinks beneath their weight.

52. Culler, *Imaginative Reason*, 84.

53. Honan, *Matthew Arnold: A Life*, 229.

54. Langbaum, *Mysteries*, 88.

55. Stange, *Poet as Humanist*, 167.

56. In *The Cultural Theory of Matthew Arnold* (Berkeley: University of California Press, 1982), Joseph Carroll lists "The Buried Life" as one of "the poems that in theme and imagery group themselves around 'Empedocles' " (21).

57. Riede, *Betrayal of Language*, 195.

58. Jacques Derrida, *Of Grammatology*, ed. and trans. Gayatri Spivak (Baltimore: Johns Hopkins University Press, 1976), 20.

CHAPTER 5. HISTORY

1. This remark by Schopenhauer is quoted in Carl A. Raschke, "Schopenhauer and the Delusion of Progress," *Schopenhauer Jahrbuch* 85 (1977): 76.

2. For a fuller treatment of the historicist Arnold, see Fraser Neiman, "The Zeitgeist of Matthew Arnold," *PMLA* 72 (1957): 977–96; Peter Allan Dale, *The Victorian Critic and the Idea of History* (Cambridge: Harvard University Press, 1977), 91–168; A. Dwight Culler, *Victorian Mirror*, 122–51; and especially David DeLaura, "Matthew Arnold and the Nightmare of History," *Victorian Poetry*, Stratford-upon-Avon Series, 15 (1972): 37–57.

3. Culler, *Victorian Mirror*, 123.

4. Ibid., 124–25.

5. DeLaura, "Nightmare of History," 41.

6. DeLaura proposes a similar qualification to Arnold's emerging historicism in "Matthew Arnold and the Nightmare of History": "Certain poems of the 1852 volume suggest a new willingness to accept history, but nevertheless always with the characteristic Arnoldian doubleness of effect" (53).

7. Culler, *Imaginative Reason*, 130.

8. Riede, *Betrayal of Language*, 77.

9. Earlier critics have offered similar comments on the historicizing of Ober-mann. John P. Farrell describes Arnold's strategy in "Stanzas in Memory of the Author of 'Obermann' " as the "conversion of his Alpine hero into a master of his-torical consciousness" (" 'What You Feel, I Share': Breaking the Dialogue of the Mind with Itself," *Essays and Studies* 41 [1988]: 54). In *Matthew Arnold: The Poet as Humanist*, Stange remarked on how atypical Arnold's treatment of Senan-cour (in essentially these terms) is: "In a manner that seems uncharacteristic of Arnold, Senancour's literary significance is made to depend entirely on his topical-ity, on the peculiar relevance of his work to modern feeling and suffering" (730).

10. Riede, *Betrayal of Language*, 77.

11. Culler, *Victorian Mirror*, 124.

12. Carlyle, *Sartor Resartus*, 168.

13. Ruth Pitman, "On Dover Beach," *Essays in Criticism* 23 (1973): 119—an essay that provides a useful summary of the debate on this "vexed question."

14. Pitman, "On Dover Beach," 120.

15. R. H. Super, *The Time-Spirit of Matthew Arnold* (Ann Arbor: University of Michigan Press, 1970), 27.

16. William Cadbury, "Coming to Terms with 'Dover Beach,' " *Criticism* 8 (1966): 126.

17. Holland, *Dynamics*, 117.

18. Dorothy Mermin, *The Audience in the Poem: Five Victorian Poets* (New Brunswick, N.J.: Rutgers University Press, 1983), 107. Of the predominantly pessi-mistic readings of "Dover Beach," the best are Murray Krieger's " 'Dover Beach' and the Tragic Sense of Eternal Recurrence," in *The Play and Place of Criticism* (Baltimore: Johns Hopkins University Press, 1967), 69–77; and Riede, *Betrayal of Language*, 195–202.

19. Holland, *Dynamics*, 123.

20. Miller, *Disappearance*, 253.

21. Ibid.

22. Freud, *Inhibitions, Symptoms, and Anxiety*, 119.

23. Quoted from Arnold, *Poems*, 257.

24. Holland, *Dynamics*, 127.

25. Ibid., 126.

26. See Honan, *Matthew Arnold: A Life*, 233–35.

27. Culler, *Imaginative Reason*, 4–5.

28. Arnold, *Poems*, 278.

29. Buckler, *On the Poetry*, 102.

30. Madden, *Matthew Arnold: A Study of the Aesthetic Temperament*, 63.

31. Culler, *Imaginative Reason*, 7.

32. This account from the diary of Fanny Lucy is quoted by Honan, *Matthew Arnold: A Life*, 239.

33. Murray sees in the poem a "tension between the attractions of the contem-plative life and the insistent call to the active life that the Victorian age made to him and that his new career, which he would be starting in barely a month, would come to symbolize" (*Life of Matthew Arnold*, 118–19). But he does not explain why he thinks Arnold would represent those engaged in the contemplative life as children.

34. The concluding coda to "Stanzas from the Grande Chartreuse," with its un-explained reversion to childhood, has produced less discussion than one might have expected, certainly less than its counterpart in "The Scholar-Gipsy." But

both Culler and Madden have read in it a pull toward death at poem's end. Culler describes the childen as "all dead," since "[t]heir protective glade is a 'close of graves' " (*Imaginative Reason*, 27). Madden, who regards the poem's "emotional impulse" as "a longing for freedom from the intolerable pressure of inner tensions," believes that "since this cannot be secured through choice, the speaker turns instinctively to the peace to be found in death" (*Matthew Arnold: A Study in the Aesthetic Temperament*, 74).

35. For a detailed account of Arnold's interest in mesmerism in connection with "The Scholar-Gipsy," see Culler, *Imaginative Reason*, 178–80.

36. This phrase appears in a sentence from Glanvill that was incorporated by Arnold into his own explanatory note to the poem. See Arnold, *Poems*, 357.

37. Culler, *Imaginative Reason*, 182.

38. Culler, in fact, chooses the famous penultimate line of "Ode to a Nightingale" as an epigraph for his chapter on "The Scholar-Gipsy" in *Imaginative Reason*, 178. For a searching and sensitive examination of Keats as precursor poet for Arnold in "The Scholar-Gipsy," see William A. Ulmer, "The Human Seasons: Arnold, Keats and 'The Scholar-Gipsy,' " *Victorian Poetry* 22 (1984): 247–61.

39. In *Imaginative Reason*, Culler provides a detailed account of the structural parallels that link "The Scholar-Gipsy" (especially the first part) and "Ode to a Nightingale" (183–85).

40. Ulmer offers the fullest discussion of the immortality of "The Scholar-Gipsy," treating its "status" as "psychological, not ontological" and concluding that "Arnold redefines the idea of immortality as a metaphor for constant dedication and wholeness of self" ("Human Seasons," 159).

41. For a discussion of Keats, immortality, and metaphysics, see my essay "Noumenal Inferences: Keats as Metaphysician," in *Critical Essays on John Keats*, ed. Hermione de Almeida (Boston: G. K. Hall, 1989), 292–317.

42. But we need to exercise caution in not being too literal-minded when adopting Culler's useful categories. As Hamilton aptly puts it, the scholar-gipsy seems "a stray, but not a reveller" (*Gift Imprisoned*, 160).

43. Leon Gottfried, *Matthew Arnold and the Romantics*, 116–50.

44. As early as 1862, in "Maurice de Guerin," Arnold had already said that in Keats "the natural magic is perfect" (*CPW*, 3:334).

45. Riede, *Betrayal of Language*, 142. In arguing that the scholar-gipsy we are given in the first half of the poem is fundamentally different from the scholar-gipsy of the second half, Riede follows the lead of Culler in *Imaginative Reason* (188).

46. G. Wilson Knight, "The Scholar-Gipsy," in *Matthew Arnold*, ed. Harold Bloom (New York: Camden House, 1987), 65. The one notable exception in this regard is A. E. Dyson in "The Last Enchantments," *Review of English Studies* 8 (1957): 257–65.

47. *The Aeneid of Virgil*, trans. C. Day Lewis (Oxford: Oxford University Press, 1952). All quotations from the *The Aeneid* are from this edition.

48. Culler, *Imaginative Reason*, 191. The complaint that the presumably elucidating simile and the referent to it are finally ill-matched goes back as far as the end of the last century and George Saintsbury's concession of defeat in his efforts to explain their relationship: "No ingenuity can work out the parallel between the 'uncloudedly joyous' scholar who is bid avoid the palsied, diseased *enfants du siècle*, and the grave Tyrian trader who was indignant at the competition of the merry Greek and shook out more sail to seek fresh markets" (*Matthew Arnold* [Edinburgh: Blackwood & Sons, 1899]), 42.

49. In "Arnold's 'Scholar Gipsy' and the Crisis of the 1852 *Poems*," *Modern*

Language Quarterly 45 (1984): 144–62, William Oram notes this connection, though he draws a somewhat different inference from it than I do: "[T]he Greeks recall the 'Sons of the world' from whom the speaker turns in 'Stanzas from the Grande Chartreuse' (161)—a race whose 'exulting thunder' betrays a spiritual emptiness" (159).

50. Langbaum too suggests that these "joyous Greeks could stand well enough for modern men of *action*" (*Mysteries*, 60).

51. The order of composition for the three major works completed within months of each other in 1853—"The Scholar-Gipsy," "Sohrab and Rustum," and the preface to the *Poems* of 1853—must remain conjectural. In her editing of the poems of Arnold for the Oxford Authors series, Miriam Allott, in *Matthew Arnold*, ed. Miriam Allott and Robert H. Super (Oxford: Oxford University Press, 1986), presents the order of composition as the preface, "Sohrab and Rustum," and "The Scholar-Gipsy," but complicates that chronology by reminding us that "Arnold was contemplating ['The Scholar-Gipsy'] as early as 1848" (545).

52. Arnold, *Poems*, 420.

53. This last phrase is taken from the title of a 1908 essay by Freud, " 'Civilized' Sexual Morality and Modern Nervousness," in *Sexuality and the Psychology of Love*, ed. Philip Rieff (New York: Collier Books, 1963).

Works Cited

Allott, Miriam. "Arnold and Marguerite—Continued." *Victorian Poetry* 23 (1985): 125–43.

Anderson, Warren. *Matthew Arnold and the Classical Tradition*. Ann Arbor: University of Michigan Press, 1965.

Armstrong, Isobel. *Victorian Poetry: Poetry, Poetics, and Politics*. London: Routledge, 1993.

Arnold, Matthew. *The Complete Prose Works*. Edited by R. H. Super. 11 vols. Ann Arbor: University of Michigan Press, 1960–1977.

———. *The Letters of Matthew Arnold: 1829-70*. Edited by Cecil Y. Lang. 3 vols. Charlottesville: University Press of Virginia, 1996–99.

———. *Matthew Arnold*. Edited by Miriam Allott and R. H. Super. Oxford Authors series. Oxford: Oxford University Press, 1986.

———. *The Poems of Matthew Arnold*. Edited by Kenneth Allott and Miriam Allott. London: Longman, 1979.

———. *The Yale Notebooks*. Edited by S. O. A. Ullman. Ann Arbor: University of Michigan Press, 1989.

Baricelli, Gian Pierro. *Giacomo Leopardi*. Boston: Twayne, 1986.

Baum, Paull. *Ten Studies in the Poetry of Matthew Arnold*. Durham, N.C.: Duke University Press, 1958.

Berlin, James A. "Arnold's Two Poets: The Critical Contrast." *Studies in English Literature* 23 (1983): 615–31.

Bristow, Joseph. " 'Love let us be true to one another'; Matthew Arnold, Arthur Hugh Clough, and 'Our 'Aqueous Ages,' " *Literature and History*, 3d ser., 4 (1995): 27–49.

Buckler, William. *On the Poetry of Matthew Arnold: Essays in Critical Reconstruction*. New York: New York University Press, 1872.

Cadbury, William. "Coming to Terms with 'Dover Beach.' " *Criticism* 8 (1966): 126–38.

Carlyle, Thomas. *Sartor Resartus: The Life and Opinions of Herr Teufelsdröckh*. Edited by Charles Frederick Harrold. New York: Odyssey Press, 1937.

Carroll, Joseph. *The Cultural Theory of Matthew Arnold*. Berkeley: University of California Press, 1982.

Coleridge, Samuel Taylor. *Biographia Literaria; or Biographical Sketches of My Literary Life and Opinions*. Edited by James Engell and W. Jackson Bate. In *The Collected Works of Samuel Taylor Coleridge*. 2d. ed. Vol. 7. Princeton: Princeton University Press, 1983.

Collini, Stefan. *Arnold*. Oxford: Oxford University Press, 1988.

Compton, Allan. "A Study of the Pyschoanalytic Theory of Anxiety: I. The Development of Freud's Theory of Anxiety." *Journal of the American Psychoanalytic Association* 29 (1972): 3–44.

———. "A Study of the Psychoanalytic Theory of Anxiety: II. Developments in the Theory of Anxiety since 1926." *Journal of the American Psychoanalytic Association* 20 (1972): 341–94.

———. "A Study of the Psychoanalytic Theory of Anxiety: III. A Preliminary Formulation of the Anxiety Response." *Journal of the American Psychoanalytic Association* 28 (1980): 739–73.

Coursen, Herbert R. " 'The Moon Lies Fair': The Poetry of Matthew Arnold." *Victorian Poetry* 4 (1964): 569–81.

Culler, A. Dwight. *Imaginative Reason: The Poetry of Matthew Arnold*. New Haven: Yale University Press, 1966.

———. *The Victorian Mirror of History*. New Haven: Yale University Press, 1985.

Dale, Peter Allan. *The Victorian Critic and the Idea of History*. Cambridge: Harvard University Press, 1977.

Danahy, Martin. *A Community of One: Masculine Authority in Victorian Britain*. Albany: State University of New York Press, 1993.

Dawson, Carl. *Victorian Noon: English Literature in 1850*. Baltimore: Johns Hopkins University Press, 1979.

DeLaura, David J. "A Background for Arnold's 'Shakespeare.' " In *Nineteenth-Century Literary Perspectives: Essays in Honor of Lionel Stevenson*, edited by Clyde de L. Ryals. Durham, N.C.: Duke University Press, 1974.

———. "Matthew Arnold." In *Victorian Prose: A Guide to Research*, edited by David DeLaura. New York: Modern Language Association, 1973.

———. "Matthew Arnold and the Nightmare of History." *Victorian Poetry*, Stratford-on-Avon series, 15 (1972): 37–57.

Derrida, Jacques. *Of Grammatalogy*. Edited by and translated by Gayatri Spivack. Baltimore, Md.: Johns Hopkins University Press, 1976.

Dyson, A. E. "The Last Enchantments." *Review of English Studies* 8 (1957): 257–65.

Empedocles. *The Poem of Empedocles: A Text and Translation with an Introduction by Brad Inwood*. Toronto, Buffalo, London: University of Toronto Press, 1992.

Farrell, John P. " 'What You Feel, I Share': Breaking the Dialogue of the Mind with Itself." *Essays and Studies* 41 (1988): 45–61.

Fenichel, Otto. *The Psychoanalytic Theory of Neurosis*. New York: W. W. Norton & Co., 1945.

Freud, Sigmund. *The Standard Edition of the Complete Psychological Works of Sigmund Freud*. Edited by James Strachey and Anna Freud. 24 vols. London: Hogarth Press, 1955–68.

———. "The Most Prevalent Form of Degradation in Erotic Life." In *Sexuality and the Psychology of Love*. Edited by Philip Rieff. New York: Collier Books, 1963.

Frye, Northrop. "New Directions from Old." In *Fables of Identity: Studies in Poetic Mythology*. New York: Harcourt, Brace and World, 1963.

———. Foreword to *Romanticism Reconsidered*, edited by Northrop Frye. New York: Columbia University Press, 1963.

Gay, Peter. *Education of the Senses*. Vol. 1 of *The Bourgeois Experience: Victoria to Freud*. Oxford: Oxford University Press, 1984.

———. *Freud: A Life for Our Time*. New York: W. W. Norton & Co., 1988.

———. *The Tender Passion*. Vol. 2 of *The Bourgeois Experience: Victoria to Freud*. Oxford: Oxford University Press, 1985.

Gibson, Mary Ellen. "Dialogue on the Darkling Plain: Genre, Gender, Audience in Matthew Arnold's Lyrics." In *Gender and Discourse in Victorian Art and Literature*, edited by Anthony H. Harrison and Beverly Taylor. De Kalb: Northern Illinois University Press, 1993.

Gottfried, Leon. *Matthew Arnold and the Romantics*. London: Routledge & Kegan Paul, 1963.

Graff, Gerald. *Beyond the Culture Wars: How Teaching the Conflicts Can Revitalize American Education*. New York: W. W. Norton & Co., 1992.

Greenberg, Robert A. "Patterns of Imagery: Arnold's 'Shakespeare.' " *Studies in English Literature* 5 (1965): 723–33.

Grob, Alan. "Noumenal Inferences: Keats as Metaphysician." In *Critical Essays on John Keats*, edited by Hermione de Almeida. Boston: G. K. Hall, 1989.

Hale, Nathan G., Jr. *The Rise and Crisis of Psychoanalysis in the United States: Freud and the Americans, 1917–1985*. New York: Oxford University Press, 1995.

Hamilton, Ian. *A Gift Imprisoned: The Poetic Life of Matthew Arnold*. London: Bloomsbury, 1998.

Hardy, Thomas. *Jude the Obscure*. Edited by Norman Page. New York: W. W. Norton & Co., 1978.

Harrison, Anthony. "Matthew Arnold's Gipsies: Intertexuality and the New Historicism." *Victorian Poetry* 29 (1991): 365–83.

Holland, Norman. *The Dynamics of Literary Response*. New York: W. W. Norton & Co., 1975.

Honan, Park. *Matthew Arnold: A Life*. New York: McGraw-Hill, 1981.

Houghton, Walter E. "Arnold's 'Empedocles on Etna.' " *Victorian Studies* 1 (1958): 311–36.

Janaway, Christopher. *Schopenhauer*. Oxford: Oxford University Press, 1996.

Johnson, Wendell Stacy. *The Voices of Matthew Arnold: An Essay in Criticism*. New Haven: Yale University Press, 1961.

Keats, John. *The Letters of John Keats*. Edited by Hyder Edward Rollins. 2 vols. Cambridge: Harvard University Press, 1958.

Ker, W. P. *The Art of Poetry: Seven Lectures*. Oxford: Oxford University Press, 1922.

Kermode, Frank. *Romantic Image*. London: Routledge and Kegan Paul, 1957.

Knight, G. Wilson. "The Scholar-Gipsy." In *Matthew Arnold*, edited by Harold Bloom. New York: Camden House, 1987.

Knoepflemacher, U. C. "Dover Revisited: The Wordsworthian Matrix in the Poetry of Matthew Arnold." *Victorian Poetry* 1 (1963): 17–26.

Krieger, Murray. " 'Dover Beach' and the Tragic Sense of Eternal Recurrence." In *The Play and Place of Criticism*. Baltimore: Johns Hopkins University Press, 1967.

Laing, R. D. *The Divided Self*. New York: Pantheon Books, 1969.

Langbaum, Robert. *The Mysteries of Identity: A Theme in Modern Literature*. Chicago: University of Chicago Press, 1983.

Leopardi, Giacomo. *A Leopardi Reader*. Edited and translated by Ottavio M. Casale. Urbana: University of Illinois Press, 1981.

Locke, John. *An Essay concerning Human Understanding*. Edited by Andrew Seth Pringle-Pattison. Oxford: Oxford University Press, 1956.

Machann, Clinton. *The Essential Matthew Arnold: An Annotated Bibliography of Major Modern Studies*. New York: G. K. Hall & Co., 1993.

———. *Matthew Arnold: A Literary Life*. New York: St, Martin's Press, 1998.

Madden, William. "Arnold the Poet." In *Matthew Arnold: Writers and Their Background*, edited by Kenneth Allott. Athens: Ohio University Press, 1976.

———. *Matthew Arnold: A Study of the Aesthetic Temperament in Victorian England*. Bloomington: Indiana University Press, 1967.

Magee, Brian. *The Philosophy of Schopenhauer*. Oxford: Oxford University Press, 1983.

McGann, Jerome J. "Matthew Arnold and the Critical Spirit: The Three Texts of *Empedocles on Etna*." In *Victorian Connections*, edited by Jerome J. McGann. Charlottesville: University Press of Virginia, 1989.

Mermin, Dorothy. *The Audience in the Poem: Five Victorian Poets*. New Brunswick, N.J.: Rutgers University Press, 1983.

Miller, J. Hillis. *The Disappearance of God: Five Nineteenth-Century Writers*. Cambridge: Harvard University Press, 1963.

Morgan, Thaïs. "Rereading Nature: Wordsworth between Arnold and Swinburne." *Victorian Poetry* 24 (1986): 427–39.

Murray, Nicholas. *A Life of Matthew Arnold*. London: Hodder and Stoughton, 1996.

Neiman, Fraser. *Matthew Arnold*. Boston: Twayne, 1968.

———. "The Zeitgeist of Matthew Arnold." *PMLA* 72 (1957): 977–96.

Nietzsche, Friedrich. *The Will to Power*. Translated by Walter Kaufmann and R. J. Hollingdale. Edited by Walter Kaufmann. New York: Random House, 1967.

Oram, William. "Arnold's 'Scholar Gipsy' and the Crisis of the 1852 *Poems*." *Modern Language Quarterly* 45 (1984): 144–62.

Oxenford, John. "Iconoclasm in German Philosophy." *Westminster and Foreign Quarterly Review* (spring 1853): 388–407.

Pitman, Ruth. "On Dover Beach." *Essays in Criticism* 23 (1973): 109–36.

Pratt, Linda Ray. "Empedocles, Suicide, and the Order of Things." *Victorian Poetry* 26 (1988): 79–90.

Raschke, Carl A. "Schopenhauer and the Delusion of Progress." *Schopenhauer Jahrbuch* 85 (1977): 73–86.

Ray, Linda Lee. "Callicles on Etna: The Other Mask." *Victorian Poetry* 7 (1969): 309–20.

Riede David. *Matthew Arnold and the Betrayal of Language*. Charlottesville: University Press of Virginia, 1988.

Roper, Alan. *Arnold's Poetic Landscape*. Baltimore: Johns Hopkins University Press, 1969.

Ryals, Clyde de L. *A World of Possibilities: Romantic Irony in Victorian Literature*. Columbus: Ohio State University Press, 1990.

Saintsbury, George. *Matthew Arnold*. Edinburgh: Blackwood & Sons, 1899.

Schopenhauer, Arthur. *Parerga and Paripolemona*. Edited by E. J. F. Payne. Vol. 2. Oxford: Oxford University Press, 1974.

———. *The World as Will and Representation*. Translated by E. J. F. Payne. 2 vols. New York: Dover Publications, 1958.

Shakespeare, William. *Hamlet*. In *Complete Works of William Shakespeare*, edited by David Bevington. 4th ed. New York: HarperCollins, 1992.

———. *King Lear*. In *Complete Works of William Shakespeare*. Edited by David Bevington. 4th ed. New York: HarperCollins, 1992.

Sibley, Gay. "A Matter of Ellipsis: Love, Strife, and the Pressure for Specialty in Matthew Arnold's 'Empedocles on Etna.' " *Nineteenth Century Prose* 16 (1988–89): 53–78.

Sophocles. *Oedipus at Colonus*. Translated by Robert Fagles. New York: Viking Press, 1982.

Stange, G. Robert. *Matthew Arnold: The Poet as Humanist*. Princeton: Princeton University Press, 1967.

———. "The Victorian City and the Frightened Poets." In *The Victorian City*, edited by H. J. Dyos and Michael Wolff. Vol. 2. London: Routledge and Kegan Paul, 1973.

Stone, Donald. *Communications with the Future: Matthew Arnold in Dialogue*. Ann Arbor: University of Michigan Press, 1998.

Suleri, Sara. "Entropy on Etna." In *Matthew Arnold*, edited by Harold Bloom. New York, New Haven, Philadelphia: Camden House, 1987.

Sundell, M. G. " 'Tintern Abbey' and 'Resignation.' " *Victorian Poetry* 5 (1967): 255–64.

Super, R. H. *The Time-Spirit of Matthew Arnold*. Ann Arbor: University of Michigan Press, 1970.

Tennyson, Alfred Lord. *The Poems of Tennyson*. Edited by Christopher Ricks. London: Longmans, 1969.

Tillotson, Kathleen. "Dr. Arnold's Death and a Broken Engagement." *Notes and Queries* 197 (1952): 409–11.

Tinker, C. B., and H. F. Lowry. *The Poetry of Matthew Arnold: A Commentary*. London: Oxford University Press, 1940.

Turner, Paul. *Victorian Poetry, Drama, and Miscellaneous Prose*. Oxford: Oxford University Press, 1989.

Ulmer, William A. "The Human Seasons: Arnold, Keats, and the 'Scholar-Gipsy.' " *Victorian Poetry* 22 (1984): 247–61.

Vida, Elizabeth M. *Romantic Affinities: German Authors and Carlyle, A Study in the History of Ideas*. Toronto: University of Toronto Press, 1993.

Virgil. *The Aeneid*. Translated by C. Day Lewis. Oxford: Oxford University Press, 1952.

Wallace, Jennifer. "Translations in Arnold's *Empedocles*." *Essays in Criticism* 45 (1995): 301–23.

Willey, Basil. *The Eighteenth-Century Background: Studies in the Idea of Nature in the Thought of the Period*. London: Chatto and Windus, 1940.

Wymer, Norman. *Dr. Arnold of Rugby*. London: Robert Hale, 1953.

———. "Dr. Arnold's Death and a Broken Engagement." *Notes and Queries* 197 (1952): 503–4.

Zietlow, Paul. "Heard but Unheeded: The Songs of Callicles in Matthew Arnold's *Empedocles on Etna*." *Victorian Poetry* 21 (1983): 241–56.

Index

Allott, Kenneth, 43, 93, 95, 110, 137, 140, 227 n. 2, 228 n. 23
Allott, Miriam, 233 n. 24, 239 n. 51
Anderson, Warren, 90, 97, 229 n. 5, 230 n. 13, 232 n. 22
Armstrong, Isobel, 30
Arnold, Frances Lucy (wife; née Wightman), 113, 132, 226 n. 50, 233 n. 24
Arnold, Jane (sister), 109–12, 232 n. 14
Arnold, Mary (sister), 233 n. 24
Arnold, Mary Penrose (mother), 196–97, 220
Arnold, Matthew: biographical background of, 108–14, 118–19, 194–96, 198, 208, 210, 228 n. 14, 233 n. 24. Works: *Balder Dead*, 217–18; "The Buried Life," 36, 97, 147, 150–61, 188, 236 nn. 51 and 56; "Byron," 30–32; *Culture and Anarchy*, 151, 220; "Destiny," 36, 51, 85, 131; "Dover Beach," 15, 18, 19, 22, 41, 45, 47, 48, 68, 135, 138, 148, 164, 171–84, 221; *Empedocles on Etna*, 18, 34–38, 40, 45, 52, 55, 68, 77–79, 82–83, 87–105, 129, 140, 147, 157, 158, 166, 215, 221, 231 nn. 15 and 17; Callicles in, 38, 45, 88–90, 101, 102, 203, 230 nn. 10 and 12; *"Empedocles on Etna," and Other Poems*, 184; *Essays in Criticism*, 220; "A Farewell," 122–23, 144–50; "The Forsaken Merman," 39, 45, 47, 48, 116, 138; "The Future," 22, 41, 184–89; "Human Life," 31, 34, 35, 41–44, 47, 48, 79, 85, 86, 136, 144, 148, 215; "In Harmony with Nature," 30; "In Utrumque Paratus," 87; "Isolation. To Marguerite," 44, 69, 77, 129–36; *Last Essays on Church and Religion*, 28; "Lines Written in Kensington Gardens," 128; "Maurice de Guerin," 238 n. 44; "Meeting," 120–

25, 147; "Memorial Verses," 128; "Memory Picture, A," 119–20; *New Poems* (1867), 18; "New Sirens, The," 39, 114–18, 228 n. 23, 232 n. 22; *Merope*, 217–18; "Mycerinus," 35, 65–74, 135, 228 nn. 14, 15, and 23; "Obermann Once More," 163, 179; "Parting," 118, 125–29, 151; *Poems* (1853), preface, 17, 203, 205–7, 215–17, 220, 221, 230 n. 9, 239 n. 51; "Resignation," 21, 31, 34, 36, 40, 45–46, 54, 73, 75–87, 93, 111–12, 121–22, 128, 129, 137, 147, 148, 152, 156, 187–88, 198, 218, 228 n. 3, 232 n. 14; "Rugby Chapel," 218–19; "Scholar-Gipsy, The," 21, 22, 41, 64, 69, 79, 164, 166, 189, 198–216, 219, 221, 239 n. 51; "Self-Dependence," 91, 130, 131; "Shakespeare," 54, 60–65, 165,166; "Southern Night, A" 218; *Sohrab and Rustum*, 215–16, 217, 220, 221, 239 n. 51; "Stanzas from the Grande Chartreuse," 22, 41, 164, 189–98, 212–14, 237 n. 34; "Stanzas in Memory of the Author of 'Obermann,' " 20–22, 24, 41, 164–71, 193–94, 197, 237 n. 9; "The Strayed Reveller," 203; *"The Strayed Reveller" and Other Poems*, 21, 54, 75, 165, 166, 227 n. 1; "Study of Poetry, The," 200; "Summer Night, A," 35, 41, 44–45, 47–53, 68, 91, 116, 130, 157, 173, 215, 226 n. 50; *Switzerland*, 119, 233 n. 24; "Thyrsis," 218, 219–20; "To a Friend," 36, 76, 165, 175; "To a Gipsy Child by the Sea Shore," 21, 31, 40, 54–60, 63, 65, 69, 79, 227 nn. 1, 2, and 5; "To Marguerite-Continued," 30, 36, 45, 47, 48, 69, 73, 77, 79, 85, 100, 136–44, 173–74, 221, 235 nn. 44 and 48; "To the Duke of Wellington," 167–68;

246

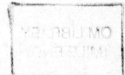